Chicken Soup
for the Soul.

Random
Acts of
Kindness

D0038734

Chicken Soup for the Soul: Random Acts of Kindness
101 Stories of Compassion and Paying It Forward
Amy Newmark

Published by Chicken Soup for the Soul, LLC www.chickensoup.com
Copyright ©2017 by Chicken Soup for the Soul, LLC. All Rights Reserved.

The publisher gratefully acknowledges the many publishers and individuals who
granted Chicken Soup for the Soul permission to reprint the cited material.

Front cover illustration courtesy of iStockphoto.com/Mike_Kiev (©Mike_Kiev)
Back cover and interior illustration courtesy of iStockphoto.com/brozova (©brozova)
Interior photo of Amy Newmark courtesy of Susan Morrow at SwickPix

Cover and Interior by Daniel Zaccari

Distributed to the booktrade by Simon & Schuster. SAN: 200-2442

Publisher's Cataloging-In-Publication Data
(Prepared by The Donohue Group, Inc.)

Names: Newmark, Amy, compiler.
Title: Chicken Soup for the Soul : random acts of kindness : 101 stories
    of compassion and paying it forward / [compiled by] Amy Newmark.
Other Titles: Random acts of kindness : 101 stories of compassion and
    paying it forward
Description: [Cos Cob, Connecticut] : Chicken Soup for the Soul, LLC
    [2017]
Identifiers: LCCN 2016960915 | ISBN 978-1-61159-961-9 (print) | ISBN
    978-1-61159-260-3 (ebook)
Subjects: LCSH: Kindness--Literary collections. | Kindness--Anecdotes. |
    Compassion--Literary collections. | Compassion--Anecdotes. | LCGFT:
    Anecdotes.
Classification: LCC BJ1533.K5 C45 2017 | DDC 177.7/02--dc23

PRINTED IN THE UNITED STATES OF AMERICA
on acid∞free paper

25 24 23 22 21 20 19 18 17   01 02 03 04 05 06 07 08 09 10 11

Random Acts of
Kindness

101 Stories of Compassion
and Paying It Forward

Amy Newmark

Chicken Soup for the Soul, LLC
Cos Cob, CT

Changing the world one story at a time®
www.chickensoup.com

Table of Contents

❶

~Miracles Happen~

❷

~Just the Right Words~

❸

~One Good Deed Deserves Another~

❹

~One Little Thing, One Big Difference~

❺

~Who Helped Whom?~

❻

~Never Too Young to Help~

❼

~It Takes a Village~

8

~The Joy of Giving~

9

~Above and Beyond~

10

~Eye Opening Kindness~

⑪

~Holiday Helpers~

Chapter 1

Random Acts of Kindness

Miracles Happen

Nothing is black or white, nothing's "us or them."
But then there are magical, beautiful things in
the world. There's incredible acts of kindness and
bravery, and in the most unlikely places,
and it gives you hope.
~Dave Matthews

Some Kind of Miracle

*In this world it is not what we take up, but what
we give up, that makes us rich.*
~Henry Ward Beecher

Her name was Jean. She taught first grade. She drove a sputtering old Volkswagen Jetta with dull blue paint and frayed bucket seats. As a single mother with one young son, she found that the car served her needs. It wasn't the speediest vehicle, but Jean was never late to work. In fact, each school day she was the first teacher to arrive and the last teacher to leave.

Jean took great care to plan instruction, create assessments, and decorate her classroom. Parents in the neighborhood would beat down the principal's door to have their children assigned to her class. Jean could teach a mouse to read, and all her students passed into second grade with advanced vocabularies and language skills. Needless to say, she was a gifted teacher.

One August, the faculty returned from summer break to see Jean drive up to school with a carload of children. Two sisters in high school had found themselves living in a dangerous environment. They did not want to enter foster care. They asked the caseworker to contact their first grade teacher. Jean lived in a modest home with her son. Yet, she took the sisters in. One of the girls even had a baby. Jean welcomed the baby into her home, too.

Packed with children, the little blue Jetta sputtered onward. Each day, even though Jean took her son and daughters to school and shuttled the baby to daycare, she was still the first teacher in the school parking lot.

During lunch, while faculty members exchanged life stories in the teachers' lounge, Jean never complained about her new responsibilities. She did, however, speak about her car. With three new bodies to transport, the Jetta was too small. It burned oil. Jean needed something new. She wanted a van.

In the teachers' lounge, Jean shared that a new van was not in her budget, especially with three new children in her home. Like a good friend, I listened to her concerns. There was nothing that I could do. At the time, I was a young teacher who lived at home with my mother. I did not have any disposable income. But in my heart I wanted to help Jean purchase a van to accommodate her growing family.

I don't know how the idea came to me. But one day during lunch, I did not go to the teachers' lounge. Instead, I sat at my desk and typed a one-page letter to *The Oprah Winfrey Show*. I shared Jean's story. I told Oprah that Jean was a pillar in our school. Her influence as an educator was so great that two high school girls remembered her kind spirit when they were faced with foster care. They hoped for the impossible and they got it — their first grade teacher welcomed them into her home. And though her resources were limited, Jean made sacrifices to care for the girls as if they were her own.

A month passed. One morning the principal called Jean into his office. He wanted her to attend a "teachers' conference" in Chicago. She had two days to pack. Jean made arrangements for childcare and flew to the Windy City. A limousine driver dashed her away to Harpo Studios for a surprise taping of *The Oprah Winfrey Show*.

Oprah's topic for that day was generosity. Midway through the taping, she called Jean to the stage. Oprah hugged the dedicated teacher and explained she had received a letter expressing her need for a van. The audience listened to the details of Jean's story and clapped for her. Then Oprah announced that Jean would receive a new Chrysler van for her family. Cheers filled the studio and Jean trembled with disbelief. She was speechless, but her tears expressed her overwhelming gratitude.

The year was 1999. Six hundred miles away, I watched the joy of it all from the television in my living room. Jean's big heart taught me many lessons that year. I learned that as we satisfy the needs of others, God supplies our needs. I learned that the simplest acts (like writing a letter) can require a daring faith. And nothing is impossible. Miracles happen every day.

~Alice Faye Duncan

Finding Peace

All God's angels come to us disguised.
~James Russell Lowell

heard her tiny body hit the wall before he slammed shut the bathroom door. She sounded more like a child than an eight-pound dog when she cried out. That sound pierced the wall that separated us. On the other side, my heart was pounding in terror.

My stalker was inside my home, raping me. And all I could hear was my heartbeat, his rancid breathing, and my little dog's sudden silence.

I was bleeding from places on my body I could no longer feel. She was whimpering, in the soft delicate way she had whimpered when we first met.

I had rescued her from the colorful alleyways of Venice Beach, on a Sunday evening vibrant with music, laughter, and the other sounds — those of discontent — that fill Los Angeles after dark. She was curled up in a shadowy corner, lying atop discarded debris and broken glass, ignored and alone.

At first I thought she was a large rodent, but it was her huge ears that drew me closer. I saw that she was a tiny dog, trembling from her infected wounds, the worms that had invaded her empty belly, and, most of all — fear.

Had I not found her when I did she would have died right there in that rat-infested alley. Had I not found her when I did, I would have died too — of sadness, self-loathing, and the bondage of memory that kept me prisoner. It was destiny. We were waiting to find each other.

After she recovered at the local vet, she came home to me. The first few months were challenging. She hid beneath my bedroom dresser, never allowing me to touch or cuddle her in any way. I simply slipped a bowl of water and kibble in front of her hiding place each morning, and opened the French doors that led to my gated yard for her to relieve herself. I was content to know that she was safe. It was enough that she had a home, that she was loved, and that she had given me both a challenge and a purpose.

That frightened little dog was a mirror to my brokenness. I understood her lack of trust. I had stopped trusting too after I walked in on my husband naked in the bathtub with the babysitter. I hid from intimacy in darker places than she could ever squeeze her tiny body into.

But one day, after months of hiding, I woke to find her on the pillow next to my own. From that day forward, we were inseparable, until my rapist ripped us apart.

He had a tattoo on his hand of an Om. Ironic, because I had named her Om Shanti. "Om" is a vibration often defined as the sound of creation. And "Shanti" means "peace."

For years we clung to one another. She was my very best friend. She was the only living being who truly saw me, and still cared, without pretense, when I walked into a room. She was the pulsating-with-life reflection of God that I trusted with all of me. She was the wag at the door that welcomed me after long days, and her smile at the end of the leash reminded me that life was still unfolding outside my home and outside my head. She was the friend who licked my tears when life demanded more than I had to give.

When the ambulance arrived, Shanti was freed from the bathroom. The policeman who found her said she was too swift; he tried to catch her but could not. The front door had been left open, and Shanti was last seen chasing behind the ambulance that carried me away on the busy streets of Los Angeles.

When I finally was released from the hospital I spent each waking moment posting signs outside and online in search of my best friend. I couldn't breathe without her, couldn't heal, and couldn't sleep.

A month or so went by and I had given up hope of ever seeing her again. I was pulled from a sedated sleep when the phone rang. It was a woman from Boston, 3,000 miles away, who just so happened to be going through missing pet announcements when she read my story. She said the mental image of this poor rescued dog chasing an ambulance led her to call and that she felt compelled to help me search. Her name, she said, was Angel.

One week later Angel called again. "I don't know if it's your Shanti," she said, "but there is a dog with the same huge ears wearing the red collar you described, but without any tags, in a kennel in the city of Downey." Downey was 150 miles from my home. Although I knew it was an impossibility, there was something in the spirit of her voice that gave me hope — that restored a semblance of my faith and propelled me to drive the distance.

I walked into the kennel shaking, and handed the flier and pictures of Shanti to the woman behind the desk.

"There's a dog here that fits this description," she said. "A nurse from a hospital in Los Angeles found her hiding under a bush. But apparently she was headed out here that night, so she brought the dog with her and dropped her off the next morning. If you'll follow me, I can take you back to her. I do hope she's yours. The poor thing is scheduled to be put down by end of day."

As I turned the corner I heard her yelping with excitement. It was her! It was Shanti. I had found her 150 miles from home. She jumped into my arms and I fell onto the floor. She was climbing on my head, wagging every part of her body, and I was laughing and crying at the very same time. We had rescued each other again. And we had both survived to love another day.

The drive home was the very first time I truly exhaled since the trauma. I cried out in gratitude and awe to God until I reached my front door. I immediately ran to the phone to call Angel. When I dialed her number, the automated response said, "The number you have dialed is a non-working number; please check the number and dial again."

~Piper M. Dellums

Room for a Turkey

Genuine kindness is no ordinary act,
but a gift of rare beauty.
~Sylvia Rossetti

was brushing my teeth getting ready for bed when the phone rang. *This cannot be good*, I thought as I hurried to see why I was summoned so late at night. My mind quickly ran through the list of family members that might need my help, but the voice on the other end of the line was only vaguely familiar.

"Lindy, this is Leslie," she said. "I hope I didn't catch you sleeping."

I didn't know Leslie very well, so I was a bit dumbfounded that she would be calling me at eleven o'clock at night. We had children of similar ages and occasionally spoke with each other at various community events, but to say we were friends was a stretch. I assured her that I was still up and asked what she needed. I was afraid it might be something really dire to cause her to reach out to someone she barely knew. Instead, she asked me a most peculiar question.

"Do you have room for a turkey in your freezer?" she asked.

We had lots of room in our freezer. In fact, we had too much room. My husband's business had taken a downturn and we were pretty much at the bottom of our food supply.

"Sure," I responded, "Did your freezer break down?"

"Not exactly," Leslie replied, "but if you will give me directions to your house I will explain when I get there."

This was certainly odd. I told my husband that Leslie was coming over and needed to use our freezer. "Our freezer? Now?" Tom asked. "We hardly know her." I didn't have an explanation for him, so I just shrugged my shoulders.

We quickly changed back into blue jeans from our nightclothes and scurried to meet her outside so the doorbell would not wake our four children.

Pulling up the driveway was a huge freezer truck. Leslie stepped down from the passenger side and explained that her husband serviced a small grocery store that had just lost its lease. They had to empty all the freezers before midnight that night. Leslie and her husband thought it was a shame to just throw all this good food into a Dumpster so she began to go through her list of contacts, dropping off food to anyone she could think of who might be willing to take it.

When she put the turkey in our freezer Leslie noticed that it was pretty empty. "Is it okay if we just fill this up?" she asked. "We have a few more turkeys and some other items." Ours was the last place they planned to stop and anything left would have to be discarded.

While Leslie's husband was bringing in a load of food he noticed a smaller freezer that we also had in the garage. "If that works," he said, pointing to the freezer we had planned to donate, "plug it in and we can fill that, too!"

The four of us walked back and forth between the truck and our freezers carrying armloads of frozen foods. In less than an hour we had filled both freezers in the garage and even the small freezer space in our refrigerator inside the house!

Still not fully understanding what had just occurred, I asked her, "When will you be coming back for all this?"

Leslie just laughed. She rearranged the blocks of food for extra space and wedged one last Butterball in place. Then she shut the freezer door and wiped the frost from her hands. When she turned to face me she replied, "We don't want it back. It is yours to eat, to share, to enjoy! We have been delivering food since 5:00 p.m. and have exhausted our list of contacts. That's the end of it! Thanks for helping us out." Then she and her husband climbed back into their truck, waved goodbye and backed down the driveway.

"For helping *them* out?" I said out loud. Tom and I watched them drive away and then just looked at one another. What had just happened didn't seem real. Even though it was midnight, we were compelled to go back into the garage and look in the freezers. We opened one freezer door and counted four big frozen turkeys. In the other freezer there were three more. Stacked around them were pizzas and freezer meals, vegetables and desserts. These were the expensive, convenient foods that we never bought but often longed to try. Our freezers were so full there was no space left, not even for an ice cream bar!

Leslie had no idea that we were in such a tight financial spot that we struggled to buy groceries. It was not something that Tom or I shared with anyone. My eyes filled with tears because I knew that God had heard the concerns of my heart and was meeting our needs in a miraculous, surprising way. Having plenty of food for my family was a huge stress reliever during a difficult time.

Over the next several months we ate well and shared turkey with friends, family and neighbors. By the time the freezer food finally ran out we were back on our feet. Our income had surged and buying groceries was no longer a problem. We blessed someone else with our now empty extra freezer.

I admit that I still startle at late night calls, assuming the worst, but then I remember that summer night when an acquaintance called. She had a smile in her voice when she asked, "Do you have room for a turkey?"

~Lindy Schneider

Miracle Mike

There are two ways to live: you can live as if nothing is
a miracle; you can live as if everything is a miracle.
~Albert Einstein

"**S**top worrying, Dad! The car is *fine*. I'm going!"
Famous last words from a stubborn eighteen-
year-old version of myself as I flew out the door
to go to my first college party.

The year was 1996 and I was just finishing up my first semester
of community college. I had opted to get the first two years of general
education classes under my belt at the more affordable community
college before transferring to a university in my junior year. The closest
community college was thirty minutes away, so I lived at home with my
dad and commuted. Thus, since a commute was going to be involved,
I had to have a car. After a few months of borrowing my dad's vehicle,
we had finally decided it was time for me to own my very first car.

I was frugal (and so was my family) so we headed straight to the
used car section. I found what I thought was a great deal on a cute
little car, but my dad had his doubts from the start. He wanted to get
it thoroughly checked out before we agreed to purchase it, but not
me. I was in a hurry.

"Daaaad. We can't give every car the third degree. Let's just pick
one already. I want *this* one…"

So, he gave in. Yes! The cute little car was mine!

And no sooner had we driven off the lot than the problems started.

First, the constant overheating. Next, the knocking sound coming from the engine. But oh no — I was not to be deterred. Not Miss Fancy Pants College Girl. I had my own car! So, the needle went to the "H" every now and then? Big deal! I just wouldn't look at it. So, there was a pesky little sound coming from the engine? Hey — I could just turn up the radio. Problem solved!

So, here I was, smack in the middle of ignoring a multitude of warnings, heading out the door to a Friday night party in my college town. I had been looking forward to it for weeks and had been shocked that my dad was allowing me to go. But as the night arrived, along with an unexpected winter snowstorm, my dad started having second thoughts. The snowy roads combined with the problems that were plaguing my car were enough to make him speak up. But I was not listening. I was an *adult*, thank you very much. I was not about to miss that party.

So, off I went.

I swung by and picked up my friend Carrie and the two of us started on our thirty-minute drive in the snow. Just as we hit a long stretch of somewhat deserted highway, the inevitable finally happened. My precious little cute car spit and sputtered its final breath… and died. Luckily, I had just enough time to coast to the side of the highway, just barely over the line onto the shoulder, before it came to a complete stop. And there we were. Two eighteen-year-old girls stranded on the side of the road on a snowy dark night. Now, remember, this was 1996 — this was before we all had cell phones. There was no whipping out the cell and calling Dad for help. No, we were stuck. Really, really stuck.

We started looking around to see if there were any houses nearby. Of course it was too dark to see anyway, but having driven this stretch of road so many times in the past few months, we knew that we had managed to break down in the least inhabited portion of the drive. Walking to get help was not going to be an option. So, we decided to do the only thing we knew to do. We got out of the car and started trying to wave down passing cars.

After having no luck whatsoever, and starting to freeze in the frigid temperatures, we piled back into the car. We hadn't sat there long before — oddly — a truck pulled over to the side of the road in front of us. Looking back, it never occurred to me how strange it was that he knew to stop. We were no longer standing outside the car and there were obviously no lights on inside the car since everything had stopped working. How did he even know there were people in the car needing help? Regardless, there he was. And boy, were we grateful.

Of course, we were hesitant at first to climb into a stranger's truck. At this point, however, we were cold and desperate. The warmth of the truck was too inviting to pass up. As we climbed inside, the first thing we noticed was a picture of what we assumed to be his beautiful wife and two smiling kids taped to his dashboard.

He introduced himself as "Mike" and asked where we were headed. We explained our situation and where we were headed and, as luck would have it, he was heading that very way and would be glad to drop us off. We felt immediately at ease with Mike. He had a jolly laugh and had us giggling along with his family stories by the time we arrived at our destination. As we piled out of the car, we asked Mike if there was anything we could do to repay him. His only answer? "Just be careful, girls. Listen to your dad next time." And with a wink, he drove away.

Had I told him that my dad had told me not to drive that night? I couldn't remember. I didn't think I had... but surely I must have. How else would he have known? I shook off the thought, and headed in to the party. I made the dreaded call to my father to explain the situation. Since it was so late and travel was so treacherous, we decided to stay at our host's house for the night. My dad would pick us up in the morning when the weather had cleared. In the meantime, he would call the tow truck and have the car removed from the highway.

The next morning, my dad picked us up and we drove to the tow lot to get some personal belongings from the car. As we pulled into the snow-covered lot and rounded a curve, my jaw dropped open. I couldn't believe what I was seeing. There, under a thin layer of new snow, sat my car.

Demolished.

I was floored. What? What had happened? My father gave me "the look," to which I immediately responded, "I didn't do that, Daddy! It didn't look like that when I left it, I promise!"

Of course, I was wasting my breath telling him that. Obviously, anyone could see that I hadn't been in the car. Why is that? Well, for one thing, the driver's side was smashed in. You couldn't even see the steering wheel anymore — it was hidden beneath a mangled pile of metal that used to be my precious little cute car.

After a few phone calls and information from the tow truck driver, we learned that after Mike picked us up off of the side of the road, a driver had fallen asleep behind the wheel of a U-Haul truck, veered off the road, and smashed into my car, totaling it. The U-Haul driver, seeing that no one was in the car and realizing that his own vehicle was still in good driving condition, drove on and stopped later down the road to call in the incident. And here's the kicker. After a review of the police report and the U-Haul driver's statement, the estimated time of impact was able to be determined. The time? Approximately two minutes after Mike had picked us up off the highway.

Two minutes.

A mere two minutes later and my friend and I would have been sitting huddled in that car trying to keep warm as the U-Haul plowed into us. There is no doubt in my mind that we would have not survived the impact.

After discovering what happened, Carrie and I asked around to try to find Mike. We described his vehicle to everyone we knew. We even paid for a small ad to be placed in the newspaper asking him to come forward so that we could give him our proper thanks. No one ever turned up.

No one had ever heard of Mike.

I sit here eighteen years later reflecting on that night and I wonder. Somewhere down deep inside, I do believe in miracles.

And I'm certain my Mike was one of them.

~Melissa Edmondson

One Small Gesture Can Reap Huge Blessings

For it is in the giving that we receive.
~Saint Francis of Assisi

On more than one occasion I have pulled up to the drive-through window at Starbucks and the cashier has said, "No charge! The person in front of you is 'paying it forward.'" What a nice way to start the day. I always wish I could run after that person to thank him or her.

Consequently, I always watch my rearview mirror to see if someone I deem "worthy" of that gesture is behind me. Once in a while I do, and I feel like a naughty schoolgirl who just got away with something when I pay for their coffee. I trust my generosity is appreciated although that is not why I do it. Giving in secret is much more rewarding—and fun!

That particular morning, I glanced in my rearview mirror when I got to the drive-through window to pay. An attractive middle-aged woman was driving a shiny sports car with the top down. I could see her gold jewelry glistening in the sunshine. I smiled to myself thinking, *No way does she need me to buy her coffee!* I imagined she had more money than she knew what to do with, but then that voice shouted in my heart: *Pay for her coffee.*

Are you kidding me? I shouldn't have been buying a special coffee for myself, let alone a stranger. My finances were tight and I was already feeling guilty for spending cash on my *own* coffee.

I cringed, but I told the cashier, "Please put the red convertible's order on my tab." As soon as I said it, I felt relief. I knew I had been obedient to that little voice and that was all that really mattered. I paid the server and proceeded to the parking lot. I had a quick errand to run. When I got back to my car, the red convertible was parked next to mine.

"Hi," the lady said. She was gorgeous and reeked of money. "I want to thank you for the coffee this morning. I never expected that."

"You're welcome. I was just 'paying it forward.'" I smiled and started to get into my car.

"Do you have a minute?" she asked.

I nodded and she proceeded to cry. "I don't know why I am telling you this but I need you to know how much I appreciate that cup of coffee this morning."

"There's no need to thank me. I was happy to do it." I felt a twinge of guilt, as I wasn't being totally honest.

"My husband and I may have to declare bankruptcy. Our business partner swindled us out of all our holdings and left us in the cold. This could not have come at a worse time as we lost our son to cancer last month. He was only twenty-six years old. Our hearts are breaking and we aren't thinking clearly. I blamed God and asked Him why He didn't care. I told him it was not fair and there were moments when I didn't know if I could go on. I needed a sign that He still loved us and that everything would work out. When you bought my coffee this morning, I knew that was my sign. I had no idea God cared enough to tell a stranger to buy my coffee. Thank you ever so much. I will never forget this, especially if I am feeling alone."

Now I was the one who was fighting back tears. I told her that I could relate on both counts. We, too, had recently lost our son, and we had also lost our business to partners who stole it from us. I shared how God does indeed care and He would mend her broken heart.

We chatted for a few more minutes, exchanged phone numbers and set up a coffee date.

I sat in my car for a few minutes, visibly shaken. I believe I gave her much more than a cup of coffee that morning. I will be her friend and her confidante. I will lend support — she will know she is not alone.

Next time I am in the drive-through and feel the urge to pay it forward — there will be no hesitation.

~Carol Graham

The Journey
Back from Gone

Hope is the companion of power, and mother
of success; for who so hopes strongly has
within him the gift of miracles.
~Samuel Smiles

happily snacked on a rare Lunchables between the two sets of sliding doors at Kmart, trying to stay warm. My black fake leather coat and spiked hair didn't do much to keep me warm in the Michigan blizzard, but I wasn't allowed to go back to the homeless shelter until 5:00 p.m. I hunkered down so the store manager wouldn't see me as she passed; she knew I was a homeless teen trying to keep warm and would call security to shoo me away.

There had been a time when I was a privileged boarding school student, and for all appearances, I had everything going for me. Beneath my family's smiling Christmas card, though, lay abuse, fear and control. When I graduated high school, my father put me in a Catholic seminary to keep track of me. Too afraid to defy him, I began classes in the seminary he chose. On the second weekend, I had my first drink, then was drugged and raped. After my discharge from the hospital, the school asked me to withdraw.

I had no other choice. I flew home.

That Halloween, I mustered up the courage to tell my father what had been done to me. He played with his fingers, not looking at me as

I wept, recounting as much detail as I could so he understood it wasn't my fault. His expression was inscrutable. After I finished delivering my message, there was a long pause before he spoke.

"Let me get this straight. As of right now, you have run away from home, picked up smoking of all things, drank alcohol and now you've slept around? You have screwed up your life in every way except using drugs, but I suppose you'll go for that, too, soon enough."

He kicked me out. Numbly, I found an apartment on the crime-ridden side of town. Eventually, I met the neighbors, who were hardened addicts. My drug use with them escalated into a full-blown addict lifestyle in less than a month. "I'm too far gone," I would tell myself any time someone told me I needed to fix my shattered life.

After nearly a year of silencing my pain and rage with every substance I could hustle into my body, I experienced a miracle. Lying on a filthy couch in front of the television with a newly emptied needle playing between my fingers, a children's services commercial began. A parade of children excitedly told the camera what they wanted to be when they grew up. Confused by the high, I waited for my turn to announce what I wanted to do. Dark panic crept across my heart as I realized I didn't remember what career or life goals I'd had. The realization sobered me quickly from my high and I began to plan.

I decided to join the military. When I told my parents, they chuckled at me. I quit drugs cold turkey and my new hope tempered the withdrawal. My roommates, however, grew concerned that I would soon be an informant and threw me out with only a sad little backpack containing two changes of clothes. All at once, I was a homeless teen addict with little more than a wisp of hope.

I checked into a homeless shelter after begging my father fruitlessly for help. He had laughed again, enjoying the moment and telling me I would never survive on my own. For years, his derisive chortles would fuel me to push through the months of rape, beatings and sometimes starvation following that final conversation with him.

As I sat, content to warm myself and eat my Lunchables in the safety of Kmart, a woman dressed in a long, teal coat stopped by on her way out of the store.

"Have you had anything real to eat? You're so thin. Let me get you something better than that."

It was the first time I'd been spoken to with kindness in years, and I nearly fell out of the handicap cart I was occupying. The manager spotted me and came over.

"I told you to leave! Unless you are buying something, you can't loiter here. Next time I see you, I am calling the cops."

I was too ashamed of my clearly homeless state to accept the kind woman's offer so I quickly scrambled out into the blizzard. Out of the corner of my eye, I saw a gang member waiting by a corner to jump me. I doubled back and took her hand.

I don't remember her name, but that woman changed my life. She ignored the stares from all sides as she led me to a table in a nice restaurant. She asked me about my passions and goals, and when I told her I was trying to join the Air Force, her face split into a warm smile. She believed in me; beyond my spiked hair, cheap hoop earrings and the piece of string I utilized as a belt, she saw potential. "Maybe I'm not actually too far gone." I thought. The realization was as fresh and life-giving as each course she ordered for us.

The moment we stepped out of the restaurant, the sounds of honking cars coupled with shouts from the alley grounded me. I fell from cloud nine and the dignity I had gained smashed onto the sidewalk. Suddenly full of shame, I fled. I never saw her again.

The mysterious woman had given me a new addiction: hope. For the next two months, I coordinated with a recruiter and went through military enlistment processing.

In April 2010, I left for basic. I went through rigorous counseling and physical training, but the most powerful transformation was left on my growing heart by a parade of one soul after the next, tossing love into the abyss of my self-worth with the same message: "You're not too far gone."

The love that was heaped into me over the years began to spill over; finally I had an abundance to share as well. I began to teach life skills classes to homeless teens. On occasion, friends would ask me how my heart could handle seeing so much brokenness and despair.

"No one is too far gone" had become my mantra.

Six months ago, I decided I wanted a bag of Fritos. Locking up my house, I hopped in my car and rolled to the corner store. What I found changed my life.

The cashier, who was trying to sell a teen girl, panicked and asked if I could take his "friend" to the homeless clinic. She was collapsed on the floor by the register. Not comprehending the situation, I asked the girl if she was all right. Her clothes were caked stiff in filth and bodily fluids. In spite of the meth sores encircling her lips, she looked to be around fifteen years old.

I packed her into my car, assessing the situation. She was too ill to go to the clinic, I decided. She introduced herself as Paloma before passing out. I rushed her to the hospital.

For the sake of her privacy I will say only this: Statistically, she should have died from the profound abuse that made her so ill. I lived with her in the hospital for a week. As she improved, word spread and soon she had a stream of visitors, filling the holes in her heart with love. They joked with her, played with her hair and supplied her with clothing sporting her favorite bands. During her last night in the hospital, I kissed her goodnight on the forehead and turned to leave for the evening. Her sweet voice piped up: "Night Mom. I love you."

Paloma is now my daughter because I know no one is beyond hope. I placed her in a nearby transition home where she has counseling and tutoring to help her learn to read and write. She loves to play with our puppy and cranks the car radio with the same smile as any other kid. Last month, as we drove to a hiking trail, she filled me in on the latest drama with her new friends. One of the friends she described made me nervous, and I worried she would cause trouble for Paloma. Cautiously I asked her if she felt the girl would do well in the home. Her smiling answer, for the hundredth time in my life rocked my world: "Mom, no one is too far gone."

~Skye Galvas

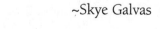

Future Restored

*Love and kindness are never wasted. They always
make a difference. They bless the one who receives
them, and they bless you, the giver.*
~Barbara de Angelis

M y pillow was saturated in tears that winter night. An
e-mail from my college's financial aid office was still
showing on my computer screen. I did not have the
money to return the next semester.

My roommates were comparing their new class schedules, strategizing how to share textbooks, and calculating nap schedules into their new class line-up. They were another step closer to their dreams.

I was packing *my* dreams into boxes, along with blankets, pillows and towels. My dad helped load my belongings into his faded blue pickup truck and I hugged my friends goodbye. There were a mixture of well wishes and hopes for my return, but I was confronting the prospect that my departure was permanent.

As the New Year passed, my social networks were filled with my friends' hopes for the school season. They were returning to school and I was at home. I didn't realize how lonely it would feel.

It was the first official day of classes. I woke to the ring of the phone downstairs. As my father talked on the phone, I started searching for jobs in my area. Now that I wasn't in school, I would need to start paying back my school loans.

The fact that I would not be returning to school became real.

Ever since I had packed my things, there had been this small hope that maybe something miraculous would happen. But as I searched the job listings, I knew it was because I had given up hope. No hero was going to swoop in and save the day.

The clunk of the phone being hastily placed into the receiver and the thundering of my dad's footsteps pulled me from my self-pity.

"Pack up your stuff, you're heading back to school!"

My father's face was flushed as he grabbed a suitcase.

"That was the financial aid office. Someone donated $5,000 and paid the remainder of your spring tuition."

"But Dad, I'm not signed up for any classes!"

A big boyish grin spread on my dad's face.

"Your professors have made room for you. Your first day of class is today. Now get your stuff packed, we gotta move!"

In the ensuing chaos of throwing an assortment of clothes, bedding, and shower needs back into the pale blue pickup truck, my dad explained that the donor was unknown and had just paid off my tuition that morning. My professors had been notified and made a schedule so I could continue to graduate on time. I called my roommates and they cheered and said they would get my side of the room cleared and ready for my arrival.

It wasn't until I was sitting in my first class three hours later, with the pen and notebook we had bought at a gas station on the drive back to school, that I realized that I was actually back. The miracle I thought wouldn't come… came. It was just a little late getting here.

I never learned who paid for my return, but whoever you are, you were my miracle. Thank you.

~Nan Rockey

The Gift Card

Help one another; there's no time like the
present and no present like the time.
~James Durst

The year 2014 had been financially difficult for me. Aside from social security, my only other source of income was writing. During the last six months of the year, several of my manuscripts had been rejected and the idea well was running dry. I suffered a series of health problems; my twelve-year-old car needed a new battery, tires and brakes; the water heater and furnace both quit working; Christmas was just around the corner and my checking account was looking alarmingly anemic. Upon opening one of my Christmas cards, I discovered a gift card along with the note: "Buy something special for yourself."

There was no signature on the card nor return address on the envelope. All of a sudden, ideas began pouring into my head. I could buy a new pair of winter boots, a digital camera or that printer I'd been needing. Maybe I'd buy some of the DVDs I'd been wanting. Wow... this would MAKE my Christmas. Feeling both pleased and oddly embarrassed, I set the card aside until I could figure out who might have sent it.

Along with several other organizations, our church sponsors a food pantry. Local grocery stores provide bread, cereal, eggs, beans, canned goods and produce. Once people register, they can come in and take whatever they need. Everything is free. As I was helping distribute food two weeks before Christmas, I noticed a forlorn-looking woman approaching my counter. She wore a stained T-shirt, threadbare jeans and a denim jacket that showed signs of recent mending. As she placed a bag of dried pinto beans and a small onion into a plastic grocery store bag, I asked if she was shopping for her family.

"No," she replied, "just me." There was obvious sadness in her voice but also a need to tell someone her troubles. "My daughter and her family live in Florida and my husband died a couple of months ago. I was thinking that maybe I'd get some tortillas and beans for Christmas dinner. My husband always liked pintos."

"What was his name?" I asked.

"Jack." She started telling me all about her husband: his crooked smile, the color of his eyes, the years he spent driving a big rig to support the family and the way he enjoyed going to church, especially on Christmas Eve. As she spoke, tears trickled down her cheeks. "This will be my first Christmas without him. We never had a lot of money but now there isn't even enough to buy our grandchildren Christmas gifts."

Searching in my apron pocket for a tissue, I discovered the gift card and handed it to her, saying, "Here — maybe this will help — Merry Christmas."

At the New Years' service, our pastor read the following letter forwarded to him by the food pantry:

Dear friends at the food pantry,

Two weeks ago, I felt as if life wasn't worth living. My husband, Jack, drove an 18-wheeler for a living. On his way home from Colorado three months ago, he ran into a sudden rainstorm on the Interstate. The driver in the car in front of him lost control on the slick pavement and started swerving from lane to lane. In order to avoid hitting the car, Jack drove his truck into a ditch. It overturned and he was killed. I later learned that the people in the car, a mom, a dad and a two-month-old baby, were on their way to visit family in Texas. Jack saved them all.

I was devastated. In all our twenty-three years of marriage, Jack had never wanted me to work. After his death, I tried to find work but, without skills, no one wanted to hire me. When what little money I had left after burying Jack ran out, I started going to the food pantry. Two weeks before Christmas, I came to buy the ingredients for what I thought might be my last dinner — pinto beans and tortillas. However, one of the volunteers handed me a gift card. There was no value printed on the card but I hoped it would be enough to buy my grandchildren a few small gifts. Imagine my surprise when I went to the store and found out the card was worth $500. The unexpected money allowed me to buy Christmas presents for my grandchildren and enough groceries to fill my pantry. Feeling encouraged, I signed up for a call center training program and will begin working in less than a month.

Someone once told me that God always provides. Up until the day I walked into the food pantry, I had begun to doubt that. However, that day, He not only provided, He did it in a way that changed my life. If it had not been for the volunteer and her generous gift, my Christmas would have been quite different. I wouldn't have a full pantry and I wouldn't be looking forward to starting a career and earning a living and my future wouldn't look as good as it does now. I thank that volunteer, the food pantry and all the people who reach out to help people in need. God bless you all and have a wonderful new year — I know I will.

A grateful friend

Most times, we don't learn the end results of our seemingly random acts of kindness, but once in a while, we do. Either way, our reward comes not from the knowing but from the doing.

~Margaret M. Nava

Snow Angel

The best way to find yourself, is to lose
yourself in the service of others.
~Mahatma Gandhi

couldn't believe it was snowing. It never snowed in Ohio this early. When I first drove to Cincinnati to stay with my friends for Thanksgiving, we were having perfectly warm fall weather. Now I was heading into what would become known as the Blizzard of 1977.

My friends begged me to stay a few more days, but I declined. I couldn't remain motionless. It was during the quiet, the stillness, that I felt overwhelmed by emotions, consumed by thoughts of him—Sargent Charles Anderson. My husband. My soul mate and protector, the one and only person who would never leave my side. We had been married only a month before he was taken from me, killed in a helicopter crash during a military training exercise.

I had just passed Columbus, the halfway point between Cleveland and Cincinnati, when the weather turned worse. The flakes joined the land and sky into a blurry white void and my car was skidding all over the highway.

My mind turned inward and I thought of Chuck. He never failed to amaze me. Somehow, he could make any situation right. I wished he was with me, but no matter how much I needed him, he would never be there.

But I still had my son, eight-year-old Sam. I looked at him in the back seat. I needed to find a place to stop. Then, through the white haze, I saw our salvation — a green sign reading "Rest Area." At last, someplace we could wait out the storm.

I pulled in, noticing the car's gas needle nearing empty. It didn't matter as long as we had someplace warm to stay. I parked in the lot and left my son sleeping in the back seat as I went to check inside.

As I trudged through the snow toward the brown pavilion, something felt wrong. There were no lights on. I went to the door, only to find it locked. The only rest stop for miles and we couldn't get in. My heart sank. Whatever strength was holding me together since my husband's death, disappeared. I collapsed into the snow and wept.

That's how he found me. He knelt down and asked, "What's wrong?"

Between sobs, I choked out, "My husband's dead. He died in a helicopter crash."

"Overseas?" he asked.

I nodded weakly.

"I read about it in the newspaper."

I looked up at him in disbelief. How could this man possibly know what I was talking about? Then he added, "I flew helicopters in Vietnam."

Slowly, I regained my composure. He told me he was a truck driver for Fazio's Supermarkets on his way north. He was behind schedule and had to get back on the road, but he asked if there was anything he could do to help. I told him my car couldn't make it through the snow. He suggested I follow behind his rig since the eighteen-wheeler would pack down the snow. It didn't work. My car went off the road before we left the on-ramp.

He climbed out of his cab and forced his way through the snow to my car. He helped me out first, and then turned to retrieve my son. He stopped, momentarily startled.

"He has crutches?" he asked in disbelief. Sam was temporarily using crutches as the result of a sprained ankle.

His bewilderment lasted only a moment as he lifted Sam from the car and carried him to his truck. He drove us to the nearest hotel.

He pulled up to the hotel's front door, stopping right in front of a sign that read, "No Semi-Trailer Trucks." After Sam and I were settled in our room, he turned to leave, reminding me he had a schedule to keep. I don't know why he decided to pull over at that rest stop when he did, where he came from, or how he knew of my husband's death. I only know that at the moment I needed him most, somehow, it seemed like my husband was still watching over me. I thanked the truck driver for all he had done for us, but there just didn't seem to be words to say how truly grateful I was.

As he opened the door to leave, he hesitated. Turning, he looked at me and said, "I never knew why I got out of Vietnam alive. But now I know — it was so I could be here tonight to help you." He closed the door and I never saw him again.

~Gloria Anderson Goss

Chapter

2

Random Acts of Kindness

Just the Right Words

*Beginning today, treat everyone you meet as if
they were going to be dead by midnight. Extend
to them all the care, kindness and understanding
you can muster, and do it with no thought
of any reward. Your life will never
be the same again.*
~Og Mandino

The Cool Guy
on the Plane

Kind people are the best kind of people.
~Author Unknown

A

t this point in my son's life, *The Cat in the Hat* is everything to him. He has the book, the movie, the T-shirt.
As we arrive at Burlington International Airport he
runs to the gift store and demands I purchase *Dr. Seuss
Pops Up* for $24.95. I comply because I hope that this may be the one
thing that will get us through the TSA security check, onto the plane,
and to Chicago without a meltdown.

We board the plane, and I feel like every head turns to us at that
moment, looking at us with a feigned politeness. I know what they
are thinking: "Oh great, it's a family. Please, don't sit in the aisle next
to me." In my head I can even hear the flight attendant saying, "You
can feel free to store your... child in the overhead compartment or
the space beneath the seat in front of you."

We find our seats. My son sits by the window, my wife in the
center, and I take the seat on the aisle. I see this "cool guy" get onto
the plane, a man about my age. He is wearing a concert T-shirt, ripped
jeans, and I can hear that he's listening to punk rock from the 1970s
on his iPhone. This guy represents who I was as a traveler before I
had a child. He takes the aisle seat directly across from me. I want to
say to him, "Look, Cool Guy, you might think you are going to relax

and enjoy this flight, but you are part of my family for the next 1400 miles, so strap in, it's going to get bumpy!"

We take off.

Planes are not designed with children in mind. There is no ball pit, no playground, and an iPad can be entertaining for just so long. To keep my child occupied, my wife and I take turns walking him from the pilot's cabin to the tail. We hit turbulence over Buffalo and need to take our seats. The plane is shaking; my son's ears begin hurting from the drop in cabin pressure, and he has a meltdown. This is a child who has difficulty with crowded social situations and excessive stimulation. My wife and I can do nothing but hold him and live through this moment.

I look over at Cool Guy, and he is staring at me, trying to pour a rum and Coke. I want to say, "Look, Cool Guy, I am sorry if we are ruining your time on United Airlines, but we have a crisis here, and if anyone on this plane needs to drink, it's me!"

My son falls asleep from exhaustion. And that wave of exhaustion flows over my family. I just sit there, listening to the hum of the engine and staring blankly at the SkyMall catalog shoved into the sleeve of the seat in front of me, hoping we will start our descent into Chicago soon.

Then, I feel something hit my shoulder.

It's Cool Guy. He hands me two single serving Bacardi Silvers and a Diet Coke and says, "You need this more than I do." I pour the rum into the Coke and that sweet taste of Puerto Rican rum and bitter aspartame is the most soothing drink I have ever had.

We start talking and he tells me that he grew up in Vermont and now lives in Los Angeles. He works in "the business."

"You're brave to take a kid on a plane," he says. "I have three kids, and I won't drive them from Long Beach to Malibu. Does your son have autism?"

"Yeah," I say and I tell him about some of the difficulties, and some of the triumphs.

He doesn't say, "That must be hard" or "You're a great dad." He just listens to me, allowing me to feel human for just a few minutes. He turns what is the most horrible flight of my life into the most memorable flight of my life.

Whenever I have a heartfelt conversation with someone I am never going to see again I want to say something like, "May the Universe treat you well," but I never end up saying anything that poetic and goofy. Instead as we landed in Chicago, I said "Hey, if you're ever in Vermont again…"

He stops me, smiles and says, "I'll stay in a hotel."

Then, my family and I enter Chicago O'Hare International Airport. My son promptly finds a bookstore and demands I buy him a second copy of the same book I'd bought him two hours earlier in Vermont.

Thank you, Cool Guy, may the Universe treat you well.

~Michael Ray Kingsbury

A Ride to the Future

*Just remember — when you think all is
lost, the future remains.*
~Bob Goddard

Spring 1968. I'm standing on the shoulder of a not-busy-enough road outside of Cortland, New York trying to hitchhike back to campus seventy-five miles away, deep in a sophomore slump. I haven't been to classes in two weeks and I'm contemplating dropping out.

A car heads in my direction as I hold up a cardboard sign with "Oneonta" scrawled on it. As the car approaches, the driver looks at me, then away. He drives past me. I don't blame him or others who have driven by in the last two hours. Why would they pick up a bearded, longhaired stranger wearing ragged cutoffs and a black sweatshirt turned inside out? I lower my sign. I think about packing up my belongings when I get back to my dorm. I decide that college is artificial, disconnected from real life and real people.

"Hey, buddy," someone shouts. A rusty, brown Rambler sits idling roughly across the road headed in the opposite direction. "You go to college in Oneonta?"

"Yes," I say. "Oneonta State. Why?"

"Wait a minute," the driver says. He turns his car around and pulls to the shoulder in front of me. I walk over to the driver's window and see a woman holding a baby sitting beside him.

"Been here long?" he asks. He has a full beard and black-rimmed glasses. His ratty cap and soiled denim shirt tell me he has just come from work.

"A couple of hours," I say.

"It's getting late," he says. "Traffic's thinning out." He glances at his watch and turns to the woman next to him. They exchange a knowing look.

"Get in," he says. "We'll drive you."

"Are you sure?" I ask. "You were headed in the other direction."

"We're just out for a ride," he says. "We don't mind driving you."

The seat behind the driver is filled with an empty car seat, baby stroller and assorted bags of baby supplies. I walk to the passenger's side of the car and climb in. My feet straddle a black metal lunch pail and an oversized steel Thermos. I can't believe it. This man is going to drive me an hour and a half out of his way and then drive back again.

"I'm Aaron," he says. "This is my wife, Sylvia, and my son, Zack."

"Hi," I say. "I'm Dave."

I settle in as Aaron and Sylvia decide on the route. They agree quickly, and we're off.

"Like I was saying," Aaron says. "Today I got home from work and Zack was fussing and Sylvia was stir-crazy, so I decided to take them out for a ride. And here we are on our way to Oneonta."

"If you don't mind my asking, what kind of work do you do?" I ask.

"I work at a truck assembly firm," he says. "I bolt down truck beds. The job don't pay much, but the work's hard." He laughs. His face appears drawn and haggard in the rearview mirror. He seems to be only a year or two older than me.

For a few minutes we ride in silence. I am content to look out my window at the rolling hills of dairy farm country. Farmers on tractors plow swaths of dark furrows. Aaron and Sylvia talk softly to each other, mostly about Zack: when he'll wake up, when he had his last bottle. Their voices merge with the engine noise and the whine of the transmission.

"So what are you taking in college?" Aaron asks. Our eyes meet in the rearview mirror. The question is innocent, but I know it will lead to others.

"English," I say. "Secondary education."

"So you're going to be a teacher?"

"Yes." I am surprised how quickly and definitively I answer.

"That's fantastic!" he says. "Did you hear that, Sylvia? Dave's going to be a teacher."

"I did," she says. Zack wakes and fidgets. Sylvia unbundles him and helps him stand on her lap. She looks briefly over her shoulder at me and then at Zack. "We need good teachers. Don't we Zack?"

I am taken back by this enthusiasm for a career I had chosen by default.

"You got brothers and sisters?" Aaron asks.

"Two older brothers, one younger sister."

"They in college, too?"

"No. I'm the only one."

"So, you're the first one in your family to go to college?"

"I guess so." I hadn't thought about it before.

"Wow! Your parents must be proud of you."

"I suppose."

"You suppose!" he says. "Being the first one in your family to go to college is a big deal."

I am slightly miffed by his tone. I look out my window in silence.

"Don't mind Aaron," Sylvia says. "Aaron's dream was to be the first in his family to go to college, but he couldn't afford to go." She points to a bag next to me. "Would you please hand me a bottle from that bag, Dave?"

I unzip the bag containing several bottles and hand one to her. She cuddles Zack again and feeds him.

"You have quite an opportunity," Aaron says. "Your future is bright."

As we drive on, Aaron asks me about college life. I tell him about living in the dorm, eating in the cafeteria, my instructors, and campus events. I am surprised that I paint a positive picture of my experience. As we drive closer to campus, I begin to doubt my decision to drop out. What was I thinking?

The sun is setting when we arrive. I have Aaron drop me off at the back entrance so it will be easier for him to follow his route home.

I empty my wallet and pockets and hand him $5.83, enough for gas. He protests, but I insist. As we say goodbye, he shakes my hand. I feel calluses and strength as I thank him again.

" Look," he says. "If we don't help each other, who will help us?"

As the car starts to drive off, Aaron rolls down his window and shouts "Hey! Maybe Zack will have you for a teacher someday."

"I'll keep an eye out for him," I say.

"Might be a while," he says.

I watch the car rumble up the hill and wait until the taillights disappear. I'm cold, I am out of money, and I'm two weeks behind on my schoolwork. But for the first time in my life, I see my future in front of me, and I am filled with a sense of purpose. I salvage my sophomore year, finish college, and go on to a successful teaching career. Aaron and Sylvia don't know it, but they didn't just give me a ride back to campus, they gave me a ride to my future.

~David Brigham

12

Dinner Is on Us

We rise by lifting others.
~Robert Ingersoll

My husband Mike and I wanted to celebrate our wedding anniversary in style. We made reservations at our favorite restaurant, but when we arrived our table wasn't ready. Mike looked at the waitress and said, "We'll wait in the bar area. Please come to get us when our table is ready."

"Of course," she replied.

We walked toward the two open seats at the far end of the bar. Mike pulled out a stool for me at the same time the man next to me scooted over to give me room to slide in. I smiled my thanks.

"I'm here on business. Can you suggest some interesting things to do locally when I have some time off?" the man seated next to me asked.

Mike and I immediately shifted our attention to the stranger. We love our adopted hometown and quickly suggested half a dozen fun activities that he might do when he wasn't working. As we turned back toward each other, the stranger asked us a few follow-up questions and we were suddenly drawn into a full-blown conversation.

Within minutes we were on a first-name basis. The stranger's name was Bill. He said that he was a mechanical engineer from out of state who was hired to work on our local hospital's expansion plan. Mike was a mechanical engineer at the time, too. The two men had plenty to talk about. Seconds turned into minutes and strangers turned into friends.

When the hostess approached us to let us know our table was ready, we said goodbye to Bill.

"We're out to dinner tonight to celebrate our wedding anniversary," I said as we got up to follow the waitress to our table.

"Wow! I really appreciate you both taking the time to talk to a stranger then," Bill said. "You could have ignored me and you didn't. Happy anniversary!"

The evening sped by as Mike and I reminisced about our wedding and all the changes in our lives since that day. We also talked about meeting Bill. We marveled at how quickly strangers can become friends. Soon, though, we had to get home. Mike signaled our waiter for the bill. Instead, the waiter smiled and handed us a note:

Thank you again for talking to a stranger. I really appreciate your kindness. Dinner is on me.
Bill

Astonished, we looked at the waiter.

"Yes," he said, nodding his head up and down. "It's true. He paid your bill."

Mike and I walked back to the bar to thank Bill, but his seat was empty. Nothing like that had ever happened to us before. We marveled at Bill's kindness. And we never forgot his generosity.

Years later, as I sat at an outdoor restaurant waiting for Mike to arrive, the hostess seated an older woman at a table next to me. I recognized her from earlier in the day. The first time I saw her she was sitting on a bench on the boardwalk. She was all alone and crying. Concerned, I had sat down next to her.

"Do you need any help?" I asked. "Are you okay?"

"No," she said. "My husband and I had a massive argument. And he stormed off. I'm afraid he'll never come back."

I didn't know what to say, but I sat with the woman, handing her tissues, until she stopped crying.

Now, I was startled to see the same woman sitting at the table next to ours for dinner. I said, "Hello. How are things going with you?"

The woman looked at me and I saw the flash of recognition in her eyes. She leaned toward me and whispered, "Thank you for being so kind earlier today. I'm hoping my husband shows up. I left him a message, asking him to meet me here for dinner so we could talk."

At that moment Mike arrived. As I stood up to kiss my husband hello, I whispered to the woman, "Good luck! I hope everything works out for you."

Mike and I enjoyed our dinner and the colorful sunset. At one point I heard a chair scrape behind me. I hoped the noise meant that the woman's husband had arrived.

After Mike paid our bill and we rose to leave, I glanced at the table next to ours. Sure enough, the woman and her husband were deep in conversation and they were holding hands. As we wended our way through the tables toward the exit we passed our waitress. I asked Mike to stop.

"Do you see the couple sitting at the table where we were seated?" I asked the waitress.

She nodded her head yes.

"We'd like to pay for their dinner. As a surprise."

"I was just about to take them their check," the waitress said and handed it to me.

Mike looked at me, puzzled, as I paid their bill and wrote on an extra message on the receipt:

Wishing you many years of happiness together.

"Here you go," I said.

The waitress smiled and walked toward the couple, note in hand.

"What was that all about," Mike asked, as I looped my arm through his.

"Remember Bill? We're paying it forward," I said as we walked down the boardwalk toward our hotel.

~Darlene Sneden

13

Are You Okay?

*Kind words can be short and easy to speak
but their echoes are truly endless.*
~Mother Teresa

n my two-year-old son's "I-am-going-to-start-crying-soon voice" he said, "Mommy, I'm hungry." We were at the drugstore to pick up some medicine for him, and the day had already been hectic. In fact, the past few weeks and months had been hectic.

Quite frankly, as I stood there looking down at his trusting eyes that expected me to magically provide food, the thought of taking another trip in and out of my hot, non–air conditioned car to pick up fast food or to even head back home and prepare something made me feel like crying. I was hungry as well, but sometimes it was easier to do without food than to endure the extreme Arizona heat in my hot car.

I tried to explain to him that we could go back home after we were done here and get lunch, but that solution wasn't quite fast enough for him, not that I blamed him. Always the inventive one, he quickly found the solution as we walked down the aisle to check out.

"Look, Mommy! Let's get some sandwiches. And we can get something to drink, too!"

Perfect solution, of course! Why didn't I think of that? Perhaps it was the outrageously inflated prices on the sandwiches: three to four dollars a sandwich as compared to a ninety-nine cent cheeseburger at McDonald's. Or, it could have been the fact that this particular solution still consisted of finding somewhere to eat it, since the drugstore didn't exactly have chairs and tables available.

However, it was the only solution that would provide food quickly, and my toddler *did* need to eat, so I gave in and shelled out the extra money for sandwiches and cold juice. Once outside, we deliberated on where we should eat them. My son, of course, was all about eating *now*, but neither one of us had any desire to sit in the hot car any longer than we had to. The quote to fix my air conditioning was over a thousand dollars, and as a divorced, single mom who was attempting to go back to college to get my degree, that kind of money just wasn't floating around.

"Let's eat it outside, Mommy! It can be like a picnic!" my son said excitedly. It was late afternoon at least and there was some shade near our car. After touching the sidewalk, I decided it was cooler than our car would be, so we proceeded to plop down and have our "picnic" on the drugstore sidewalk.

As we sat there eating, I noticed a middle-aged lady pull up in a nice car. She was dressed nicely, like a professional businesswoman. I found myself admiring her calm air and businesslike poise, wondering if I would ever reach that state, or if I would be forever stuck in frumpy, grumpy single mommy status. She looked over at us and smiled as she got out, and I noticed her keep looking back the entire time she was walking into the drugstore. I thought she was just admiring my son. As a mother of a talkative baby, you get used to strangers ooh'ing and aah'ing over your child, so I thought nothing of it.

Not too much later, as we were finishing up our meal, she came back out. She looked at us again, smiling in a friendly manner as she went to her car, but she kept looking back and seemed to be debating something.

Apparently making up her mind, she approached us. I prepared myself for some comment about us not needing to eat outside the drugstore, perhaps an invitation to her church (I got those a lot), or any other type of random event. I was not, however, prepared for what she did say.

"Are you okay?" she asked me. "Do you need anything?" It floored me for a moment, but then I managed to recover from my surprise and stammer a response.

"N-no, we are okay." I mentally begged forgiveness from above for the little white lie. "Thank you though," I remembered to say then as I gathered my thoughts together. Oh, the things I could have said. Of course I wasn't okay, nor did I know if I would ever be. I had entered the world of single motherhood in extreme poverty and was barely surviving from all the stress. We weren't even living from day to day, but from moment to moment. But to my mind's eye, there was so much wrong that not any one thing could be singled out to tell someone. Besides, I did not want to impose on anyone. I realized then how it might look as we sat there on the sidewalk, eating food from a drugstore cooler. Perhaps she thought we were homeless. Perhaps she thought our car broke down.

She hesitated at my answer. "Are you sure?" she asked then, as though giving me another chance if I needed it. I nodded and thanked her again, and she left, though seemingly reluctantly, and with a friendly wave and smile.

It was such a small thing, really — only a few minutes in a vast array of time. Yet, that was eight years ago and I have never forgotten it. For despite my supposedly large family and circle of friends, I was alone in my journey, alone in a sea of troubles and despairs in an all-consuming life of stress. Those who knew me did not make offers to help, or ask if I needed anything.

But this perfect stranger took the time to stop and care. The memory has stayed with me through many years of turmoil and strife, in a mind so filled with stress that most memories don't bother to hang around. This small act gave me hope that perhaps not all mankind is thoughtless and cold, and perhaps there was hope for us yet. Every time I get discouraged about the world and people, this memory brings me yet another ray of hope and keeps me going just a little bit longer, all because one stranger took the time to ask, "Are you okay?"

~May Hutchings

14

A Small and Trivial Incident

We ourselves feel that what we are doing is just a
drop in the ocean. But the ocean would be less
because of that missing drop.
~Mother Teresa

took the letter out of its special box, the letter that I'd held in my hands so many times that it's amazing the typewritten words are still visible. It was written in 1966, a lifetime ago, during the Vietnam war.

The writer was the owner of a beauty salon in Columbus, Ohio who spotted a young Air Force officer in a sportscar drive through a busy intersection where two elderly women were having trouble crossing the street. The young officer did a U-turn, parked his car, and got out to help those two stranded women.

"Even though this was such a small and trivial incident to possibly himself and the public which may have viewed him, I think this gentleman is a fine example of the caliber of men representing our United States military either here or overseas," said the writer.

He included the car's license plate number and mailed the letter to the commanding officer of nearby Lockbourne Air Force Base. The letter found its way into the officer's personnel file and eventually found its way to me.

The letter is precious to me because that Air Force officer was my stepbrother and best friend, Mitch. He was one year older than me, and we'd been raised together since we were young. From the day our parents married, I spent every day with him, first playing together as kids and then double dating as teenagers. When Mitch left for the Air Force Academy, I cried for weeks. When he came home on his first leave, I hugged him so hard that I almost broke his ribs.

I wasn't surprised to learn of Mitch's kindness. We were brought up to be kind, to be polite, and to think of others, and the boys in our family were required to treat all women with respect. Mitch opened the car door for his dates, and sometimes even for me. When a woman entered the room, Mitch jumped to his feet and offered her his chair.

Mitch's kindness was more than just good manners. It was ingrained in his nature. He taught me to row a boat, tried patiently to teach me to play tennis, and helped me learn to drive, without becoming short-tempered with his nearsighted, uncoordinated kid sister.

Now, as I re-read that decades old letter, I pictured Mitch as he was in 1966: twenty-one years old, an average looking skinny young man whose only distinguishing features were his ears. Dumbo ears stuck straight out of his head, looking even larger because of the military haircut. I imagine him approaching those ladies, stranded on the street corner, addressing them as "ma'am," offering an arm to each of them, and escorting them across the street.

After I read the letter, I carefully put it back into the special box. Inside the box were all the letters Mitch wrote to me over the years, the little gifts and cards he sent, and the newspaper clippings of his marriage, awards, and promotions.

Also inside the box was the telegram that was hand-delivered to our parents on May 22, 1968, informing them that the C-130 that Mitch was flying over Laos was overdue, and that he was missing in action. The POW bracelet I wore is in the same box. Years later, the wreckage of the plane was found. Mitch and his crew had crashed in flames in the mountains of North Vietnam. Everyone was killed instantly. The names of the crew, who flew together and died together, are etched side by side on the Vietnam War Memorial in Washington, D.C.

Mitch has been gone forty-eight years, but I know that the kindness he showed that day lives on and has multiplied, and will be multiplied, in ways I cannot imagine.

And because of the kindness of that long-ago business owner, who took some of his time to write, I have his priceless letter that will be handed down to my children and grandchildren, and to future generations, so that they can get a glimpse of the uncle they never knew.

You see, no act of kindness is ever small and trivial.

~Josephine Fitzpatrick

15

Sunshine State

How beautiful a day can be when kindness touches it!
~George Elliston

Growing up knowing that I was different was not easy. The realization that you're gay creeps up on you and then one day you recognize the lie that you've been living. My sudden realization came in high school.

I went to school in Florida with kids who made their distaste for gay people known and it scared me every day. I quickly understood what being gay meant. It meant living a lie. I had to restrain myself from being me, making sure to not be too flamboyant, or talk in an effeminate way, or comment on someone's cute shoes, or hold my partner's hand in public.

In many ways this is what led to my depression. My parents tried talking to me, but as a teen, talking to my parents didn't feel like an option. Looking back now, I wish I would have said something. They asked if I wanted to see a psychologist and I told them no. Nobody really wants to talk about the problems they have.

I struggled every day, trying to suppress my true self, and as a result I became more depressed. Being a naturally happy person, I hid away the "depressed me" when I was around people, but that façade cracks so easily. I would make fun of myself to make others happy, make them laugh, keep them entertained, while beneath the surface I thought about my own death.

Making others laugh made me seem like a happier person. But

during this constant battle to appear normal, I found myself losing ground. I couldn't pretend anymore and I found myself arguing constantly with my friends, pushing them away by accident, which only made my depression worse.

In the tenth grade life got harder. I saw other kids come out to their families and get kicked out. I loved my family and never wanted to lose them because I was gay. So I didn't tell them who I really was.

I thought about suicide but it never became a real possibility until my best friend dropped me. She had decided that being friends with me, a gay boy, would hurt her chances of getting a boyfriend. For days I cried. I dreaded going to school alone, with absolutely no friends. I felt as though I had lost everything important to me because I was gay.

One evening, after a particularly rough day at school, I found myself shopping with my mom. I remember walking through the noisy crowd of teenagers, feeling them glare at me like I was a freak. I heard them whisper to each other, talking about what I wore, how I talked. It was like a nightmare come true. My mother was very perceptive and knew I was having a bad day and quickly tried to take my mind off it by shopping.

I dragged myself through the store right behind her, leaning on the cart, looking defeated. I couldn't do it anymore. I was planning my suicide for later that week.

As my mother searched the aisle for dinner, an elderly woman shuffled up beside me pushing her cart. She was short, had close-cut white hair, and her skin was wrinkled and freckled from too much time in the sun. Her eyes were steely gray. She reached her hand out to touch my cheek.

"It gets better, child," she whispered as she lay her wispy fingers on my disheartened face.

She gave me an empathetic grin and shuffled away, pushing her buggy full of toilet paper and milk. I swallowed hard and turned to my mother. I sputtered, asking if we could leave as tears began to run down my face. When we got into the car I lay down in the back, sobbing into the rough fabric of the seat.

I never really believed in fate, but some things are too surreal to be coincidence. That woman saved my life, and ever since then, her message has stuck with me. No one asked her to reach out to a stranger and tell him it gets better. No one asked her to save a life. All she did was say four words. She never knew me, she didn't know my name, or the weight I carried, and she will never know how big an impact those four words made. I wish I knew who she was so I could tell her how much she has changed me for the better.

I began to volunteer with hospice after that, hoping I would see her somewhere, just for the opportunity to thank her for being alive. But that is the thing about fate; it takes you by surprise and in its wake leaves lasting impressions. Sometimes you don't even know its name.

~Mike Ford

16

The Sign

To teach is to learn twice over.
~Joseph Joubert

had a secret. I had been contemplating the decision for some time but hadn't discussed it with anyone. I didn't know where I would go, but there was this yearning inside of me to leave. Fifty percent of teachers leave the profession by their fifth year. I was in my fourth year as an English Language Arts teacher and I was ninety percent certain I was about to become part of that fifty percent.

I kept praying for a sign to stay. Although many students liked my class and I had received hundreds of letters from former students expressing the impact my influence had on their lives, I still didn't feel like what I was doing mattered.

It was nearing the end of what I had come to think of as my last year. A senior named Lyric who was my teacher aide asked if I could meet him and another student named Ari for dinner to discuss how to prepare for college. I agreed and didn't think anything of it.

It was on a Saturday evening and my schedule for that day was already packed. I attended the funeral of a student that morning and then spent the next four hours at the boys' basketball banquet where I was a varsity assistant coach. By the time the banquet ended I had about an hour to get to the dinner. I was so tired and emotionally drained from the funeral that I almost called Lyric to re-schedule. But I had promised so I got in my car and headed to the restaurant, still in my suit from the funeral.

As I was walking up to the restaurant I saw Lyric, Ari, and Sal, another former student, all dressed up, too.

I asked Lyric, "Why are you guys so dressed up?"

He responded with, "Follow us and you'll see."

The three of them led me to the outside patio where there was a long table full of some forty students, all dressed up. They yelled, "Surprise!"

I had never been more confused and stunned in my life. My brain was trying to process this. My birthday wasn't for another month.

As each student came up and hugged me, I kept asking, "What is this for?"

And they kept saying, "It's for you."

I was dumbfounded. "For what? What did I do?"

I was acting the same way that I had about all the thank-you letters I had received. I didn't know how to accept my students' appreciation.

Lyric and Ari settled everyone down and made a toast: "Mr. Schultz, you have made all of us feel loved. You have made all of us feel like we mattered. We are doing what you've taught us to do. We are being leaders and we want you to know that you are loved, too, and that you matter."

You could have filled up all their glasses with the tears I was fighting back. I was floored and speechless. And it's pretty difficult to make an English teacher speechless.

For four years I had ended every class, every day, with these parting words: "Be kind to yourself and be kind to each other."

My personal motto that I had put on the wall of my classroom, on dog tags that I gave to every student, and on the back of the T-shirts of my basketball players is: Love larger. Give greater. Be kinder. Elevate others.

As I glanced at every face down that long table, I finally saw what I had been teaching transformed from words into action. Their kindness crushed the barricade around my heart and I was finally able to receive love.

All these students, from different grades and different classes, had gotten together, organized this event, kept it a secret, and pulled off the biggest surprise of my life. In doing so, they elevated my life and saved my career.

These wonderful young leaders pulled all their money together and paid for the meal and made the reservation to have the whole back patio reserved for us. I'm so happy I didn't cancel.

Every person at that table gave me a handwritten letter and some kind of gift. The star baseball player gave me the game ball from his first save. The All-American, CIF Champion wrestler, ranked third in the state, gave me the first championship belt he ever won. The track star gave me one of his medals. Another gave me a book and another a pen. And so on. The gifts kept coming and these students became my teachers. They instilled in me this lesson: Our lives matter most in the moments we let others know how much their lives matter.

More than the physical gifts they all gave me, the most valuable gift they collectively gave me that night at the dinner table was making me feel like I mattered. They had no idea just how much this meal meant to me. For so long I was criticized for teaching kindness and talking about love in the classroom, and for so long I wondered if my critics were right. Was I making a difference? Do high school students really care? As the meal went on and the stars came out, these teenagers turned my critics into crickets. I now knew what I had been doing mattered in the biggest way.

A month later I was voted Teacher of the Year by the student body. I definitely had received my sign to stay.

At graduation the Teacher of the Year has to give a speech. It was here that I revealed my secret for the first time — that just a few months earlier I was planning to leave the profession because I thought what I did didn't matter. Then I told the story about those wonderful teenagers who surprised me with a meal, and I told the audience what they served me: a banquet of love.

~Steve Schultz

17

It's Just Your Turn

No matter who we are, no matter how successful,
no matter what our situation, compassion is
something we all need to receive and give.
~Catherine Pulsifer

had assured my husband that I could attend my first doctor visit after the birth our child, Robert, on my own. I knew he was worried he had already taken too much time off work. Besides, I was confident I could handle it. I had stocked the diaper bag and included extra supplies in the car just in case. I had even worked out the timing so I could stick to Robert's schedule by feeding him in the parking lot before my appointment. That way he would be ready for a nap when I needed to head in. My plan went smoothly and I was feeling pretty good when I walked into the office.

I was informed at check-in that the doctor had been out earlier that morning for a delivery and was running late. No problem, I thought. I found a spot in the crowded waiting room off in the back corner where I could set my things and my now sleeping baby.

All was well for about fifteen minutes. Then, Robert woke up very upset. A dirty diaper, I thought. I gathered up supplies and trekked to the bathroom down the hall. Once there, I realized that wasn't the problem. I went back to the waiting room with Robert still crying. Maybe his tummy was bothering him? After ten minutes of pacing the room and patting his back he was still not happy. Could he possibly be hungry again? Nervous about breastfeeding for the first time in public,

I gave it a shot. No good. It actually seemed to make him angrier. I couldn't figure out what was wrong and how to fix it. I considered leaving, but assumed they would call us back soon.

Over the next hour, I repeated the process again and again. Changing the diaper. Pacing the waiting room. Patting his back. Trying to feed him. Changed, paced, patted, and fed. I was exhausted and flustered and near tears. I knew we were disturbing the rest of the women in the waiting room but I had no idea how to fix the situation.

Feeling a bit hopeless, I went to the front desk to inquire about rescheduling. I was willing now to call this whole visit a bust. I was assured that I would be called in just a few minutes. Turning back to the waiting room I got a full view of the others there. All had impatient looks on their faces and I was overwhelmed with embarrassment. Robert was still fussing and had been nearly the entire time we were there. What kind of mother was I if I couldn't get my infant to settle down?

Nervously, I began pacing and patting again. An older woman who had been quietly reading a book caught my eye. "I am so sorry," I blurted out. "I'm not sure what is wrong."

The woman's face softened as she laid her book on her lap. "Oh, sweetie," she said. "Please don't worry about it." Looking around the room, she added, "We have all been there. It's just your turn."

It was one of the kindest things anyone has ever said to me. Perhaps, too, one of the wisest observations on parenting. With her simple words, she had assured me that my current crisis would pass. Sure enough, it did. Moments after, I was called back to the exam room. Twenty minutes later I was headed home with a happily sleeping baby in his car seat.

After seven years and two more kids, that phrase remains a maxim of mine. Toddler throwing a fit in the aisle at Costco? "It will pass. It's just your turn." Kid having trouble at school? Take a deep breath. You can figure out a solution. "It's just your turn." Visit to the emergency room? You can handle this. "It's just your turn."

We tend to only hear about the best parts of people's lives. What they post on social media or say at a play date are the stories they choose to tell. It doesn't always reflect their real challenges and if it does, like my story above, it is told after the fact when some resolution has been reached. When you are smack dab in the middle of the drama it can be hard to imagine getting out of it and tempting to assume that everyone else has it easier than you.

The truth I learned that day from one woman's kind words is that every tough situation will eventually come to an end. Every problem has a solution if you give yourself time to figure it out. Challenges aren't a mark of bad parenting so much as they are part of life. Accepting that "it's just your turn" and approaching those challenges with a positive attitude is what matters. And, maybe too, remembering that some kind words to someone who is struggling can make a real difference.

~Elizabeth Moursund

18

Mirror Mirror on the Wall

She opens her mouth with wisdom, and the
teaching of kindness is on her tongue.
~Proverbs 31:26

When the Weinberg family from Baltimore lost their mother, Mrs. Chana Weinberg, in January of 2012, they observed the traditional Jewish custom of mourning for a period of seven days. Hundreds of people came to comfort them. Besides being a remarkable woman on her own right, Chana was also the wife of the late Rabbi Yaakov Weinberg who was the Dean at Ner Israel Rabbinical College of Baltimore, a prominent Jewish high school and post high school that currently boasts over 950 students.

A couple in their sixties walked in and sat down together in front of the mourners. The husband, a prominent community figure, related the following story:

"My father was a Holocaust survivor. He worked in the girl's school in Baltimore doing maintenance. He was a bitter man, always noticing the bad in other people and in all situations. He would curse often. The students and staff in the school understood how his past had affected him, as did many of the people at the time, and merely took in his insults. They understood that there was little that could be done.

"One day, I went to the school to help my father out. I was four years old at the time. My father was complaining how I was unable to assist him with his work since I was such a fool. Mrs. Weinberg was passing by and heard these comments. She came over to my father and asked if she could borrow me as she needed some assistance in a classroom."

"'I don't know why you would want an idiot like him,' my father said, 'but if you really need him, you can take him.'

"Mrs. Weinberg took my hand and we walked down the hallway. We passed by the women's bathroom and she took me inside. She picked me up onto the counter and we stood side by side looking into the mirror.

"'What do you see?' Mrs. Weinberg asked.

"'I see that I am standing next to you,' I replied.

"'Look again,' she said, 'what do you see?'

"'I see a boy,' I said.

"'What type of boy do you see?' she asked.

"I replied, 'I see a stupid boy. A klutzy boy. A bad boy.'

"'That's interesting," Mrs. Weinberg said, 'I don't see that at all. First of all, I see a very handsome boy.'

"I perked up at that comment.

"She continued. 'I see a very smart boy.'

"'And most of all,' she concluded, 'I see a very good boy.'

"'Mrs. Weinberg then took out of her purse a pocket make-up mirror, a paper and a pen. She wrote the following on the paper, which she stuck onto the mirror: What does Mrs. Weinberg see?'

"'I took that mirror all over with me,' this man at the mourner's house continued. 'And whenever I heard hurtful words I would take out that mirror, look at those words your mother wrote, and look into the mirror. I was not shaken at the slightest because I was confident that I truly was a genuine individual; a good boy. I never got angry.'"

As the man concluded his speech, he reached into his pocket and pulled out a pocket make-up mirror. He opened it up. Inside there was a paper. If you looked closely you could see in faint writing the words:

"What does Mrs. Weinberg see?"

~Avi Steinfeld

Chapter 3

Random Acts of Kindness

One Good Deed Deserves Another

Compassion is not a relationship between the healer and the wounded. It's a relationship between equals. Only when we know our own darkness well can we be present with the darkness of others. Compassion becomes real when we recognize our shared humanity.
~Pema Chödrön, The Places That Scare You: A Guide to Fearlessness in Difficult Times

19

Just When I Needed It

Give yourself entirely to those around you. Be generous
with your blessings. A kind gesture can reach a
wound that only compassion can heal.
~Steve Maraboli, Life, the Truth, and Being Free

"Look, Mommy, look!" Jimmy had a hopeful smile. He was holding a plastic package filled with green army men. "Can I buy these, please?" I returned his sweet smile and told him that he could put his treasure in the shopping cart along with the food and other necessities that we were buying. I watched as all three of my children — Steven, age eleven; Ana, age eight; and Jimmy, age five — chose a few small items to keep them occupied in the car during our long ride from Georgia to New Hampshire.

My heart ached, even as they happily picked out their new toys and activity books. This trip was monumental, and I was both excited and terrified. After divorcing my husband of sixteen years, I was taking the children back home to my family.

The children were happily chattering about their new toys as we stood in the checkout line. As I watched our purchases add up on the register, I started to get nervous. It was obvious that the running total I had been calculating as we shopped was wrong. We would have to put back all the children's toys and activity books.

Tears were clouding my eyes as I told the children I wouldn't be able to treat them after all. They didn't say a word, but their crestfallen faces broke my heart. Ana ran her hand down her pony's mane one last time before she removed it from the conveyor belt. My children were losing their father, their friends, their home, and even their cat.

Suddenly, a petite woman with dark brown hair and two young children of her own stepped in front of me. Because of my tears, I was barely able to see the forty dollars she placed in my hand. When I realized what she was offering, I started to protest, but she put her hands over mine and said, "I've been in your shoes before. Please buy those things for your children."

At that moment, I felt her sincerity and it comforted me deeply. I cried once more, but this time it was tears of relief. I hadn't realized how much strain and loneliness I had been feeling, and how worried I was about the children's loss. This woman may have been human, but, to me, she was an angel.

All I could do was thank her over and over. After I paid the cashier, I tried to give this generous woman the change, but she refused to take it. Her kindness overwhelmed me.

That good-hearted woman had no idea that she changed my life that day. From that point forward, I hoped for the chance to do the same for someone else one day when I could.

Then one day the children and I were shopping in Walmart. We found ourselves in line behind a mom whose infant was sleeping in a car seat in her shopping cart. She was in the same pickle I had been in: she had more items than cash and she was struggling to choose what to buy. My heart went out to her and I knew I wanted to help. When I saw that one thing she had to give up was a bag of red apples, something so simple and nourishing, I didn't waste a moment.

Steven was ahead of me in line, so I asked him to tap her gently on the arm. When she turned I said, "If you will allow me, I'd really be happy to pay for your order."

She stared at me for a moment in disbelief. Then her eyes widened and she replied, "All of it?"

I smiled and answered, "Yes, because a few years ago I was in need and someone did the same for me. Please let me do this for you."

Still looking shocked, she thanked me and added her discarded things back onto the conveyor belt. I could see the weight lift from her shoulders and it brought me such joy. After it was paid for and bagged, the young mother gave us a big smile and another heartfelt thank-you. She left the store with a spring in her step that day. My children and I had quite a bit of springiness, too, along with a strong desire to continue paying it forward.

~Jennifer Zink

20

The Boomerang Effect

*If we all do one random act of kindness daily, we just
might set the world in the right direction.*
~Martin Kornfeld

It had been a horrible day, and it didn't get any better when I went to the grocery store. If I had parked any farther away I would have been in a different shopping center. And then the store aisles were crowded, and littered with abandoned carts, so I just grabbed a couple of essential items and went to the checkout. There I found long lines and cashiers who seemed to be chatting with each other.

I was considering whether I should just put my items down and leave when an elderly gentleman said, "You don't have much. Why don't you just go in front of me?"

"Thank you, but that's not necessary. You don't have much either," I said, looking at his cart. He was obviously shopping for one.

"I insist," he said and backed his cart up to make room for me. I didn't have a cart, and the gallon of milk I was holding was both cold and heavy, so I didn't wait for the offer to come again. I stepped up and put my items on the belt.

I finally moved forward and the clerk, without a single word of acknowledgement, rang up my items. I asked for a scratcher lottery ticket as well. Reluctantly he complied. First he couldn't get the case open and then he accidentally canceled the transaction and had to ring it all up again. I gave a weak smile to the nice gentleman who had been so kind to me, certain that by this time he was thinking about that old adage that no good deed goes unpunished.

When the transaction was finally completed I turned and handed him the ticket.

"Oh, no," he said, shaking his head. "You don't have to do that."

"I know. But I really needed a kind word today." I laid it down with his items. "If you win a million bucks, look me up," I said with the first smile that had graced my face that day and starting walking toward the door.

"I will!" he called out, laughing. "Did you see that?" I heard him ask the clerk. "She just gave me a lottery ticket!"

It was a one-dollar scratcher. If he won, he certainly didn't win much. But that made no difference to him. My gesture of appreciation and acknowledgement meant as much to him as his gesture of kindness did to me. As much as that seemed to be the highlight of his day, he has no idea how much he improved mine simply by noticing a fellow human being who needed a little bit of kindness and letting me cut in front of him in the checkout line.

For the rest of my day it was as if a cloud had been lifted. Suddenly I found parking spaces where I needed them, traffic lights turned green as I approached intersections, and the world seemed to be a little brighter.

I hope he won, because I know that I did!

~Beki Muchow

21

Floating Through Traffic

There is no angry way to say "bubbles."
~Author Unknown

At my friend's wedding, we were given little bottles of soap bubble solution in place of rice or birdseed. When the bride and groom emerged from the building after the ceremony, we greeted them with a delightful shower of bubbles.

I loved my little party favor, so when I stopped at a red light on my way home, I took it out and blew bubbles out the window of my car. I watched the bubbles as they floated on the breeze, and I saw the man in the car next to me grinning and laughing as the bubbles swirled around his car.

From then on, whenever I was stopped at a red light or stuck in traffic at the bridge on my way to work, I'd blow bubbles. Sitting in traffic probably isn't high on anybody's "good time" list, but I soon realized that I was looking forward to my daily rush-hour backups.

I loved the way people responded to the bubbles. Kids waved. A guy on a Harley honked his horn. Teenaged girls in a bright blue Beetle with pop music blasting from their radio cheered. A group of guys in a construction van gave me two thumbs up.

I loved it so much that I started carrying bottles of bubble solution in my car so I would never run out. I got a new bottle, one with the wand attached to the cap, so the excess solution wouldn't drip on my car or me. I was becoming quite the bubble connoisseur.

One hot day I was driving to a friend's house, and traffic on the freeway slowed to a crawl as cones moved three lanes into two, and on ahead, two into one. Cars were jockeying for position — pushing and crowding to get ahead. People were honking, and you could almost feel the tension in the air. I was about ten cars away from the spot where two lanes would merge into one when the traffic came to a standstill the way it does when there's an accident ahead. I waited a minute or two, but we were definitely not moving... so I pulled out my bubbles and began to blow. After a minute I noticed a couple in a car just about next to mine had rolled down their window, waving to get my attention. "That is the BEST!" the man shouted.

I had just bought some small refill bottles earlier that day, and they were sitting in a bag on my passenger seat, so I held up a bottle and yelled back to them: "Want some?" The woman squealed, "YES!" as the guy looked around — seeing that the cars still were not moving — and jumped out of his car toward mine. I tossed the bottle to him and he quickly ran back to his car. Soon we were blowing bubbles in tandem.

When the traffic started moving again, my bubble-blowing buddies yelled "Thank you!" and waved me on ahead.

I thought that was the highlight of my bubble blowing adventures, until a few weeks later, en route to work and backed up at the bridge once again, I inched toward the tollbooth. When I got there, I held out my money, and the toll collector waved me on: "He paid for you," she said as she indicated a car that had just pulled away from the booth. "He said thanks for the bubbles."

I still carry extra bottles in my car, and I've given out many more when stuck in traffic jams over the years. While I use EZ Pass at the tollbooths now, I still don't mind little traffic jams. It's amazing what an effervescent effect those little soap bubbles can have.

~Deb Cooperman

22

Table Talk

Technology is notorious for engrossing people so
much that they don't always focus on balance
and enjoy life at the same time.
~Paul Allen

As we get out of the car our son announces, "Phones stay in the car."

"I know, I know," growls our twelve-year-old granddaughter.

"Why do you always have to tell us that?" grouses her fifteen-year-old brother.

Our son's wife winks at us. "He's reminding Grandma and Grandpa," she says. "They may not know our rules."

She goes on to explain: "We have a family rule that no one may bring their cell phone or iPad or tablet—well, anything electronic, to the table."

We lock our phones in the car. I suspect we'll have to wait for a table since the parking lot is crowded. We do. Even though the restaurant is filled with families, there is little noise. All I hear are a few quiet conversations and the ding of forks on plates.

After a few minutes we're led to our table. Maybe it's because my husband and I don't eat out often, but the quietness unnerves me. Where are the whiny kids? The teen versus dad arguments? The mothers yelling at their kids? The loudmouth braggadocios? And then I look around. Everyone, even the young kids, is staring at some kind of screen.

The silence is broken when the six of us sit down. We start talking, sometimes having multiple conversations. The waitress stands patiently and waits for our orders. Once our food comes, we continue to chat. It's not that we haven't seen each other for a long time — we have — it's just that a lot has happened in the week since we were last together.

An elderly couple at the table next to us are finishing their dinners and conversing quietly. I notice that they shoot us a few glances, and wonder if our constant chatter is annoying them, but I don't mention it to the others. They must have left, because the next time I look two women are sitting at the table. They scan their menus and then their iPhones.

Of course, the kids want dessert. We sip our coffee while they scoop every last morsel into their mouths. My son signals the waitress for the check.

She hesitates when she brings the black vinyl folder to our table and I assume she's confused about whether to give it to my husband or son. The half-smile on her face turns into a huge grin when my son's reach surpasses his father's, and he snags the check.

He reaches in his pocket for his wallet and takes his time finding the right credit card. The smiling waitress continues to stand there, which makes me wonder why she appears so happy.

My son opens the black vinyl folder — it's empty. "You forgot the check," he tells her.

"There isn't one," she says with a giggle. She pauses for a few seconds before saying: "Someone else paid your bill — and the tip too."

"Why?" asks our son, his wife and myself in unison.

"They loved that no one was connected," she says. "They loved watching you guys talk. The woman went on and on about how nice it is to see a family eating and talking instead of looking at 'electric games' — that's what she called them."

For a change everyone at our table is at a loss for words.

Then we all start talking at once. My son's voice rises above the others. "Where are they?"

"We want to thank them," adds his wife.

One Good Deed Deserves Another | 71

"Oh, they left after you ordered dessert," the waitress says. She lifts her chin indicating the table next to us, the one where the elderly couple had been sitting.

We spent the next fifteen minutes discussing this goodness and came up with a plan. The next time either of us sees a family eating at a restaurant without looking at anything electronic, we'll pay it forward, just like what happened to us. The kids are adamant that they'll want to stick around to see this family's reaction; the grown-ups differ. The one thing we agree upon though, is this… first we need to find this family.

~Polly Hare Tafrate

23

A Good Bet

*If you light a lamp for somebody, it will
also brighten your path.*
~Buddha

Our New Jersey home was near a thoroughbred race
track, but we had never been there together. We
lived a frugal life — carrying lunch to work, skipping vacations, and staying in. But it was our fif-
teenth wedding anniversary, so we decided to splurge this one time.

I had grown up with horses and racing. My father, a successful
textile executive, was a one-time racehorse owner, and my mother had
always loved to cheer me on at horse shows. I had a magical twenty-
first birthday at this track with my parents and siblings. We reserved
the best table at the track's gourmet restaurant, and I ran through a
few hundred dollars in an hour making bets.

Those extravagant days were long gone though. Since retiring and
moving to Las Vegas, my father had lost a sizable chunk of his fortune
watching dice, not horses, disappoint him.

Now I was back at the track for another special occasion, with
my husband. We chose a chic Italian restaurant near the track and
arrived early enough to dawdle over dinner. We ordered appetizers
and soup and entrées, and even a glass of wine each. Halfway through
our very delicious dinner, Frank and I noticed that the two diners at
the table to our right seemed to be looking for something under their
table and all around. The elegantly dressed woman appeared to be in

her late seventies, and her much younger male companion looked like he might be her son. The woman kept touching her ear.

"Did you lose an earring?" I asked.

The woman shook her head and looked worried.

"My hearing aid," she said. "My son finally convinced me to get it this week, and it's so expensive, and…" she trailed off. "My son's eyes are better than mine, but he can't find it either."

No waiters seemed to be helping, and the other Saturday night diners seemed to be purposely ignoring the small commotion.

Frank stood up immediately. "Let me look," he offered. "You never know, maybe a fresh eye will spot it."

"Oh, it's very small, and it's the same color as the floor," the woman said, adding, "I don't want to bother you."

"That's okay, let me try," Frank said, and dropped to a crouch, moving a few inches at a time, eyes and hands sweeping back and forth.

The woman sat down slowly, rubbing her back. Her son was tracing his foot back and forth away from the table and back. Meanwhile, I stood over their table, scrutinizing, moving the cutlery, using a fork to look under the bread in the basket, running my hand over the tablecloth, shifting the plates.

"Thank you so much, you two," the woman said. "But I'm afraid it's lost forever. Your dinner's getting cold; please don't worry."

I saw tears forming in her eyes. Soon, her son sank back into his chair, too. But Frank kept looking until one of them thanked him again, and he too, finally sat down to finish eating.

Ten minutes later, as we finishing our entrées, the mother and son were sipping coffee, silent.

"I'm going to take one more look," my husband said, lowering himself back to the tile floor. "You never know, it may have rolled a lot further away." In his only pair of dress pants, Frank crawled from table to table, moving his hand slowly one way and then the other, over patches of floor.

Soon, the manager appeared. The woman explained, and he left again, not offering any assistance.

A moment later Frank stood up, peering at something clasped

between his thumb and forefinger. He extended it toward the woman. "Is this it, Ma'am?"

It was.

"Oh yes, oh my yes!" she exclaimed, clutching his arm, half-hugging him. Her son shook Frank's hand and added his thanks. She continued, "How can I ever thank you? You've saved me a lot of money and a lot of worry! That's a mitzvah, you know."

I didn't know the meaning of that expression until I looked it up later on, but I knew she was saying my husband had done a kind thing. If you knew my husband, I thought to myself, you'd know that this is nothing out of the ordinary.

"Please let us buy you coffee and dessert," she offered. "I'd like to thank you properly."

Frank shook his head, and so did I. "No thanks, I'm just glad you found it. I know what it's like to have to pay for something like that."

"Well, we're very grateful," the son said.

We all exchanged goodbyes, and they left. Frank and I ordered coffee and dessert, lingered and talked. I could tell he felt good about helping.

When we asked for the bill, the waiter shook his head and explained, "That's been taken care of, sir, tip and all. The people who were at the next table said it's a thank-you gift."

Giddy, and a little embarrassed, we headed to the track. We'd missed the first few races, which meant we didn't have to pay the entry fee. We watched a few races, betting two dollars here and five dollars there, mostly choosing based on horses' names and not their records. We were mostly losing but it was fun.

Then we looked over the horses in the final race and one name caught our eyes: Lady's Gratitude.

We hadn't had to pay for our anniversary dinner, so I said, "Let's go for it." We plunked down twenty dollars on Lady's Gratitude.

Frank's determination to find that stranger's hearing aid was matched by that long shot filly's. She won by a nose, and the payout on our twenty-dollar bet was 250 dollars. It was a memorable anniversary and it's a treasured story we've told many times since. More than that, it reaffirmed that an act of kindness, especially coupled with a bit of perseverance, is never wasted. And sometimes, it gets you yet another anniversary gift — in our case, new patio furniture.

~Lisa Romeo

24

Noted and Seconded

Act as if what you do makes a difference. It does.
~William James

've been a youth group leader at my church for a number of years. One of the kids' favorite activities is called ARK night, with ARK standing for Acts of Random Kindness. A couple of times a year, on a Sunday night, we venture out into our community to perform kind acts for others.

We split into small groups and complete assignments around town. One group typically goes downtown to where the homeless population congregates and hands out sandwiches and cold water in the summer, and hand warmers and hot bread in the winter. Sometimes a group makes posters and goes to local police and fire stations to say thank you. We often have groups visit nursing homes and hospitals to share a smile and conversation with the patients.

One time, the group I was chaperoning left Post-it notes with positive messages on the windshields of all of the vehicles in the visitors' parking lot at the hospital. The hope was that someone who was sad or worn out after visiting a patient would be cheered up by our note.

We had spent the first part of the evening at our church, with the kids writing positive messages on their Post-it notes, things like "God loves you," "Keep smiling," "We are praying for you," and "Have a nice day." One girl had curvy, beautiful handwriting and she decorated the corners of her notes with pretty multi-colored hearts.

After the kids left their notes on all those cars, one girl said to me,

"We didn't see one single person. How will we know that our notes made a difference?"

"We'll just have to trust that they did," I said. Normally, the kids could see the reactions of the people they were helping, and I could tell they were frustrated by the lack of interaction with people during this assignment. I wondered about it, too. Would the notes cheer anyone, or would they be tossed aside like the advertisements that are sometimes left on car windshields?

Monday morning I was scrolling through my Facebook feed and I found a post by a friend of mine who was going through a rough patch in her life. She described a series of not so pleasant things that had happened to her over the weekend. "But then," she added, "I was hurrying to work this morning and stopped quickly at the drive-through bank to make a deposit. There, on the side of the kiosk, was the nicest little note. It made my day." She included a photo of the note.

It was one of our sticky notes! I recognized it immediately from the curvy little hearts around the edges and the nice message: "God loves you, have a nice day." I have no idea how that note traveled from the hospital parking lot clear across town to the drive-through lane at the bank, but I'm pretty sure that it must have cheered some stranger's heart enough for him or her to want to pay it forward to another stranger. I smiled and couldn't wait to tell the youth group. Mission accomplished.

~Jill Haymaker

25

The Driver's License

*If we have the opportunity to be generous with our
hearts, we have no idea of the depth and
breadth of love's reach.*
~Margaret Cho

t had been a typical busy day at Frank Family Vineyards in Napa Valley. As I was closing up I noticed a driver's license in the cash register drawer. There was a note with it explaining that someone had found it in the women's restroom.

I had almost finished counting the register receipts when the phone rang. It was a woman named Christine Lewis, and she was the mother of the young woman who had left her driver's license behind. She said they were returning to San Francisco and had just started across the Golden Gate Bridge when her daughter realized she had left it. She was flying back to New York the next morning at 6:30 a.m. and needed her driver's license to board the plane.

Christine said they were meeting friends whom they hadn't seen for several years for dinner in San Francisco. She asked if there was anyway I could hide the driver's license on the property; they would drive all the way back up to Napa after dinner to retrieve it.

I could have left the license under the front door mat of the tasting room, but I thought about what a bad way it would be for them to end their day after having such a great experience here in Napa Valley. And then I asked, "Where are you staying in San Francisco? I don't have anything planned tonight. Go ahead and meet your friends for dinner. I will put your daughter's license in an envelope and leave it at the front desk of your hotel."

Christine asked me where I lived. When I told her that I lived ten minutes from the winery she was surprised. After all, San Francisco is an hour and a half away, so it would be a three-hour round trip.

The phone was silent and then she asked, "You would do that?"

I said, "Sure, I don't have anything planned tonight." I hung up the phone and a few minutes later it rang again. It was Christine asking if there was someplace they could meet me halfway. I told her not to worry about it. They should just meet their friends.

I locked up the building, stopped at my house to change my clothes, and then started my drive to San Francisco. I had just passed Rutherford Grill when my cell phone rang. It was my good friend, Babs. She wanted to know if I would like to go to dinner. I told her, "I would love to go to dinner!"

Babs said, "Where do you want to go?"

I said, "How about the City?"

She said, "The City, you mean San Francisco, on a Thursday night?"

I told her I was driving there to drop off someone's driver's license and if she wanted to go with me, I would turn around and pick her up in St. Helena and I would explain everything to her on our way.

When Babs and I were almost to San Francisco, Christine called and asked if we would come by the restaurant where they were eating dinner instead of dropping off the license at their hotel. They wanted to thank me personally and her husband wanted to pay me for my gas. I told her I would stop by the restaurant, but I absolutely would not take any money.

When Babs and I walked into the restaurant, almost everyone started clapping. A young woman ran up and hugged me. I instantly recognized her from the picture on the license. The looks on their faces were priceless and I received lots of hugs. The husband wanted to pay me and again I declined. He then insisted on buying dinner for us.

After the family left, Babs and I sat at our table sipping wine. She was quiet for a few minutes and then she told me that this restaurant had a special meaning for her. Her oldest son, who had passed away a few years earlier, had his graduation dinner there. It was bittersweet for her, but she was glad to be there again. What a coincidence, that we had ended up in this restaurant that held special memories for her. It was a fitting end to a beautiful day.

~Pamela Schock

26

Kindness Gives Back

Carry out a random act of kindness,
with no expectation of reward, safe in the
knowledge that one day someone might
do the same for you.
~Princess Diana

had a quick thirty-minute layover in Detroit before heading home to Toronto. After rushing up the jetway I embarked on a brisk walk, knowing that my gate was on the opposite end of the airport. I got there with five minutes to spare and stood waiting for "Group 3" to be called.

I was tired and had a coaching call scheduled for an hour after I was set to get home. I guess you could say that time was of the essence. But then I heard the announcement: "It seems we have overbooked the flight. Would anyone care to volunteer to stay for the later departure?" There were 100-plus people and not a single person volunteered.

The next flight was in four hours, at 7:30 p.m. I looked around and saw businessmen needing to get home for work, moms needing to get home to see their kids, kids needing to get home to see their friends, and more importantly, I saw people that needed to be helped. Even though I wanted to be home just as much as anyone, something inside me said that I should volunteer. I should extend some kindness to this group of strangers. The gate attendant had said that the flight couldn't board until someone volunteered.

I picked up my bag and approached the desk. I said, "I volunteer as tribute!" The gate attendant smiled and understood the reference to *The Hunger Games*.

As she was processing my ticket, I looked around at all the passengers who could now board their flight and I was happy that I had been able to help. The attendant handed me my boarding pass for the later flight and then said, "This is for your kindness." She handed me another piece of paper and I saw that it was a seven-hundred-dollar voucher to fly anywhere in the world during the next year!

I got to my new gate and took a seat next to a power outlet so that my laptop would make it through the extra four hours. I rescheduled my coaching call. And then I got a lot of work done, which was a wonderful silver lining.

When my flight started boarding, I was surprised to discover that my new boarding pass was for a seat in first class. I boarded the plane, and I thought about how grateful I was for everything that had happened, and how it was all because of the ripple effect of kindness. I gave with the intention to serve others, with no thought of reward, and that kindness was returned to me with an upgrade to first class and a big voucher for future travel.

~Juan Bendana

27

Walk a Mile in Your Shoes

One shoe can change your life.
~Cinderella

September 11, 2001 was a glorious morning in New York City. I was working in my studio as a kaleidoscope of rays from the sun glimmered and reflected through the glass skylight over my head. When was a day so perfect?

"Boom," a blast, a roar suddenly froze me to the spot. I looked out the window, anticipating a sun shower. What else could explain such an unearthly sound? I thought of the childhood fairytale with Chicken Little running through the town, screaming, "The sky is falling, the sky is falling."

A few minutes later, the phone rang. It was my husband: "A plane just hit one of the towers at the World Trade Center."

"I heard it," I answered, unruffled, as though it was just another day in turbulent New York City. I live in Brooklyn Heights, just minutes away from downtown Manhattan across a bridge. It's no surprise that I would have heard the crash.

"It must have been a small plane going into the tower. Maybe the pilot had a heart attack or lost his way," I conjured up, visualizing in my mind, a private plane hitting the side of the tower.

I turned the television on to get the details. A second plane, an enormous aircraft, was crashing into the second tower.

"Oh my God," I shouted, recalling how years ago Orson Welles went on the radio with a fictional Martian invasion news story that had listeners believing it was true. But this wasn't that. I had heard the explosion, seen a plane go into the tower. Now the commentator was speaking of another plane that had hit the Pentagon. I stood paralyzed, not able to process what was happening.

My husband's voice brought me back to the moment. "They're closing all the offices in my building and, apparently, much of Manhattan. I'm coming home."

Little did we know that all means of commuter transportation in New York City were being shut down. Thousands of people were walking for hours over bridges, through the tunnels, on highways, to get to their homes. Those who lived too far away slept at friends' houses, in offices, in the train stations.

My home in Brooklyn is on Clinton Street, a direct path to and from the Brooklyn Bridge. My neighbors and I stood outside our houses, watching the barrage of people coming our way.

"Can I help you? Can I help you?" we repeated over and over again, offering bottles of water. Since so much of the debris from the explosions sheathed city streets, many of the people were covered from head to toe with soot, like mummies in dreamlike states. They were exhausted and stunned.

A young woman in a bright red dress was painfully hobbling down the street in her high heels. I was wearing a pair of old yellow flip-flops and stepped out of them to give them to her. "Please take these. You'll be so much more comfortable." She hesitated, but then gratefully accepted my meager offering.

"Thank you, oh thank you." She put her hand on mine. "I don't think I could have made it all the way home in these," she said, pointing to the red and black high heel shoes, that she must have carefully matched to her dress that morning. What matched no longer had much importance. She slid her feet into the yellow flip-flops, with a big sigh of relief. "Aah. I'll return them, I promise."

"There's no need. Keep them." I touched her arm as I answered. "I have others, they're just cheap plastic flip-flops."

That night, the sandals were returned and back on my doorstep. The following day, the bell rang and my new friend Anna stood at my door with a bouquet of yellow roses. "Yellow roses are for friendship," she said as she offered them to me.

I invited her in and we spoke for quite a while about life and what mattered and what went to the top of our life pyramids. "My mother wants to meet you," she said with a smile.

I laughed and asked, "Why, does your mother want to know where I bought the flip-flops for $1.99?"

We laughed and she took on a more serious tone. "My mother wants to meet the lady who stepped out of her shoes for me." Her gratitude felt disproportionate for what I considered the smallest gesture on my part. But I suppose, on that day, no gesture or kindness seemed insignificant: a state of grace had come over New York City.

Our city came to a complete halt for a few days. The frantic nature of our lives changed. We were scared and humbled, and focusing on the essentials. ˆ It was a time for reflection, compassion and ultimately, gratitude that we could depend on each other. We could be kind. The unimaginable had happened and we were witness to it and pulled together in spite of it.

A few months later, a letter came to me from Anna. Her appreciation was limitless. It was a gift certificate for a local restaurant that we both loved, and with it a note:

I will always remember you for your kindness on that terrible day, and it was an honor to walk a mile in your shoes.

~Linda Holland Rathkopf

Chapter

4

Random
Acts of
Kindness

One Little Thing,
One Big Difference

*No kind action ever stops with itself. One kind action
leads to another. Good example is followed. A single act
of kindness throws out roots in all directions, and the
roots spring up and make new trees. The greatest work
that kindness does to others is that it makes
them kind themselves.*
~Amelia Earhart

A Wise Friend

*All that is valuable in human society depends upon the
opportunity for development accorded the individual.*
~Albert Einstein

This story begins one late afternoon in Carl's back yard, in Detroit, Michigan. We were sixteen years old. We had just finished playing stickball, and I was about to get on my bike to go home.

"Wait a minute," Carl yelled.

He ran into his house and came back with a book for me to take home and read. All he said was, "See if you like it."

I said absolutely nothing. I hated school because I hated reading. I kept the book for a couple of weeks and then returned it unread. Carl never asked me if I liked it or not.

During the following two years Carl lent me three more books. The last one was *Martin Eden* by Jack London. Each time I returned them unread.

A few days after graduating from high school, Carl asked, "Benny, what college are you going to?"

"I'm not going to college."

"Why not?" he asked.

"Because my father can't afford the seventy-five dollars for tuition."

"Is that it?" Carl asked.

"Yes," I said.

I lied. I had no intention of going back to school now that I was out.

The following day Carl knocked on my door and handed me a check for seventy-five dollars from his father.

"I think that should do it." he said.

Once again I was in shock. What could I say, except thank you? Because I was working full-time in my brother's bakery, I enrolled in two classes at Wayne University in Detroit part-time at night.

Halfway through the semester, and after receiving failing grades on exams and essays, I decided there was no way I would ever become a decent student and get satisfactory grades. I dropped out of college and continued working in the bakery.

By now, I was twenty years old. Carl had just finished his second year at Swarthmore College in Pennsylvania and had come home for summer break. Once again we got together to have a good stickball game in his back yard.

After the game, he took me aside and asked, "So Benny, what are you doing these days?"

I hesitated and sheepishly answered, "I'm working in a slaughterhouse butchering cows."

Once again he asked me why I wasn't going to college. This time I told him the truth.

"I hate school and I hate reading."

It was 1954, a year after the Korean War ended, and the military draft was still a requirement. Carl suggested that I volunteer for a couple of years and this would give me time to think about what I wanted to do with my life.

After failing a written exam to get into the Navy, I was accepted into the Army. After basic training, I spent the next eighteen months in a heavy mortar infantry company in Neckarsulm, Germany.

Two years later I was honorably discharged. I had no more of an idea what I wanted to do with my life than when I went into the Army.

After mustering out of the Army, I returned home to Detroit where I tried to get my old job back at the slaughterhouse, but no jobs were available.

I took my mustering-out pay and drove to Los Angeles, California, to visit my younger sister who had run away from home at the age of seventeen.

While in California for only two weeks, I met a young lady who told me to take advantage of the GI Bill. I took her advice and drove back to Detroit and took the Veterans Administration's aptitude tests. After recognizing my lack of reading skills, they suggested I go to a trade school where they taught radio and TV repair.

This time I took the suggestion and ran with it. The GI Bill covered all costs.

By the time I graduated, I was twenty-three years old. I hadn't spoken or written to Carl for over four years.

On January 11, 1958, with just one month to go before receiving my diploma, I had a blind date. On January 22nd, I asked her to marry me.

A few days after we got married, a wedding gift arrived in the mail from Carl. It was a book.

I opened up the book and inscribed on the inside were the words:

TO THE WASSERMANS ON THEIR WEDDING DAY.
Carl

The book was *Martin Eden*, by Jack London, the last one he had lent me six years earlier.

"What a waste," I said, "It will never get read."

But then, the more I thought about it, the more I realized that Carl was trying to tell me something. I decided to phone him so he could tell me. No one answered.

"What do you have to lose?" my wife asked. "Carl took the time to send it to you; you might as well take some time and read it. Once you've read it you can do anything you want."

A couple of days later I started to read the book, which had 411 pages and no pictures! There were many words on every page that I didn't understand. I decided to buy a dictionary. By the time I finished reading the book, which took me over two years, I recorded the definitions of 747 words in the margins.

Now I understood why Carl wanted me to read the book. The main character, Martin Eden, had my own poor educational background, but managed to educate himself and become a published author.

For the first time in my life there was a glimmer of hope that I, too, did not have to remain ignorant the rest of my life.

Once the world of books opened up to me, it became a road of exhilaration and excitement at the turn of every page. Only those who have been buried so deeply in ignorance, and have been able to see the light by reading books, can possibly understand the thrill of becoming enlightened. My life would never be the same again.

What happened to my wise friend, Carl? That teenager, who took such an extraordinary interest in a kid from the other side of the tracks, went on to graduate from Harvard Law School and became a civil rights attorney. He was still caring for the less fortunate. Within a few more years he was a member of the Detroit City Council. And then, in 1978, at the age of forty-four, Carl was overwhelmingly elected to the United States Senate from the State of Michigan. He went on to serve for thirty-six years, elected to six terms by his constituents.

In 2007, Carl Levin, the teenager who showed such kindness, agreed to write the foreword to my first published book, *Presidents Were Teenagers Too.*

~Benny Wasserman

29

Lost in Translation

Appreciation can change a day, even change a life.
Your willingness to put it into words is
all that is necessary.
~Margaret Cousins

As a recently arrived English teacher in Japan, I often found interesting little souvenirs to send home to family and friends. I was just exiting the post office one day when a middle-aged woman stopped me. She was wearing an apron over her blouse and had a sun visor on — a typical housewife's outfit — and when she held some papers out to me I unthinkingly took them.

"Did I forget something?" I asked. Perhaps I had dropped a letter or postcard on my way in. But when I looked down at what was in my hands, I saw they were stamps. The woman had handed me stamps.

"Here," was all I could understand with my limited Japanese. "They're yours."

I hadn't bought stamps that day. It had to be a mistake. "These aren't mine," I tried to tell her. "I didn't buy these."

"They're for you."

I held them out, confused and distressed in the post office parking lot, caught in what I thought was a translating error on my part. Did she find them and want me to turn them in? What was happening?

Panic must have shown on my face, because another woman approached. Even shorter than the first, she smiled behind her glasses.

"She says, for you," she said in fractured English. "She give them to you."

I stared at the bundle of stamps.

"Present," my interpreter added. "She say 'present.'"

"Present," the first woman echoed in Japanese, looking anxious, but pleased.

What could I do?

I said thank you, thank you very much, in English and Japanese, and smiled. I said I would put them on postcards to my grandfather. The woman smiled back and the interpreter nodded before bustling away, her work finished. I bicycled home with my head in the clouds, trying to go over that conversation again, then sat on my apartment floor and stared at the stamps. Three thousand yen in stamps, more than thirty dollars' worth. A present from a perfect stranger.

For nearly a year I stuck those stamps on every birthday card, every postcard, every note home. To my grandfather, yes, and my parents and brother and sister, each one sent without delay because I had a little bundle of stamps in my kitchen drawer ready and waiting to be used.

How did she know what I needed? Did that woman have a child living abroad who she wished would write more often? Had she hosted a homesick student once? Had she heard me stumbling through conversations at the post office desk and hoped to spare both the staff and me future troubles?

Or had she simply decided that what someone so obviously far away from home needed most was a little bundle of stamps, to send postcards home? A small kindness to make this growing world a little less lonely?

I went to that post office forty or fifty times more before moving away, but I never saw that woman again. She gave me more than she knew that day; she gave me a little piece of home.

~Stephanie Hunter

30

Valet Service Extraordinaire

*Kindness is tenderness. Kindness is love, but perhaps
greater than love... Kindness is good will. Kindness
says, "I want you to be happy."*
~Randolph Ray

We were headed to the nationally famous Blue Owl
Restaurant, in historic Kimmswick, Missouri, to
celebrate our sixtieth anniversary. On Valentine's
Day, the restaurant offers a sweetheart dinner
that is well worth the price. We had decided to indulge ourselves.

The weather report had called for freezing rain, but not until
long after midnight. We would be safely home by then. But then, as
we approached the restaurant, there was a downpour of freezing rain.
We were closer to the restaurant than home so it seemed prudent to
proceed in that direction.

By the time we arrived, the street in front of the restaurant was
a sheet of ice. The parking lot was also a sheet of ice and in front of
each entry ramp was a pool of water. I couldn't pull in and I knew,
even if I parked on the street, we would never be able to get out and
walk on that ice.

A lady walked toward us. She called out, "Were you wanting to
go in there?" She motioned to the parking lot.

I nodded and said, "We can't go in there and I don't think we can walk on the street. My husband recently suffered a stroke and I'm an amputee. I'm afraid we'll fall."

That lady happened to be Mary Hostetter, the owner of The Blue Owl Restaurant and Bakery. She said, "We have the salt truck coming any minute, but that won't do a lot of good right now."

Mary quickly came up with a plan. "Just pull the car in front of the restaurant steps and I'll walk you in. I will park your car for you and you'll be safe." I pulled the car up to the bottom of the steps. She locked arms with us, one at a time, and walked us up the steps to the door.

A few minutes later, she handed me our keys, saying, "After you have dinner and when you are ready to leave, give me your keys. I will bring your car out front and put you both back in it." I was thanking her when she quickly turned and went back to her work as hostess.

The ambiance was warm and romantic. The aroma of delicious foods wafted through the air. All the small dining rooms and tables were cheerfully decorated in red, pink, and white. Cozy would be an understatement. The smiling waitresses were dressed in long blue dresses with ruffles and white aprons. Soon the place was jam-packed.

The food was delicious, as always, and we savored every mouthful. The service was extremely attentive. We were treated as though we were the only ones in the place. We leisurely finished our food and contemplated dessert. We ordered their special chocolate-covered strawberries that were as large as baseballs. They were delicious. We finished our meal with a steaming cup of decaf coffee. Our server was kind enough to snap pictures of the two of us for our memory album. It was an absolutely perfect evening.

We got up to leave and asked the owner if she had a minute to stand with us for a picture. As busy as she was, she cheerfully put her arms around both our waists and smiled for the camera. Seeing that we were ready to leave, she held out her hand and said, "Your keys, please." I started to protest and told her we would be able to make it out okay. She pushed her hand a little closer and repeated, "Your keys, please." She left, with our keys, while we put on our coats and went to the front door. She pulled up in front of the restaurant, came back up the stairs, and repeated the drill. She walked both of us, one at a time, to the car and put us safely inside. The salt truck had come while we were having dinner and the street was looking much better.

She waved, smiled and wished us a safe trip home. She turned and disappeared back into the busy restaurant.

Mary had taken the time, on this very busy night, to make sure we were okay. I can see why she is a woman of national fame. She has appeared on many television shows. She and her restaurant have been written up in magazines and newspapers all over the United States, including O, *The Oprah Magazine*. She's very famous, and yet, she took time to reach out her hand to two total strangers on one of the busiest nights of the year.

We will never forget her kindness in the face of what could have become a disaster for us. We will remember our sixtieth anniversary dinner fondly, and with a deep respect for a wonderful, kind, and caring human being.

~Joyce E. Sudbeck

31

The Best Kind of Puzzle

To be doing good deeds is man's most glorious task.
~Sophocles

I usually did the daily crossword during my commute. But one day, on a longer-than-usual train ride, I realized I had forgotten to grab the free daily newspaper. Ugh… no crossword.

A half hour into the trip, the gentleman sitting on my left departed, leaving a copy of the *Daily News* on his seat. A hand-me-down newspaper is perfectly fine for me. I put on my glasses, pulled out my pen and opened the paper. Since the *Daily News* isn't my usual paper, I had no clue where the crossword was located and so I was browsing when pages and pages of small fine print caught my eye. It was a listing of multiple names and addresses.

Curious, I went back a couple of pages and read the explanation. It was a list of dormant bank accounts. If a person puts money into an account and does nothing for years and years, the bank designates that account dormant. The bank notifies the state, and eventually the state runs advertisements listing all the people for whom it is holding these funds. To give you an idea of the scope of this issue, New York State, where I reside, is holding $13 billion worth of unclaimed funds. You can even search the listing online in most states. If you see your name on the list, contact your state comptroller or treasurer and fill out a form. Before you know it, a check is in the mail to you.

I decided there was a reason why I forgot to bring my normal crossword puzzle that day. I made a decision to do something more meaningful than a crossword puzzle. Here was a real-life puzzle I could do. I would "puzzle out" where some of these people were and alert either them or their families about the monies.

First I skimmed for familiar names. Ding-ding, I won the first round easily. My deceased uncle was on the list. Easy to see why the bank could not reach him. However, said uncle had a son, easily reachable, and so a phone call later, my cousin knew to claim the monies.

The first set of calls were the easy ones. Most of the folks I found were those still at the same address as in the listing. Some knew they had dormant accounts but had no clue how to get the money. Some were elderly or had limited language skills and needed simple instructions on what to do.

Next I attacked the challenging ones. I scored a few hits, using LinkedIn and Facebook. I also found the obituaries of some of the folks on the list, then tracked down their heirs by using sleuthing skills. I found a young woman who had opened an account in her old college town… and then had moved cross-country to become a professional. I contacted a young man who had moved out of Manhattan when he got married, had kids, and moved to the suburbs. I met some darling seniors by phone. It was fun.

All in all, I did not spend huge amounts of time on this. I just spent a few days on it, using the time I would have devoted to crossword puzzles or Sudoku. Instead of doing crossword or number puzzles, I puzzled out the lives of random people.

It felt good, especially when one woman who I alerted about two accounts called me later that night, just to ask why I did what I did and to thank me again and again for having the *chutzpah* to call her. It truly was the best kind of puzzle for me, one that combined intellectual challenge and that nice warm feeling you get when you do a good deed for someone else.

~Goldy Rosenberg

32

The Keys of Kindness

Deeds of kindness are equal in weight to
all the commandments.
~The Talmud

t was already hot and humid when my husband left for work at six on that July morning. I waved as he pulled out of the driveway and went back inside to enjoy a couple of hours of peace and quiet before my teenagers awoke.

With a second cup of coffee swirling curlicues of steam in front of me, I sat at the kitchen table and planned my day: deposit a couple of checks at the bank, take out some cash, and maybe go to the mall to shop for a new pair of sneakers.

Sometime around noon I grabbed my purse, said goodbye to the kids, who were now in the living room watching TV, and headed for the car. In the carport next door, our neighbor Eddie was tinkering under the hood of his pickup truck. We traded hellos and a few moments of chitchat before I left in my Honda Civic.

The bank was two miles from the house. I pulled into a space in front of the glass-enclosed ATM machine and reached to turn off the ignition, but decided against it. Instead, I hopped out of the car with the engine running and the air conditioner on.

The ATM machine sucked in my card and asked for my PIN number. I typed it in and then threw an over-the-shoulder glance at the car where a multi-colored ribbon tassel hanging from the rearview mirror danced above the dashboard in the cool air. I couldn't wait to get back inside to enjoy it.

Transaction complete, I went to the car and tugged on the door handle. If ever I had an uh-oh moment, it was then. The door was locked.

The Louisiana sun was beating down on me while I stood deflated, wondering what to do. I didn't relish the thought of a two-mile hike back to the house to get the spare set of keys.

I entered the bank and took a deep breath of cool air before approaching a teller window. The young woman who greeted me listened sympathetically as I told her my problem. When I asked if I could make a call, she cheerfully obliged by showing me to the end of the counter and pushing a telephone across the polished surface.

"Hello, Fawn," I said when my daughter answered. "I locked my keys in the car at the bank, and the engine is running. Can you go next door and ask Eddie if he would bring me the spare set, please?"

Fawn came back on the line a few minutes later. The news wasn't good. Eddie was in the middle of an oil change and wouldn't be able to help for a while. I hung up and relayed my dilemma to the teller.

"You're Fawn's mother?" she asked, sounding a bit apologetic for listening in on my conversation.

"Yes, I am."

Her face lit up. "I'm Carmen. Fawn and I often work together in the church nursery. She's a wonderful person. I just love her to pieces. You must be an awesome mom."

Carmen dug through her purse, pulled out a set of keys, and held them toward me. "Here, take my car. It's the brand new Corolla parked outside facing the street. I just got it yesterday."

I was stunned. "Are you sure about lending me your new car?"

"Yes. Please, take it."

As my fingers wrapped around the keys, a hint of worry shadowed her pretty face. Clearly, letting go was a sacrifice. I was a stranger, and her car was new. She'd worked hard for it. But because of the connection we shared through my daughter, she was willing to take a chance.

"You'll drive carefully, won't you?" she asked as I stepped away from the counter.

"I will. I promise." And, I kept my promise. Fifteen minutes later I returned with Carmen's car, my spare keys, and my daughter.

"Thank you for helping my mom," Fawn said, standing before Carmen, her eyes brimming with tears.

"Oh, it was nothing."

Warmth flooded my heart as I watched the girls share a hug.

To me, the gesture wasn't "nothing." It was a huge "something." I had merited a favor based on my daughter's reputation, and I was grateful to Carmen for lending me her car. But more than that, Carmen probably didn't realize that she'd given me a gift — the most precious words a mother could ever hear: "You must be an awesome mom."

For those kind words, I will forever be grateful.

~Irene Onorato

33

The Gloves

The roots of all goodness lie in the soil
of appreciation for goodness.
~The Dalai Lama

had just returned to Canada after spending almost a month in a warm mountain valley in Mexico. I had gone to spend Christmas with my husband, who was teaching anthropology there. What a change it was being back in freezing cold Alberta.

I was scheduled to work on New Year's Day so I got up at seven and walked outside to assess the weather. The warm Chinook winds assured me that we were in for a good day. I didn't bother to retrieve my winter gloves from our other vehicle.

My first day back at work went well and as night approached I remembered the car needed gas. It felt a lot colder by the time I headed for the only gas station that was open at eight in the evening. I hadn't wanted to use that particular station because it was self-service only and it was starting to get very cold again.

I must have looked pretty funny as I tried to squeeze the gas handle with my hand in my coat pocket. There was a member of the Royal Canadian Mounted Police watching me from one of the other pumps.

I felt that I should provide an explanation. "I know I look silly, but my hands are so cold and I thought if I put my hand in my pocket I could use my coat for protection. Of course, that means I have to stand in this awkward position." I looked as though I was hugging the car.

For a moment, he said nothing. "He probably thinks I'm a real nut case," I thought to myself. Then I heard a voice and saw a pair of gloves sticking out beyond his gas pump. "Could you use a pair of gloves?"

I shut off the pump and walked over. "Oh, yes please." I replied, taking the offering and slipping my hands into the warm leather gloves.

I went back and returned to filling my tank. Then I leaned over, still holding the handle and noticed that the police officer was pumping gas with nothing to protect his own hands from the cold. I had thought he was lending me some spare gloves, not taking off his only pair.

I felt grateful for the kindness of the officer. I also felt a tad embarrassed, then worried. I suggested he take back the gloves. And he declined. "But you need something for your hands, too," I said.

"Oh, I get used to it," he responded. "Don't worry, I'm fine."

In minutes my tank was full and I thanked him, returned his gloves and went in to pay for my purchase. I felt so elated at being the recipient of his thoughtfulness. As the officer came in to pay for his own gas I smiled at him and told him how grateful I was.

He stood there and said, "It was my pleasure."

I knew he meant it. The gift was small but my hands and my heart didn't think so! What a lovely "welcome back" from the country I love.

~Margaret E. Braun-Haley

34

Midnight Delivery

We can only be said to be alive in those moments when
our hearts are conscious of our treasures.
~Thornton Wilder

"I feel so alone. And cold. And tired," I announced to the empty train platform. I glanced at my watch. It was midnight. Why had I decided to travel from Prague to Interlaken without staying somewhere along the way for a day or two? The chill in my bones on that March morning in Switzerland made me question the wisdom of making the eighteen-hour trip via three separate trains.

I was wrapping up a solo-backpacking trip across Europe during my three-week vacation from school in Grenoble, France. I wanted to get in as much sightseeing as possible since it was my first time in Europe, so I had gone as far east as Hungary and Poland, visiting ten countries in all. By the end of my journey I was weary of hauling the souvenirs I had purchased and sleeping in large hostel dorm rooms.

"What I wouldn't give for a hot bath, clean clothes, and a soft bed right now. Or even just someone to talk to." It felt a little weird speaking to the vacant station, but doing so was preventing me from falling asleep, which was important for safety reasons.

Since I still had a couple of hours before my train arrived, I tried to think of something to fill the time. I was too exhausted to read or journal. I didn't want to walk around. The restaurant was closed. I could only converse with myself for so long.

Swiveling around on the hard wooden bench I saw only vacant tracks, dark rail cars, and electronic signs with no incoming trains to announce. Most of the train cars were modern, but one series of cars caught my eye. It was the legendary Orient Express.

The dining car probably served phenomenal meals and had white tablecloths with cloth napkins. The sleepers were likely cozy and comfortable with private bathrooms that had lovely scented soaps and shampoo. A sigh escaped my lips. I returned my gaze to the empty tracks in front of me, daydreams of the Orient Express streaming through my mind.

One such dream was interrupted by a squeak and then a slam. I tensed and listened, wondering who else would be on the platform. There were footsteps behind me. They got louder and closer with each passing moment. I cautiously looked over my shoulder.

A man wearing a cornflower blue uniform strode toward me. Round gold buttons and yellow piping accented the blue. He held a single, blood red rose. I puzzled as to where he was going with a flower at that time of night. Maybe he had a girlfriend waiting for him at home.

He came to a stop beside the bench and handed me the long-stemmed flower. I held it delicately with my hands that were stiff from the cold, and gazed at the satin petals with small beads of moisture on them. Words escaped me.

"I happened to look out the window while I was working on the Orient," he said with a thick Irish accent, "and saw you sitting here all alone."

"I must be quite the sight," I said, suddenly self-conscious about my wrinkled clothes and hair that hadn't seen a shower or brush in hundreds of miles.

"You looked so lonely and cold, I couldn't help but think you needed something to lift your spirits." A gentle smile played on his lips.

"I was just thinking it would be nice to talk to someone, even for a few minutes, but a flower?" I touched a petal with my finger. "Totally unexpected. Thank you."

"My pleasure, Miss." He tapped the brim of his hat with a white gloved hand. "Safe journeys to you." He pivoted on the heel of his shiny black leather shoes and walked back to the train.

I stared at the precious gift in my hands, still trying to understand what had happened. My mind was so caught up in replaying the random act of kindness that the remainder of my wait at the station passed without notice.

When I arrived at the hostel in Interlaken, Switzerland I was dirty and disheveled from my extensive journey, but I also had a glow about me that the other residents noticed. And of course they wanted to know why a backpacker was carrying a single, long-stemmed rose.

So I recounted the tale of the angel with the Irish accent who surprised me in a deserted train station in the middle of the night, and how his kindness lifted my spirits while replacing my loneliness with joy.

~Heather Harshman

35

The Happy Little Pumpkin

*That life is to my liking which is made up of little
deeds, little sacrifices, little kindnesses.*
~Birthday letter quoted in J.R. Macduff, Birthdays

I shuffled to the end of the driveway and opened my mailbox, certain that it wouldn't hold anything interesting. After thirty-five years of marriage, my husband and I had recently separated and I had moved to a new house. The change-of-address form I'd turned in at the post office hadn't yet made its way through the system, so I rarely received anything other than mail addressed to "Occupant."

But this day in early October was different. Inside the mailbox, resting atop a grocery store flier and an ad for a pest control service, sat a pumpkin. It was bright orange, perfectly round and about the size of a softball.

"What in the world?" I muttered to myself as I picked it up. On one side was a jack-o-lantern face, drawn on with black marker. On the other, these words: HAPPY HALLOWEEN AND GOD BLESS YOU! And there was a postal sticker, meaning that this strange delivery had actually come through the mail. Who would have done such a thing? And why?

As I made my way back to the house, I couldn't help but smile a little. It had been a long time since anything had happened to brighten my day. The break-up of my marriage had been devastating. Even though I remained in the town where I'd lived for decades and was surrounded by people I knew, I felt hurt and frightened and very much alone. But in my hand was proof that someone was thinking about me, that someone cared.

I put the pumpkin on the tray in the middle of my coffee table, wondering if I would ever discover who had sent it. As the days passed and I settled into the new routine of living alone for the first time in my life, that happy little pumpkin somehow made me feel a tiny bit better every time I looked at it.

Every now and then, I would ask friends who knew I was in the middle of a painful divorce if, perchance, they had mailed me a jack-o-lantern. The answer was always a convincing no. I asked my grown children, all of whom lived in different towns. Nope, not them. I e-mailed a cousin, also recently separated from her husband, who lives clear across the country. "Did you send me a miniature pumpkin that says GOD BLESS YOU?" I wrote.

"No," came her almost-immediate reply. "But I wish I had. What a great idea!"

That little orange jack-o-lantern sat on my coffee table all the way through Halloween and Thanksgiving. In early December, when it was time to decorate for Christmas, I picked it up to throw it away. But the pumpkin was still fresh and firm and pleasingly solid in my hand. And it was still grinning at me. It seemed a shame to get rid of it. And so it nestled among jingle bells and peppermint sticks and red-and-green candles throughout the holidays.

Its happy eyes were staring at me on New Year's Day. And that's when I made a resolution that changed my life. Months ago, someone — and it was likely that I might not ever discover who — had performed an anonymous act of kindness that showed that he or she cared.

I could do the same.

In February, I mailed a box of Valentine candy with no return address to a nephew who had just lost his job. In March, I left a shamrock plant on the porch of a friend whose beloved cat had died. In April, I sent a stuffed Easter bunny to a colleague at work who had received a frightening medical diagnosis.

And so on and so on — one anonymous act of kindness, every

month of the year. Can you guess what I did in October? After learning of a neighbor whose husband had recently asked for divorce, I mailed her a miniature pumpkin, bright orange and perfectly round and about the size of a softball. On it, I drew a jack-o-lantern face.

And wrote these words: *HAPPY HALLOWEEN AND GOD BLESS YOU*.

~Jennie Ivey

36

Eighty-Seven Cents

No act of kindness, however small, is ever wasted.
~Aesop

walked through the aisles of my local Kmart, my chubby little toddler sitting in the rickety cart's seat. I'd come here for diapers, the thing we needed the most; they were the first thing I picked out. I made sure to get the most economical brand they had available.

My one-year-old son, who was admiring everything on the shelves with wide eyes and a binky in his mouth, was pretty content with just about anything. He was adorable and sweet, the kind of little boy every mother dreams about. On the way to the checkout he pointed at a bunch of bananas and the binky came loose.

"Nanas!" he cried, reaching with his plump little fingers. I pulled out my purse and opened my wallet to stare at the lonely bills: a five and two ones, with no coins. If the bananas didn't weigh too much, I had just enough cash to pay for them and the diapers. I didn't have quite enough in the checking account to cover the cost, but if it did go over I could split it up; pay part with cash and part with a check. Either way, he needed those bananas. They were good for him, and it was a healthy treat.

I grabbed the bananas, happy to see the smile on his face when I let him hold them. He tried to open one, but I told him, "not yet," and he waited patiently.

Our cashier was friendly, but as she rang up the diapers and bananas the total came to $7.87. I gave her the seven dollars in cash and started writing a check for the eighty-seven cents. It was hard, and a little humiliating, but I was going to do this for my son.

"Honey, don't worry about that," a voice said. I looked up at the lady standing in line behind me. She was blond like me, and she had a couple of kids with her. She was fishing change out of her purse. "Don't write that check," she said.

"Are you sure?" I asked. It was already halfway written. The lady smiled at me.

"I've been there," she said, handing the change to the cashier. "I've got the eighty-seven cents."

My eyes welled with tears. "Thank you," I said, trying hard not to cry in the middle of the store. "Thank you so much."

"You're welcome, honey."

I'd never met her before. Why should she help me? But she knew what real charity was, the kind of giving that has love and humanity behind it, and she was a true example of it.

I will never forget that day. In fact, whenever I have change and anyone in front of me in line is in need, I make sure to dig into my purse and provide. My son went home from the store that day with his bananas. He was exquisitely happy, as children often are, with the simplest gift. He didn't know what had happened, that I was able to save the few pennies left in my checking account for something else we might need. Instead, a beautiful woman showed me that she could care for me with this one tiny act, this one thing that would stay with me for the rest of my life. And I, in turn, will try my best to do the same.

~Amanda Adams

Chapter

5

Random
Acts of
Kindness

Who Helped Whom?

The ability to be genuinely grateful for the things
that we have and the people we love, as well as
for simply being alive and conscious, will do more
for bringing a true feeling of happiness to us on a
regular basis than almost anything else.
~Cary David Richards, The Happiness Habit

37

The Side of the Road

Time unfolds beauty, wonder, and mystery to reveal
the auspicious tapestry of life.
~A.D. Posey

I t was a steamy July morning and the air conditioner in my twelve-year-old car was operating at full blast. Curling off the highway exit ramp, I saw a car even older than mine on the side of the road, hood up and abandoned. About 100 yards farther down the rural road walked a neatly dressed young man talking on his cell phone.

A blast of hot air flooded the car when I rolled down the window and asked if the man needed some help. The young man, about the age of my own son, smiled broadly and nodded. He explained that his car had overheated. He needed to buy water for the radiator.

The nearest store was two miles away, so I offered him a ride, not convinced of the wisdom of such a gesture, but sensing it was the right choice. His bright blue eyes and grateful attitude put me at ease. Along the way he told me that his name was Stevie and he was on his way to meet college friends in a town about an hour north when the car simply stopped.

We got the water and filled the radiator but the car still wouldn't start. Several motorists stopped to help but to no avail. A tow truck was called and would arrive in an hour. Something compelled me to wait with Stevie. After all, I would want someone to help my adult children if this had happened to them.

It was too hot to stand there with the car, so we drove in my little SUV to a coffee shop where Stevie told me his incredible story.

After completing half of his first year of medical school, he was in a class where a certain type of cancer was being presented, including symptoms and ways to test for it. He went home afterward and did a self-exam that revealed he had the very disease they were studying.

Surgery and treatment followed immediately. Stevie smiled confidently at me and said, "The prognosis looks really good."

Only a few hours had passed since I had met this brave, young man. He was joyful, kind, and confident. It was stunning to learn that at age twenty-three he was not only battling cancer, but facing it with such obvious courage and optimism.

Astonished, I replied, "You are such a joy-filled person. I don't understand. How can you face a life-threatening illness at your age with such confidence?"

Stevie smiled and told me about his faith in God, the love and support of his family, and his hopes and dreams. His overheated car might have left him on the side of the road, but cancer would not.

Earlier, Stevie had called his friends, and they had agreed to drive the forty miles south to retrieve him at the coffee shop as soon as they could. It would have been okay, even normal for me to leave at that point, but the draw of his genuine personality was like a magnet and I waited with him as we continued to enjoy rich conversation. Just talking with him lifted my spirits.

Time passed quickly as we shared about our families, books we had read that had impacted us, and things we still hoped to do in our lives. We talked about things that really mattered.

When the tow truck eventually arrived, we drove back to the side of the road where his car was pulled onto the flatbed and taken to be repaired.

Escaping the heat once again, we returned to the coffee shop. Not long afterward, a small, black SUV pulled up in front of the coffee shop and three smiling people emerged. Stevie's friends embraced him and whisked him away.

The following day, in the middle of a busy Monday at work, my phone rang and I received the call no one ever wants to get. The nurse on the other end of the line was professional but detached.

She recited a line she had obviously delivered to others before me: "Your test results from last week's mammogram came back with irregularities. You will need to come in for further testing. A doctor will be there to review the results with you."

A small wave of panic washed over me and I tried to resist the temptation to jump to conclusions. I thought about Stevie and his wise perspective on cancer and life. Stevie's courage in the face of serious adversity inspired me to calm my fears and trust that I could face whatever lay ahead.

The decision to stop and help someone else had truly ended up helping me more than I could ever have predicted. The lessons learned served me well over the next few days and I began to wonder more about the encounter. Both in word and deed, Stevie showed me that it is possible to face my fears without giving in to them, to keep my focus on what I am grateful for, and to recognize that something good can evolve from something bad. Life's challenges may not be our destination but they do make our journeys more interesting. And you never know what might happen on the side of the road!

~Diane Lowe MacLachlan

38

Crossing the Gap

Those who bring sunshine to the lives of others
cannot keep it from themselves.
~James Matthew Barrie

t's 8:30 a.m., traffic at full-flow. For ten minutes I watch an elderly lady looking anxiously at the traffic, waiting to cross a four-lane priority road. She looks fragile and delicate; porcelain hands grasp each other tight to her chest. Her wide blue eyes scan for a break; there is a glint of fear in them. Her age-cracked mouth is closed firm, but the edges tremble.

A scruffy boy of ten appears next to her and says a few words in her ear. She smiles with surprise and nods with a wink. They are strangers to each other, but the trust in each is obvious.

The boy turns to the traffic holding the lady's hand and I note his little smile... he's helping.

The traffic thins... a break appears. Both say "now!" and step out, leading each other.

The old lady looks around, determined to protect her young charge. The boy clutches her hand, leading the old lady gently and safely. As they ascend the sidewalk on the other side their relief is evident.

The old lady safely guided the boy to the other side, pretending to let him help. The young boy safely got the woman across, pretending to let her help.

The two turn to each other and shake hands.

I watch with a lump in my throat and a tear in my eye, and I don't know why that is so… for I am smiling.

~Michael John Kildare

39

Out of the Blue, a Family

Friends are family you choose for yourself.
~Author Unknown

As a long-time police volunteer for the Pleasanton, California, police department near San Francisco, I got to know many of the police officers and support staff. I would often chat with Ryan, a school resource officer, at the end of his workday after he returned from one of the schools in town he was responsible for. One evening he mentioned that his rental home had become infected with black mold caused by a roof leak. Despite his repeated requests, his landlord had done nothing to remediate the mold situation.

As a result, Ryan was forced to break his lease and vacate, sending his wife Brenda and their three children to live temporarily with her parents in Idaho. He bunked at a fellow officer's home for a few weeks while he searched for a new place for himself and his family, feeling increasingly guilty over appropriating the bed of one of the officer's children.

"Well, come and stay with me," I suggested. "I live only two miles from the police station and I have a spare bedroom and private bathroom you can use."

"It could be a long time," he warned.

"I know, but it's just sitting there empty now, so what's the difference? You're welcome to stay as long as you need to."

Then the delicate question: "How much would you charge me?"

I just smiled and said, "Charge? I couldn't charge you! You have a need and I can fill that need. If it makes you feel better, you can help me with chores around the house. All the rent money you save can be applied toward a down payment on a home when you find one."

Ryan moved in a few days later and ended up staying for almost six months. He made his bed every day, straightened up his bathroom before leaving for work, and did his own laundry, grocery shopping and meal preparation. Early each morning, he moved through the house like a ninja, never once disturbing my sleep. He took out the garbage for me and helped with yard work, forbidding me to climb a ladder as long as he lived there. With the help of a sergeant friend, he even cut down an unwanted tree in my yard. He was the perfect houseguest. One day I remarked, "So, who do I send the roses to — your wife or your mother?"

Even though he was the first roommate I had ever had, we seamlessly adjusted to one another's routines and preferences, even enjoying the same TV programs. We shared similar opinions on every topic and our conversations sometimes went on until almost midnight.

He had introduced me to his wife via Facebook that first night, and she and I soon became online friends. He visited the family in Idaho a few times, with me driving him to the airport and picking him up upon his return. Although I had lived alone my entire adult life, suddenly the house felt empty during his absence.

A few months in, we got a big surprise — Ryan was named Officer of the Year by the police department. The recognition came with a gala dinner honoring him and other first responders in the county. The mayor presented him with an engraved plaque, extolling his accomplishments during the year. What a special honor that was for him! Ryan invited me to the event as it was impractical for his wife and children to fly down just for the evening.

That was in April. Mother's Day rolled around soon after, and Ryan gave me a Mother's Day card and took me out to dinner. In June I returned the kindness on Father's Day. In July, he returned to Idaho to gather his family and bring them back to the beautiful new home he had found.

Over a year has gone by since I offered my spare room, and with each passing month I feel closer to my new "blue" family. The children nicknamed me "GrAnnette," short for Grandma Annette. Given the distance that both grandmothers live from them (Idaho and Southern California), I guess I am a third grandma to them. The boys, ages eight and ten, run out to my car to greet me with hugs when I pull into their driveway. Their little two-year-old daughter squeals with glee when told I'm coming to visit. ("I'm so 'essited' to see my GrAnnette!" she says.) I've spent Thanksgiving, Christmas and Easter with them, and birthdays and family parties, too, where I met both sets of grandparents. In fact, Ryan's mother and I e-mail each other frequently. I've picked up the kids from school to free Brenda to attend to household chores, and she and I go on bargain-hunting trips together from time to time.

Ryan's four-year assignment as a school resource officer has ended and he is back to working the streets as a patrol officer. Sometimes he gets "held over" for a significant amount of time after his normal shift ends to complete an involved arrest booking or to assist another officer. Other times he has to appear in court to testify the morning after coming off the graveyard shift. Then, he stays over at my house rather than making the long drive home only to have to return to duty a few hours later.

Who knew that such a simple act as offering someone a place to stay would repay me so richly with a brand-new "family"? Over dinner recently, we reminisced about our former roommate relationship. Ryan asked if the neighbors had ever commented about his living with me, since they would see him come and go regularly. I merely smiled, saying, "I just told them I've become such a famous author (two published books and several stories in anthologies, including three in *Chicken Soup for the Soul* books) that I was forced to employ a full-time armed bodyguard."

~Annette Langer

Recycling Chivalry

Service to others is the rent you pay for
your room here on earth.
~Muhammad Ali

am a devoted recycler. Every month I bring several bags of care-fully cleaned bottles to the recycling center, pour them into blue barrels for weighing, and walk away with a few dollars per bag.

The last time I went, there was a bit of a line. A distinguished white-haired man was growing impatient with the recycling agent, who explained that the scale was not working and would have to be reset. The elderly man rolled his eyes as the clerk apologized for the delay and assured him that it would just take another minute.

The next person in line was a bearded man whose hair was so disheveled that it looked like he had been through a windstorm. His clothing was mismatched and stained and hung loosely as if he'd lost a lot of weight. He glanced up at me from behind a blue barrel filled with assorted glass bottles.

I looked behind him to see where the empty barrels were and was surprised when he grabbed one for me. "Here, you don't want to get your hands dirty," he offered with a shy smile that exposed crooked teeth and a gap from at least two missing molars on his left side. He was right about one thing. Those barrels are filthy, with enough spilled soda and beer to attract numerous bees and flies. I always come equipped with wipes and have occasionally worn latex gloves when I recycle.

Normally, when a man offers to help me carry something, I say, "I can do it" or "Thanks but I don't need any help." There was, however, a certain earnestness about this fellow that made me want to validate his contribution. I thanked him for the barrel and began to open my first bag. "I can help you with that," he offered.

Again I was tempted to tell him that I could do it myself. But then I noticed the white-haired man turning around to observe our conversation. By now, his air of disdain for the delay was obvious as he tapped one foot and folded his arms across his chest. It was the slight sneer he directed toward my chivalrous new buddy that made me accept the help that had been offered to me.

It was abundantly clear that the bearded fellow, in his ill-fitting clothes, really knew his way around the recycling center. He efficiently placed the dirty, sticky blue barrel in front of me and began to pour in my carefully cleaned bottles.

My first bag filled an entire barrel so the man rushed to get me more barrels. I was impressed by his work ethic despite the fact that he was clearly unemployed. As he started to fill the second barrel, he said, "You can go ahead of me. You must be busy and I've got all day."

I was torn. On the one hand, I was happy to wait my turn and receive a bit of spending money, and there was a certain satisfaction in seeing my carefully recycled bottles go on their way. On the other hand, this nice fellow needed the dollars I would receive a lot more than I did. And he would derive more satisfaction from the whole process than I would.

I decided to reward him for his kindness by offering him mine. The only problem was how to do it without insulting him. Finally, I hit on a plan I hoped would not seem condescending.

"You're right," I said. "I do have a dozen errands today. You could help me out by turning in my bottles for me."

He looked confused. "How will you get your money?"

"I don't really need it. I just want to get rid of the bottles. You'd be doing me a favor if you could take care of them for me."

His shy smile broadened to a wide grin and I noticed another gap on the right side of his mouth. Somehow this made him more endearing and I knew I'd done the right thing. "Okay, but I owe you one," he said.

I started to walk back to my car but turned back to assure him, "No, we're even!"

A feeling of lightness, which had nothing to do with leaving my load of bottles behind, enveloped me. I felt good. The day somehow seemed brighter than it did when I'd stepped out of my front door with my "to do" list.

Driving to the pharmacy to pick up a prescription, I thought about how little the man had, though I'd sensed no self-pity in him.

The bottles he'd brought might have been worth two or three dollars. I wondered what he could get with that: maybe a burger without the fries or Coke. On this day, at least, his options had expanded to the point that he could enjoy a good meal. On top of that, I hoped he would bask in the feeling of accomplishment that a job well done brings.

As for me, playing a small part in his momentary good fortune made my day as well. Let the dignified white-haired man spread his scowls around. I was happy to recycle the kindness offered to me by a man whose smile… while scoring low on traditional glamour scales… had become surprisingly beautiful to me.

~Marsha Porter

41

My Year of Kindness

Only a life lived for others is a life worthwhile.
~Albert Einstein

n January 2013, I decided to try something different from my typical list of New Year's resolutions. Instead, I vowed to do a unique random act of kindness every week for the entire year. I wanted to feel connected to the community around me and to help bring small moments of joy to others. Little did I know that the person I would end up helping most would be me.

I was twenty-five years old, finishing up my last semester of graduate school, with zero job prospects upon graduation. I felt isolated, living halfway across the country from my family and close friends. I had just gotten engaged to a man I loved, but whose controlling and angry behavior was growing steadily worse. Looking back, I think my kindness challenge was a way of filling up my inner reservoir, of giving to the authentic core of my spirit, week by week, until I built up enough strength to address my life head-on and make the hard decisions I needed to make.

That first week, I cleaned out my closet and gave a large bag of clothing to a women's shelter. The next week, I donated canned goods to a food pantry. I scattered lucky pennies on a playground, wrote thank-you notes, baked cookies for my neighbor, and left quarters on laundromat machines. I bought flowers for a colleague who aced her thesis defense and reached out to friends I hadn't spoken to in a while.

I didn't realize it at the time, but little by little I was weaving a web of community. And in March, when everything came crashing down—because my engagement ended and I had to move out of my apartment and the final draft of my thesis was due the exact same week—it was this community that came to my rescue, helping me find a place to stay, making sure I was safe, sending me supportive e-mails, and inviting me over for dinner.

Life had more changes in store—good things, yet still change can be hard. I was awarded a creative writing fellowship at San José State, so after graduation I moved to the San Francisco Bay area to work on a novel. I also began teaching writing classes for kids in the afternoons. I got involved in a church community and made new friends. Through all the newness and uncertainty, my weekly routine of doing random acts of kindness was a comforting anchor.

My year of kindness taught me many things. I learned that you do not need a ton of money or time to have a positive impact on the world around you—all that's required is an open heart and a little creativity. Aesop was right: "No act of kindness, however small, is ever wasted." Even small acts of compassion and joy, as simple as a smile, can make a difference.

I learned that if I'm in a sad or grumpy mood, the quickest way to turn my day around is to be kind to someone else. Being brave and putting myself out there is always worth it. Yes, it could be scary to strike up conversations with strangers and step outside my comfort zone! But I was always left with a smile on my face and a grateful connection in my heart.

Most of all, I learned faith. Time and again, I was surprised by wonderful coincidences—and kind deeds that others did for me! Whether it was a cup of coffee from a new acquaintance, a hug from one of the kids I taught, or an out-of-the-blue card from an old friend, acts of kindness never failed to boost my spirits. We truly are all connected.

My "year of kindness" officially ended in 2014, but I've continued doing random acts of kindness. Last year, I celebrated my twenty-seventh birthday with twenty-seven of them. It was my favorite birthday to date!

~Dallas Woodburn

42

A Secret Treasure

To send a letter is a good way to go somewhere
without moving anything but your heart.
~Phyllis Theroux

Her name was Amelia but everyone had called her "Poor Aunt Amelia" for so many years that "Poor" had almost become her first name. Most people thought she was a spinster but she had actually been married for one day when she was nineteen. Her husband had been arrested on their wedding night — he'd held up a store the day before the wedding. Amelia put her house up to bail him out of jail and he ran away, never to be seen again. She'd lost her husband of only a few hours and she'd lost the house she inherited from her father. She was small and shy and reminded people of a little sparrow because she always looked a bit frightened, as if you spoke too loudly she might fly away.

One Christmas I had an extra card and hated to waste it so I decided to send it to Amelia even though we had never exchanged Christmas cards before. A week after Christmas I received a letter from her thanking me. She said she hadn't received a Christmas card in years and she taped it to her refrigerator door, where she could see it every day.

I realized for the first time how lonely she must be. I lived eighty miles away so I didn't visit her, and I didn't know if anyone else did either.

I knew she didn't like talking on the phone; she said it made her nervous and most of the time she kept her phone turned off. So, after she appreciated the Christmas card so much, I decided I would send her a card or a letter once a week. I'd try to make my letters more interesting by including jokes, recipes, newspaper clippings, pressed flowers, autumn leaves, and anything else I could think of to entertain her. About once a month she'd write a note back thanking me for writing to her and telling me about her flower garden or a book she'd read.

As time went by she became more housebound, partly because of her health but mostly because she became ever more fearful. Fortunately, she could walk to the store and buy groceries and use her rolling cart to get them home. She had an old fashioned metal mailbox at her front gate and she'd watch for the mailman to see if he was going to stop or not.

Whenever I'd think about not writing or skipping a week, I'd picture her sitting in her chair by the window waiting for the mailman. I'd started out thinking that I would send her letters for a few months but it had turned into a lifelong commitment.

Then, one day, Amelia called and said she had fallen down her stairs and broken her ankle. She needed someone to stay with her just for a couple of days but if I was too busy she'd understand. I told her I'd be there in three hours and would stay as long as she needed me.

When I arrived, Amelia was in a wheelchair and looked even worse than I'd expected. She kept apologizing for bothering me and I told her she was no trouble at all. I had all the time in the world and was looking forward to a really good visit.

She told me to put my things in the east bedroom because it got the most sun and was the most cheerful room.

I took my bag upstairs and hung my clothes in the closet. I was going to put the rest of my clothes in the old dresser but when I pulled open the top drawer it was full of envelopes in neat rows. I closed the top drawer and opened the next and the next. Every drawer was filled. I pulled out an envelope and saw my own handwriting. I looked at the date — it was a letter I'd sent to Aunt Amelia six years ago, I'd put red maple leaves in the envelope; now they were brown. I looked through the drawers and found every letter and card I'd sent her for the past nine years. She'd saved them all, and there had to be about 450 of them. There was no mail from anyone else, just me.

I closed the drawers and left the rest of my clothes in my suitcase. Then I sat down on that bed and cried.

I had thought I was being kind to her by writing every week. But what she had done was overwhelming. She'd treasured each and every letter and saved them like they were the most valuable thing she owned. Because the letters were special to her, that made me special. I felt important and loved and valued. I'd never felt so needed or so appreciated. If I hadn't come to stay with her I'd have never known how much my letters meant to her.

I stayed with her until she got the cast removed. I cleaned her house, cooked and took care of her. We played *Monopoly* and worked puzzles and watched old movies on TV.

She mentioned her husband only once. She said he was beautiful—the most handsome man she'd ever seen. She said nobody understood why such a handsome man would want her, but he had, and she'd felt like the luckiest girl in the world. He was handsome and charming, but he was also weak and he couldn't face his problems so he'd run away. She hadn't heard from him in more than fifty years. She didn't sound bitter or angry, only sad that he'd left her. I had the feeling if he knocked on her door right then she'd forgive him and take him back. Amelia was incapable of holding a grudge or being angry.

When I left I promised I'd visit her once a month and she asked if that meant I wasn't going to write to her anymore. I said no, and that I'd continue writing to her once a week.

"Always?" she asked.

"Always, I promise," I said.

I'm still writing to her and I know she's still saving them.

Maybe I was kind to write to her, but her kindness was so much greater. She turned my ordinary letters into a priceless treasure, and turned my ordinary life into one that really matters.

~April Knight

43

Warmth on
a Winter's Day

*Teach this triple truth to all: A generous heart, kind
speech, and a life of service and compassion are
the things which renew humanity.*
~Buddha

I was the assistant director of a local social service agency and I had just overseen our client holiday party. Two hundred volunteers had prepared and staffed a holiday dinner for nearly 1,000 guests. For many of the agency's elderly and physically challenged clients, this was their only holiday celebration, enjoying hot meals, camaraderie and seasonal entertainment as part of an extended family. For parents, it was a chance to enjoy festive, hot meals with their children, who got to open gifts that would have been otherwise unattainable. For just a little while, our guests could set aside their daily struggles and enjoy the holiday season.

Despite the party, I was feeling glum. My own children were now in their twenties and would not be coming home for the holidays. My dearest friend was in the hospital again, having suffered a health setback. I had no plans for the holidays, other than watching old movies and dining on Chinese take-out alone. Nonetheless, I had put on a happy face for the party. That was the least I could do for our guests, who had so little, yet never wallowed in self-pity. I had so much for which to be grateful and I needed to adjust my attitude accordingly.

The party had gone smoothly and a joyous time was had by all. The volunteers had hastily cleaned up, put away the leftover food and refolded tables and chairs. After saying goodbyes and thanking each one for their extra effort on this wintry day, I found myself locking up alone. The sun would set in less than an hour and I wanted to make it home before dark.

A foot of powdery snow had fallen overnight, adding to the two feet already hemming in the Chicago sidewalks. The glistening sunshine was blinding but did little to ease the single-digit temperature and the whipping winds.

I pulled my furry hat down low on my forehead and wrapped my heavy red wool scarf around my face. With my car key in hand, I trudged slowly through the uneven path of ice and snow, struggling to maintain my balance. I pulled my car door open, turned on the ignition and waited a few minutes for the car to warm up. The street was deserted and I prayed that I wouldn't get stuck in the unplowed roadway.

As I approached the first stoplight, I noticed a man standing at the corner with two young girls. He was tall, with short black hair and no hat. His well-worn parka seemed like it had been through many a winter. The man had a brown paper shopping bag in his right hand, keeping his left hand hidden in his jacket pocket. The two children were bundled in pink jackets and matching hats, their brown eyes peeking out over the tops of their scarves. Their white boots were hidden beneath a layer of dirty slush. I wondered where they could be headed on such a chilly, gray day.

I pulled over and asked, "Are you waiting for the Main Street bus?"

"Yes, Ma'am. We've been here nearly thirty minutes so I'm hoping it will be around soon," he replied politely.

I had overheard a conversation about the Main Street bus at the holiday party. Clients were discussing the inconvenience created by the recent Sunday service elimination. Many rode this route regularly and had to find other means of transportation. Few had cars and walking was brutal on these winter days.

"It doesn't run on Sundays anymore," I told him as I got out of my car to avoid shouting. "Where are you headed?"

"Well that explains the wait. I'll have to call a cab. Thank you," he said. "We're heading home, about four miles. We were at Grandma's house helping her with holiday preparations."

For a brief moment, I heard my mother's voice in my head, reminding me to never speak to strangers and especially never, ever to offer a ride to a stranger. However, seeing this young family shivering in the cold, I felt the only option was to lend a hand and get them out of the cruel weather.

"I'm headed that way, too. Please, let me drive you," I instinctively replied. "It's too cold for anyone to be out here, and I'd be happy to have the company." I pulled out a business card and handed it to him as a way of introducing myself and establishing credibility.

"Are you sure? I don't want to put you out. Now that I know there's no bus, I can just call a cab," he replied.

"No, really, it would be my pleasure. Please. I'm going that way anyway and you'll get there faster," I insisted.

"Okay, if you're sure. Thank you, thank you so much," he said with a smile as the girls climbed into the back seat. "I'm Joshua and these are my daughters, Tanya and Toni."

"Nice to meet all of you," I mumbled. "Make sure your seat belts are on."

"You are like an angel from heaven," Joshua said. "It is so bitterly cold out there, and we were starting to lose feeling in our fingers and toes. We were able to get a ride here, but I didn't know the bus wouldn't be running today. I would like to repay your kindness in some way, but I only have our bus passes and a few holiday decorations in this bag."

"Thank you, but there is no need. I'm glad I came by at this exact time and was able to help," I replied. "After all, we are all here just to take care of each other, right?"

Slowly and carefully, I made my way through the treacherous streets. The girls chatted about the day at Grandma's and shared their Santa wish lists. Much like the clients I had served earlier in the day, I hoped Joshua and his family would enjoy a warm, joyous holiday season.

I insisted on dropping my passengers off as close to their destination as possible. The girls thanked me and gleefully called out "Merry Christmas" as they stomped up the walkway to their house. "Thank you again for being our angel. I hope kindness finds its way back to you," Joshua said as he closed the car door.

What he didn't realize was that it already had. I was blessed with an impromptu human connection, lifted spirits and a warmed heart.

~Cara Rifkin

44

A Man Named Caesar

*Unselfish and noble actions are the most
radiant pages in the biography of souls.*
~David Thomas

"Excuse me. Could you help me please?" I looked over and saw an older, gray-haired man waiting on the steps. He was near the sidewalk in front of my apartment complex.

I had never seen anyone stand there before, so it took me by surprise. I usually parked in the back lot, but that day there were no spaces available so I had parked out front.

My neighbors were walking right by him as if he didn't exist. "What's wrong?" I asked.

The man had a timid stance, with his shoulders hunched over and his hands shaking. He hesitated, then walked toward me. I couldn't help but notice his disheveled appearance. His clothes hung from his thin frame and his hair stuck out in all directions.

"My name is Caesar. I've been here for a while asking for help. People walk by, yet no one sees or hears me."

I was already running late and still needed to pack my car so I could get to my parents' on time. I was hoping I wouldn't have to call to say I'd be late again.

I looked into his eyes and knew that being there with him then was more important than being on time.

My neighborhood wasn't always the safest. I'd been afraid there before, which affected how I lived my life. I made sure I got home before dark. I installed alarms on the doors and windows, and I always checked the locks twice before going to bed. Still, I worried.

Oddly, here was a total stranger, yet instead of fear I felt only peace. In fact, the closer he came, the stronger the feeling became.

"What can I do to help?" I asked.

"I'm lost, and I don't have any money for the bus. I haven't eaten anything today, and I'm so hungry."

He looked so sad that he had to ask for help. I could feel how afraid he was. I wanted to take care of him and help any way I could.

I was lost in a different way, so I knew how hard it was to ask. I was a single mom who could no longer meet the rigors of a physically demanding and stressful job. I had ongoing health issues. I had a little savings but no income. I had my family's support, and I was grateful for that, but it left me feeling guilty and ashamed. How could I repay the kindness I'd been shown? I couldn't begin to imagine.

I gave Caesar exact change for the bus and money for food.

"Thank you," he said with tears in his eyes. "Can I give you a hug?"

I immediately said "Yes," surprising myself. Hugging was not something I often did. I usually kept to myself, especially that year when my disability and aimlessness had made me feel so bad about myself.

We reached out for each other at the same time. While we were hugging, he kept thanking me.

"Thank you. Thank you. I will go home and pray for you." He had the sweetest energy around him. As the tears streamed down his face and onto my jacket, he looked up and showed his radiant smile. Then he hugged me again.

Euphoria spread throughout my being. I was in the clouds during the whole exchange, and I found later that I was able to revisit that state whenever I thought of him. I was so down, and it was so life-changing for me to be able to help someone else for once.

Caesar kept thanking me and then he hugged me one last time.

I ran inside to get something for him to eat until he could buy food.

When I came back out, he was nowhere in sight. There wasn't a soul around. I didn't hear cars or the bus as I normally would have. I was gone less than a minute.

I went down to the sidewalk and looked up and down the block but he wasn't anywhere.

Wherever you are, Caesar, I thank you for changing my life that day. I pray that you are safe, and someone is taking care of you. I think of you and know that you are wishing the same for me.

I'm glad that back parking lot was full.

~Andrea Engel

45

Angel at Our Door

Every house where love abides and friendship is a
guest, is surely home, and home sweet home,
for there the heart can rest.
~Henry Van Dyke

The insistent pounding on the door brought me quickly from my kitchen. With three little ones down for a nap, I hurried to answer before they were all awakened prematurely.

We had just moved into the neighbourhood and I couldn't imagine who it would be. Opening the door a crack revealed an old man dressed in dirty clothing, wearing mud-encrusted rubber boots. From his hand hung a torn plastic bag.

"Can I help you?" I asked, hoping he had the wrong address.

"Would ya like to buy some fresh garden vegetables?" His voice was shaky with age but his faded blue eyes were hopeful.

"Are they from your garden?" Peering inside his shabby bag, I saw mostly dirt, with a hint of carrots.

"Yes." His voice was soft and scratchy. "And I kin get some apples from a tree in my yard. Would ya like some of those too?"

My heart softened at his neglected appearance, and I wondered if he desperately needed the bit of money he was asking for his produce. With a sigh, I gestured him in. "Please step inside and I'll get my purse."

The next day, he knocked at our door again. This time, my gregarious little four-year-old got there first. "Oh, hello. Would you like to come in for tea?" Heidi's high-pitched-voice carried an adult inflection.

Without hesitating, the old man stepped inside and held out a broken basket with several bruised apples resting at the bottom. "From my tree," he said, removing a worn cap that had seen better days. "Thought ya might like to make a pie."

There was no mistaking the wistful look in his eye.

The three of us sat at the kitchen table and sipped our tea, Heidi's cup containing a much weaker version. Sheer delight in hosting a visitor was evident in her never-ending stream of questions. "What is your name? Where do you live? Why are your clothes so dirty? Will your mother be mad at you?"

The homeless-looking man chuckled as he attempted to answer each question. His name was Mr. Locket and he lived around the corner. His wife had passed away several years before, and his children all lived far away. He was lonely. His need for companionship had sent him door to door under the ruse of selling fruit and vegetables. Ours was the only door opened to him that day.

Eventually, the cookies were gone and he struggled to his feet. Shuffling his way to the door, he turned and offered us a cheerful grin and a wave goodbye.

As I watched him limp painfully to an ancient bicycle propped against our house, my heart melted.

Once on his bike, he wobbled back down the road, perhaps a little less lonely than before. He had promised to return tomorrow, and I knew what I wanted to do.

The next day, the children excitedly awaited his visit. The table was set with china and silver, with fancy napkins folded neatly beside each plate. A small bouquet of garden flowers, picked by little hands, adorned the centre of the table. Tantalizing aromas of cinnamon and sugar filled the house as a steaming apple pie beckoned from the table.

As he entered the kitchen, he took in the efforts made on his behalf, and his eyes filled with unshed tears. He focused on the golden-crusted, sugar-topped, apple pie. Pulling up a chair beside my two little girls, he immediately seemed at home, and we watched with amazement as he devoured half the dessert.

Wiping his whiskery lips, he commented, "Yur pies sure taste a lot better'n mine!"

My curiosity was piqued. "How do you make your pies?"

"Well, I just cut up them apples and put 'em in a pan. Then I bake 'em."

I smiled. A few simple tips would help him create at least a better version.

The next day, we found a basket sitting on the step. Inside were several rosy apples.

I slipped another pie into the oven that night.

As the days wore on, Mr. Locket became a daily visitor to our active home. In his quiet and gentle way, he endeared himself to each child. I loved to peek around the kitchen door and watch as he sat in our big comfy chair with one or two little ones curled up on his lap, gazing up at him with rapt attention as he read a children's book or told a story.

Mr. Locket became an honorary member of our family. When the little ones were tucked into their beds for an afternoon nap, he would rest his weary head on the back of the chair and join the babies in slumber. He usually went home when the sun dipped low in the sky, but stayed for dinner if pie was on the menu.

Our lively family antics at the dinner table always brought a smile to his weathered face. Later, as my husband put the children to bed, I'd stand in the doorway watching this dear old friend pedal his way home in the dark.

One day he revealed a hidden passion. "Ya know, I used to go to the library and get books ta read. It helps fill in the long, quiet nights. Don't rightly feel like riding that far anymore, though. S'pose you could lend me a book?"

"That's a wonderful idea!" I couldn't believe we hadn't discussed this sooner. I loved to read, too, and I delighted in sharing books. "What if I put a stack beside your chair for you to read during your visits, and then you can take home anything you want to finish?" His answering smile said it all.

It was fun to see which books he selected and watch him disappear between the pages. He still read to the children each day, and the name "Grandpa Locket" slipped effortlessly into our conversations. Both sets of my children's grandparents lived far away, so the children missed having them attend their Sunday school concerts and Christmas pageants. Although extremely deaf, Mr. Locket was now the grandpa that came to "Ooh" and "Ahh" over each little one's part in the programs.

"Did you hear me, Mr. Locket?" Heidi would chirp.

"Well, I didn't rightly hear ya, but I know it was good!"

Heidi would beam, her tiny hand grasping his old gnarled one. The two had become best friends.

Three years after first meeting Grandpa Locket, we learned we were being moved across the country to Ontario. That night, I tossed and turned. Pink sky began to peek through the window before I'd found a gentle way to break the news to Grandpa Locket.

When he arrived that morning, I took a deep breath and blurted it out. "Mr. Locket," I began, my voice wobbling. "We're going to be moving very soon. We're all very sad. You've become a treasured part of this family and we — we — we'll miss you."

The old man's chin slowly dropped to his chest as reality hit. Moisture glistened in the corners of his eyes.

Swallowing the lump in my throat, I took his worn, calloused hands in mine. "I promise to keep in touch with you and write letters regularly. The kids will send you pictures, and I'll ship as many books as you can read." My throat tightened and I couldn't speak any more.

He nodded and softly said, "Thank you for all your kindnesses to an old man. When I was lonely, ya took me in. When I needed a family, ya included me. My life's bin happy cuz of you." He reached down and rested his free hand on Heidi's head, gazing at her as if memorizing every delicate feature.

During our last visit together, we all hugged him tightly.

Without looking back, the old man limped out the door, straddled his rusty bike, and pedalled down the road.

With heavy hearts, we watched the familiar figure disappear around the corner for the last time. As we closed the door, we knew that a part of our lives was drawing to a close and a new stage was beginning, but no matter where we were, we'd never forget this incredibly precious man.

I kept my word and wrote regularly. The kids made him pictures, and I mailed books every month. We never received a letter in return, but somehow we knew he anxiously checked his mailbox every day to see if anything had arrived from us.

About a year later, a small envelope was delivered to our home — a letter from Mr. Locket's daughter. She informed us that our dear old friend had passed away. She'd found the letters, pictures, and gifts that we had sent, carefully tucked away in one of his dresser drawers. "I'm so grateful for your loving care for my father," she wrote. "I can see how much you meant to him, too."

With tremendous sadness, my husband and I shared this news with the children. Although we grieved the loss of our friend, we also felt a sense of joy. Remembering his gentle spirit and spontaneous chuckle made us smile. And we would never forget his love for apple pie.

We still feel it wasn't just an old man who knocked on our door that day, but an angel in disguise. We're so grateful for the unexpected love that swept into our lives the moment we opened that door.

~Heather Rodin

46

Amazing Grace

When one is thankful for the blessings in their life, they
are choosing to attract more positivity and abundance.
~Michael Austin Jacobs, Change Your Perspective,
Change Your Life

first met Star twenty years ago when he was living on the streets in New York City. He earned an honest living on Astor Street, selling objects that had been discarded. He was a sober, well-dressed and soft-spoken twenty-eight-year-old African American.

"Paul," he said, "you wouldn't believe what people throw away." Everything he was wearing had been thrown out, including his perfectly fitted designer jeans. I picked up two art deco lamps displayed on his blanket, then realized I didn't have my wallet on me. On my way home to get some money I felt a tap on my shoulder. "Here, you can have them," Star said. I felt so touched that a man with so little could be so generous.

Star was sleeping in Tompkins Square Park. Two years earlier, he had come home and found his wife with another man. He moved out, and then, because he could no longer focus at work, he lost his janitorial job. When Star was three, his alcoholic father had left home. "I promised myself I would never do that to my kids, and here I went and did it."

I spent some time over the next four years helping him get off the streets. With help from my friends, Star found work and we took him back to see his kids. His two sons rushed to hug him. Star said it was the best day of his life. It was an incredible experience for me.

I saw so much of myself in Star. I still harbored resentments from my childhood, including my fear of my dad, or who I had made him out to be. I was still holding resentment for something my dad had yelled at me years before: "Wake up, you'll never amount to anything."

Star found work and a place to live for six months, but quit because his boss kept yelling racial slurs. He wound up back on the streets. When I left town a few times a month, I let Star stay in my apartment. I came back once to find my TV, VCR, and radio missing. Star had succumbed to heroin. I had no anger toward him, which surprised me. This was a momentary lapse, not indicative of who he truly was. It spoke to the pain he was in. He needed me even more now. I didn't take it personally at all. Forgiving Star and recognizing the demons that drove him also helped me to understand my own father better. I realized that his momentary lapses of temper simply revealed his pain. Both men loved me and had their own hardships to get through.

Maybe I had a lesson to learn about boundaries, but I knew Star was a good man who was lost. Humiliated, he apologized profusely. I told him our friendship was more important than my possessions.

When I met Star, all my energy had been going into my stand-up comedy career, which was daunting. I was so afraid of what I needed: to be famous, to prove myself, to pay rent. I had no time for a balanced life of vacations, relationships or sunsets. Being with Star opened my heart.

Five years after meeting Star, I moved to Los Angeles, where my career faltered. I was thirty-seven, at the lowest point in my life. I went bankrupt and I felt bankrupt, too, as if my dad was right. I learned to appreciate that my father was actually a successful man. I had been embarrassed all those years because he was a mailman and janitor and drove a ten-year-old car. But he provided for seven sons. I couldn't afford to feed a party of one.

I was down on my luck in Los Angeles when Star called. Now, he was the one on the upswing. He was a building manager, he was taking college courses, and he was back in his sons' lives and sober for four years. He said, "I can't thank you enough for all you did for me, Paul."

I teared up. If Star prevailed, so could I.

I heard my dad's words in a different light. He was right: I wouldn't amount to anything if I didn't wake up. I was doomed if I continued life with my current negative mindset. Someone once complimented my shirt, and instead of being pleased I went right to the dark side, thinking *What's wrong with my pants?* My world was dark because I kept putting out the light.

When I reconnected with Star recently, I learned that he went blind four years ago. His upbeat attitude amazed me. He said, "Paul, not once have I asked, 'Why me?' Aside from the initial shock and fear, I have a new place of gratitude, and oddly enough, I have a vision I never had. Paul, as a child my biggest fear was the dark. Can you believe that?

"Now I get around on my own, cross the street on my own. Sometimes I get help, but I can do more than I ever thought. I do my own laundry, cook my own meals. I have a new awareness. I know where every single item in my apartment is.

"While I was in rehab, a man took us out on walks, pointed out where the coffee shops were, the hot dog stands and the banks. He did this every day for two weeks. I later found out he was totally blind himself from birth. Can you believe it? Paul, that's when I knew I could handle this. I have my children in my life. I have survived so much.

"My mom raised seven kids. I could see the dirt through the floorboards in our kitchen. Get this, we had no stove; my mom would make French toast with an iron. Paul, that all prepared me to handle this. My family helps me, and my friends. I am blessed."

Just when I was getting too caught up in my career and money, Star reminded me what it's all about. Being. Being grateful. Getting in touch with the vision behind our seeing, the vision that we came into this life with and the vision that lives on.

I realized what Star had given me: He let me help him. I'm considering buying a house and mentioned it to my dad. He was thrilled. A week later I opened a letter from him with a generous check to help with the down payment.

For years I wanted my dad to apologize, not ever realizing all the good things and deeds he repeatedly has done for me, especially looking past the chip on my shoulder to continue to help me. Dad has always been there for me. And what illuminated all of this for me was a kind, homeless stranger who offered me two lamps for free.

~Paul Lyons

Chapter 6

Random Acts of Kindness

Never Too Young to Help

Every child comes with the message that
God is not yet discouraged of man.
~Rabindranath Tagore

47

A Modest and Moveable Thanksgiving Feast

Thanksgiving, after all, is a word of action.
~W.J. Cameron

We had finally decided to skip our traditional family dinner and make the pilgrimage to Macy's Thanksgiving Day Parade with our five-year-old daughter, Kerry. We never anticipated what Kerry would take away from the experience, or how it would affect our lives for years to come.

We caught the dawn train from Poughkeepsie to Grand Central along with hundreds of other excited celebrants. Like many other families we packed a small backpack with sliced turkey sandwiches and juice boxes; eating on the fly in New York City is expensive and complicated, unless you settle for pretzels and roasted chestnuts from a street vendor. Kerry was wide-eyed and a little overwhelmed. This was not your ordinary outing with Mom and Dad.

As the train pulled into the terminal, everyone rose and stood in the aisle anxiously waiting to disembark and head toward the parade route along Fifth Avenue. Rather than have our diminutive daughter jostled by the crowds, we waited until everyone had stepped off onto the pandemonium of the platform. As we walked up to the entrance to the terminal Kerry spotted a homeless woman sitting in the shadows, invisible to all except my curious daughter.

"What's that?" she asked. Linda and I looked at each other, caught off guard by the need to explain something very different than the happy scene we were about to join. During our first years of parenthood we'd discussed how we would explain such nearly ineffable topics as God, death, and eventually sex and love. But homelessness? We weren't prepared. We gave as simple and honest an explanation as we could muster and continued on to the parade.

The following year, we decided to attend the parade again. So the night before Thanksgiving we went shopping for sliced turkey for sandwiches. Again, Kerry caught us off guard.

"Can we bring some sandwiches for those people?" she asked. We knew immediately whom she meant. How could we refuse? More importantly, why would we refuse? This was a golden opportunity to honor Kerry's sense of charity. Our six-year-old daughter was teaching us an important lesson. We bought five pounds of sliced turkey, two loaves of bread and a can of cranberry sauce. What are turkey sandwiches on Thanksgiving without the tangy-sweet taste of cranberry sauce? That night we prepared and packed two-dozen sandwiches into our now overstuffed backpack.

The next morning we took the train into Manhattan again but there was a different excitement brewing in our little family. We waited until all the other families had left the train and hustled off to the parade route. Then we walked up the ramp toward the terminal, scanning the shadows. There was a homeless man sitting in the same spot as last year. We stopped and extracted the first of the little feasts from the pack. Without a word of instruction we handed it to Kerry. She walked over to the man slowly, standing still until he looked up at her. She reached out and handed the sandwich to him. Neither spoke a word. Then we were off to the parade, stopping along the way to distribute the rest of the sandwiches, except one for each of us. Somehow, no giant Thanksgiving sit-down feast ever tasted as good as those sandwiches.

Over the next decade we took a hiatus from the parade and shared the day with our families. And then, one year, our extended families couldn't get together for Thanksgiving, so we decided to resume our

Manhattan parade tradition. This time, Kerry was bringing a boyfriend along.

We were still inside the terminal when Kerry spotted the first homeless man sitting motionless in a dark corner. She extracted a sandwich and took it over to him, as usual not exchanging a word. She must have prepped her boyfriend; he wasn't as perplexed as we expected. Not only did Kerry fulfill her sense of kindness and generosity but she also passed on her good example. She's a thirty-year-old mother now with three daughters of her own. They haven't made it to the parade yet. I hope they ask us to come along when they do. There's nothing like sharing a turkey sandwich with new friends.

~Thom Schwarz

48

Kindness Is Logical

We worry about what a child will become tomorrow,
yet we forget that he is someone today.
~Stacia Tauscher

held my breath, trying not to sigh out loud. My seventeen-year-old stepson Arthur and I were leaving a holiday work function and there was plenty of leftover food that the organizers were trying to give away. Immediately Arthur honed in on a large dish of tiramisu that no one else wanted. It was enough dessert for four people, and Arthur's doctor had warned us about watching his sugar intake.

"Please, Gwen? Please?"

I gazed at my 6'2" teen batting puppy dog eyes at me, and the automatic "no" I was about to utter withered away as "Strict Mom" and "Cool Mom" waged an internal battle in my head.

Strict Mom: He shouldn't be eating that much sugar.

Cool Mom: But it's the holidays!

Strict Mom: He'll be hyper all night and then cranky tomorrow.

Cool Mom: So just tell him to pace himself and that he can't have it all in one sitting.

Strict Mom (snorting): Yeah, that'll happen.

Cool Mom: He's been handling himself very well tonight. One dessert is not going to kill him.

If it seems strange that a fully-grown adolescent boy was begging for sweets like a much younger child, there is something you should know about my kid. Arthur is autistic, and while he is extremely intelligent, he sometimes displays social quirks that cause moments of awkwardness. Like towering over me with his hands clasped and begging me to take home dessert in front of my colleagues — loudly.

"Please, Gwen? PLEASE?"

I relented. It had been a long day, and I had dragged him to this dinner because his father was out of town and I didn't want to leave him at home by himself. And even though Arthur tends to get exhausted by social situations that are not part of his regular routine, he accompanied me to the dinner and charmingly chatted with my colleagues until it was time to go home. The tiramisu, I reasoned, was his reward and a thank-you for tolerating the change in his schedule.

As we left the restaurant, Arthur clutched the dessert in his hands as he walked happily beside me through the parking lot. I tried to hurry him along when he stopped next to our car to look at something. I turned to see what had him so transfixed.

Standing about five feet away was a gentleman hunched into his threadbare jacket, stomping his feet and rubbing his hands together in an attempt to ward off the cold. Every few seconds he smiled and tried to speak to the people who were walking by without paying him any attention. At that moment, the gentleman turned around and spotted my son watching him. Before I could say anything, the man smiled broadly and spoke: "Hey man, do you happen to have any spare change?"

Arthur checked his empty pockets and then looked at me briefly. I shook my head — I hardly ever carry cash anymore. Arthur frowned and then he said something that took my breath away.

"No, I don't. But are you hungry? Do you like tiramisu?"

"Tiramisu? Naw, I don't think I've ever had it. But yeah, I'm hungry."

Arthur's whole face lit up. "Tiramisu is great! Here, you can have mine. It's a dessert that's creamy, tastes like…"

The man's eyes began to gleam as Arthur described the many virtues of this wonderful dish, and told him in no uncertain terms how he should eat it and savor its flavor. I blinked back tears as I watched the man's smile broaden even more in appreciation because I knew his joy wasn't about tiramisu.

I thought about how many people had ignored this man as he walked the streets that day. How many chose to act as if he were invisible? I had to admit to myself that I might have acted the same way. But my son? The one who just moments before had loudly begged me for a ridiculously large serving of tiramisu was now happily giving his reward away to a man because he was hungry. And he didn't just give the food and walk away. He engaged the man in conversation, perhaps the first one this gentleman had all day. He treated the man as a person, with respect, with dignity, and with kindness. The smile on the man's face told me this was the real reason for his happiness.

After Arthur finished his lecture on the proper way to eat tiramisu, the man thanked him profusely and shook his hand. Arthur smiled back at him, walked back to the car, and slid into the passenger seat. As we drove away, I looked in my rearview mirror to see the man carefully spreading out his tiramisu before him, following Arthur's instructions.

Choking back my emotions, I looked at this wonderfully quirky kid who had recently entered my life and I felt "Proud Mom" pushing her way to the surface.

"I'm really proud of you, Arthur. That was really thoughtful and I think you made his day."

His response then is the same as it is now whenever I recount this story: "It's only logical, Gwen."

Some people believe that people with autism lack empathy, that they are incapable of feeling and value logic over emotion. But we autism parents know differently. Arthur often tells me that he feels that he has *too* much empathy, which causes painful sensory overload resulting in a need to spend hours by himself in his room. And yet, he never fails to help people when he senses they are in need. My son loves to help others, and his favorite pastime is to volunteer at various charities in our community. He works hard to contribute to society in his own way and on his own terms.

I think often of that day and the lessons I learned: One, people with autism definitely have feelings and emotions just like us "neurotypicals." Two, autistics can and most definitely are empathetic to others' feelings even if they don't know how to express it. But the third lesson is perhaps the most important one of all—that being kind doesn't have to be difficult or complex.

Because as Arthur often reminds me: "Kindness is logical, Gwen. Kindness is logical."

~Gwen Navarrete Klapperich

49

Santa's Special Helpers

It is the heart that does the giving;
the fingers only let go.
~Nigerian Proverb

M y daughter and I pushed the overloaded cart up and down the aisles of the crowded store. She reached up and grabbed a game, and without asking, threw it in the cart. "Is that for you?" I asked.

"No, Santa already knows what I want. This is for my friend," she nonchalantly answered. I was proud of her. Being an only child and an only grandchild, she could have been spoiled, but instead she was caring and very giving, almost to a fault.

On the drive home, my talkative little helper was unusually quiet. Finally, she said, "Mommy, if Santa brings all the gifts, why are we buying them?"

"That's a good question," I said as I quickly tried to think of an answer.

Before I could say anything else, she yelled, "I know why. We're Santa's helpers!"

I laughed as I said, "You took the words right out of my mouth. Yes, that's exactly what we are; we're Santa's helpers."

A few days later, she came home from school quite upset, explaining, "Mommy, there's a girl in my class who's very mean to me and my friends. We talk to her anyway, and when we asked her what she was getting for Christmas, she started crying. She said she wasn't getting anything because her mother is very sick and her father doesn't have the money to pay for anything, not even food."

I calmed her down as I tried to explain that the holiday season can be a very hard time for some people, but this little girl and her family would be all right because Santa has special helpers who always help those in need.

A few days before school let out for Christmas vacation, my daughter asked if this little girl could come over to make the holiday cookies. Quite surprised, I told her that of course she could. When she came, I was happy to see the two girls getting along well and having so much fun. When we gave her new friend a container full of cookies to take home to her family, she was ecstatic. She told us she would give them to her mother for Christmas.

Later that evening, my daughter asked if she could have some wrapping paper to wrap the gifts she had gotten for her friends. I gave her a roll and went back to what I was doing. She came back and asked for more, I told her to get whatever she needed and continued what I was doing. When she came back again, I thought it was odd and asked her why she was using so much paper. She said, "Because I want the gifts to look pretty," and quickly ran back into her room.

On the last day of school, I had to leave for work extra early, so I asked her best friend's mother if she could pick up my daughter since she had quite a few gifts and cupcakes to take for the class Christmas party. I never actually saw what my daughter took to school with her.

Then, on Christmas Eve, I was wrapping gifts and noticed a few of them were missing. I looked high and low and couldn't find them. Finally, I woke my daughter and asked if she knew where they were. She said, "Mommy, I wrapped them and gave them to my friend."

I yelled. "All of them?"

She said, "Mommy, you said we were Santa's helpers!"

I said, "Yes we are, but you should've asked me if you could give those gifts away."

She started crying and said, "But you told me to take whatever I needed."

She continued, "Mommy, my friend said…"

I cut her off and yelled, "I don't care what your friend said. You're not to take anything out of this house without asking or letting me know!"

My daughter began crying uncontrollably. I told her to go back to sleep, walked out of the room, and slammed the door behind me.

So angry that I could hardly see straight, I sat in the living room taking inventory. A pair of bedroom slippers, a nightgown, a housecoat, her father's expensive cologne, stuffed animals, games, hats and gloves were all gone.

Early Christmas morning, I answered the phone to hear a woman crying. She introduced herself and thanked me over and over again for the beautiful gifts. She said if it weren't for them, they wouldn't have had anything. She told me that she was sick and was in and out of the hospital, and they couldn't afford to buy anything for the kids, not even a Christmas tree. She told me how happy the kids were with their stuffed animals, games, hats, gloves and cookies, how badly she needed the slippers, nightgown and housecoat, and how much her husband loved the cologne.

Speechless, and with tears in my eyes, I asked if I could call her back. I told my daughter about the phone call, and then we dug out our old tree and ornaments, packed some food, and took everything over to her friend's house. The mother and I fixed the family a quick dinner as the kids played and her husband set up the tree. I'll never forget their smiling faces.

Before my daughter and I left to go to my parents' house, we ate, played games and sang Christmas carols with them. We had the best time ever, and little did we know it was the beginning of an enduring friendship.

That was a long time ago, but I think that was one of the best Christmases we ever had. It changed our lives and made us see how blessed we really were. That year a tradition was started, and from then on, we have made sure to give or do something special for those in need at Christmastime.

My daughter and her friend are now grown women, and our families have kept up the tradition of spending Christmas together. I'll always be very proud of my daughter, and thankful for her generosity that year, even though I didn't initially embrace it. From her we learned the true significance of helping and giving, and we became Santa's very special helpers for life.

~Francine L. Billingslea

50

Grocery Store Giving

*I feel that the greatest reward for doing is the
opportunity to do more.*
~Dr. Jonas Salk

A few years ago, I ceased making elaborate New Year's resolutions and settled instead on a "word of the year." As I began 2014, I looked forward to how the word "gift" would frame my new year.

I planned to give a gift a day for the entire year. I also intended to keep track of the gifts in a colorful little journal that a friend had handcrafted and given me as a Christmas present.

I wanted to be intentional with my giving. Some gifts would take time to prepare and present — such as the quilt top that I sewed for months and then sent to a quilting group to turn into a sleeping bag for a homeless person. Some of the other gifts I gave came about more spontaneously, such as helping a man read a label on an item at a store when he'd forgotten his reading glasses. But either way, I always tried to be on the lookout for an opportunity to serve.

Many of my gifts in 2014 involved reading to my two sons, especially at night. If I let them talk me into reading an extra chapter aloud before bedtime, I counted that as my gift of the day. Sometimes reading a picture book before we started our homeschool day was my daily gift; other times, I read to my boys at lunch. Good stories make great gifts, and reading aloud to my children creates beautiful memories.

Twice I left a few coins on an outdoor fountain for a stranger to find and toss into the water, casting a wish into the pool along with a penny or nickel. It may have cost a few cents, but I considered it an investment in brightening another person's day. Along the way, I also brightened my own.

Other gifts I gave only once during the year, such as making a meal for a family with a newborn baby or baking a birthday cake for my husband.

One of my most repeated gifts throughout the year involved letting other customers go ahead of me in line at the grocery store. With a buggy full of food purchases and two little boys in tow, I wanted to buy my groceries and get home. But when I noticed a person standing in line behind me with only a loaf of bread or a case of bottled water, I spotted a chance to put another's needs before my own.

Throughout the year, I spoke with my children about my gift-giving, and they enjoyed hearing my stories. Sometimes my boys would ask me, "What was your gift today?" when we settled down for bedtime at night.

When my sons and I stood in line one day at the store, organic spinach and spaghetti and fruit snacks filling our cart, my older son motioned for me to lean down to him. He cupped his little hand around my ear and whispered, "There's somebody in line behind us, and he has only two things to buy."

I looked behind us to verify, and sure enough, a bearded man in a jean jacket stood there with only two items. I felt my smile stretch wide across my face as I realized that my boy had joined in on the joy of giving and wanted us to be part of that together.

I motioned to the customer behind us to take our place in line. We pulled our grocery buggy back a bit and waited a few more minutes before loading our purchases onto the counter. The few extra minutes of wait time passed with my hardly realizing it. They were minutes wisely invested.

Although this act of giving didn't qualify as something original or surprising, it remains one of my favorite gifts of 2014 — and all because I saw how my choice to give had become part of my children's lives as well.

~Allison Wilson Lee

51

On Hands and Knees

Do not be wise in words — be wise in deeds.
~Jewish Proverb

They were a group of two-year-old children running around the yard on a beautiful summer day, without a care in the world. They seemed to be embracing life in their play, making up their own games and activities, running in circles for the sheer delight of it.

The running morphed into some semblance of tag, as they all chased each other, tumbling, giggling and then getting up and tumbling again. I couldn't help but smile at their youthful exuberance.

Then I noticed a little blip marring the perfection of the scene. It was Sarah, the child from next door, the same age as those running around my front yard. The only difference was that beautiful, charming Sarah was developmentally delayed and not quite on the same level as her peers. At two years old, Sarah was not yet walking. This did nothing to temper her joy, however, and Sarah was one of the most cheerful, enthusiastic children you'll meet.

She had approached the group of children with an anticipatory smile of delight on her cherubic face, eager to participate in the fun. However, with each moment that she sat on the sidelines unable to participate in the running, her smile faded just a bit more, until she had a forlorn, abandoned look on her face.

She crawled desperately around in circles, waiting for someone to notice her, to include her. I couldn't fathom the depths of her pain, nor could I figure out what to do to alleviate that pain.

It turns out that one of the toddlers of the bunch was far wiser than I. With a quick glance at Sarah, and without missing a beat, Baruch crouched down on all fours and began crawling toward her.

"Thawah, catch me!" he shouted with his adorable two-year-old lisp. With that, he made an about-face and began furiously crawling away. Her entire countenance lit up, and in a second she was racing toward him. It took only a few seconds before the rest of the children caught on and dropped to their hands and knees, too, resuming their game of tag right where they had left off, only this time with one additional player. One deliriously thrilled player, made to feel like one of the gang despite her disabilities, thanks to the thoughtfulness of her two-year-old friend.

And I, the grown-up onlooker, having been completely blindsided by the depth of compassion and sensitivity of a toddler, couldn't keep the tears from streaming down my face.

I think of this story often, marveling at the difference one toddler made in the life of another and the difference we can all make by looking out for others, anticipating their needs and extending our kindness and compassion to those less fortunate.

And I wonder if that little boy, who is my brother, by the way, is even aware of the tremendous impact he had on his friend's life that day, of how he opened worlds for her just by looking beyond himself and getting down on his hands and knees to meet her where she was.

I marvel at the fact that it took a child to teach me the ultimate lesson in empathy and kindness, a lesson whose impact still has not diminished although this story took place many years ago. I only hope that someday I can make a difference in someone's life as profound as the one that my little brother did on that beautiful summer day.

~Devora Adams

52

A Simple Red Leaf

Every time you smile at someone, it is an action of
love, a gift to that person, a beautiful thing.
~Mother Teresa

He was there every morning, sitting motionless on the front steps of his house. His bright blue eyes seemed so far away and sad. In the morning light I could see the shadows that were etched deep within the lines surrounding his eyes.

Each morning I walked this route with my daughter to her kindergarten class. We were new to the neighborhood so I didn't know many of my neighbors. On one beautiful autumn morning, as we passed his house, my daughter piped up and called out to him: "Hi, Mr. Man!" Always the outgoing child, I wasn't surprised at her enthusiasm. But her cheerfulness soon faded when the man didn't look at her and say "Hi" back.

As we continued on our walk to school, my daughter asked why the man didn't want to say hi to her. Stumbling for words, because I didn't have an answer, I said simply, "Maybe he is having a bad day."

Once back home I tackled the breakfast dishes, and I thought about "Mr. Man." What was his story? Why did he seem so sad? I wanted to do something to cheer him up. I thought of a few ways to make his day a bit brighter, but nothing seemed special enough.

The next morning, after dropping my daughter off at school, I saw one of my other neighbors raking her front lawn. After I introduced myself, she invited me to sit and chat on her front porch for a while. I learned Theresa was a long time resident of the neighborhood. She knew everybody, and everything. She filled me in on practically every neighbor as we talked over steaming cups of coffee. Theresa had such a bubbly personality, but when I asked her about the man up the block, she got really serious. "Bob recently lost his wife in a car accident. He hasn't been the same since." She went on to tell me that Bob and his wife never had children, and she wasn't sure if he had any relatives.

The following week seemed to whiz by. I had talked to my daughter about what we could do to make Mr. Man smile. Should we bring him cookies or make him a card? With every suggestion I made, she simply said "No, not that." I asked her if she had any ideas of her own. "I will when it pops into my head!" she said confidently.

A few days later, as we approached Bob's house on our way to school, I saw him in his usual spot. My daughter called out "Hi Mr. Man!" as she did every morning, and as usual, he didn't respond. But then she ran onto his front lawn and picked up a beautiful red autumn leaf. She continued up one step and handed it to him. I held my breath.

Bob turned to her, took the leaf and smiled. As she skipped back to me, she turned to Bob, and said, "See you tomorrow, Mr. Man!" This time, he acknowledged her. In a soft gentle voice, he thanked her and said, "See you tomorrow."

From then on, Bob and my daughter exchanged greetings each morning. Bob's eyes didn't look as sad, and he would light up whenever he saw us coming. We made it a habit to leave a little early each day so we could chat with him a bit before school.

One afternoon, right before Thanksgiving, I found an envelope taped to my front door. It contained a greeting card with an illustration of a beautiful autumn tree. Inside, in perfect penmanship, it simply read: "Thank you, from Mr. Man." I couldn't wait to show my daughter.

Our friendship with Bob continued for many years. He was part of our life, coming to birthday parties and holiday dinners. But, the sweetest day is when Bob attended my daughter's high school graduation. He was older then, and it was painful for him to walk, but he wouldn't have missed that day for anything in the world.

Our memories of that graduation day still bring tears to our eyes. Bob gave my daughter a gift — a book on identifying various plants and trees. There, tucked in the pages that described an oak tree, was the leaf my daughter had given to Mr. Man when they first met. He had dried and pressed it and kept it all those years.

~Dorann Weber

53

From Five Dollars to a Wealth of Compassion

*Nobody made a greater mistake than he who did
nothing because he could only do a little.*
~Edmund Burke

As a high school teacher, I wanted to play a role in pointing my students toward a life of service. All they needed was opportunity and a little encouragement.

The Five Dollars Project was a simple exercise in mindfulness and compassion. As part of our unit on Buddhism, each student in Introduction to World Religions received an envelope. Inside were a five-dollar bill and a note: "Use this gift for good. Return and tell your story."

A church in Sherborn, Massachusetts, had recently tried the same exercise with its parishioners, and the stories of compassion were amazing. But these were high school students. Who knew what would happen?

One week after my students received their envelopes, they returned to tell their stories. Here is a sampling:

Three students took their five dollars to Dunkin Donuts. They bought hot chocolates and stood at the local bus stop in the cold, handing out drinks to shivering travelers. One student wrote, "I realized that helping others and doing good is a lot easier than I imagined. These opportunities are all around us every day."

Another student recalled the local homeless man who frequented the sub shop where the student worked. He bought the man a foot-long sub, and he wrote, "I have realized the compassion that I should and will feel toward those in need, instead of looking down on them."

One enterprising student took her five dollars to the dollar store and bought warm clothes — hats, gloves, and scarves — and distributed them to the homeless. She reported, "I felt guilty for complaining about being outside in the cold for a minute and a half, when there are homeless people walking around in the cold all day. This is when I made my decision."

Another girl bought milk and bread for her neighbors. Several students bought gifts for the Toys for Tots program. And the list goes on. From donations to the Salvation Army to childhood cancer organizations to animal welfare groups, students eagerly sought opportunities to make an impact. Many pooled money or added their own earnings to the five dollars they received to help individuals and families with holiday gifts and basic food and clothing needs.

One of the most moving stories came from a student originally from Kenya. In her native country, she had frequently helped an elderly woman who was poor and, in the student's words, "surviving on nature." The student asked her parents how she might use the money to help the woman, who was 100 years old. Together they organized a family and friends dinner to build upon the original five dollars. They raised $300 — a life-changing gift for an unsuspecting woman halfway across the globe.

As educators, we often worry about our young charges. Will lessons in character take root? Do teachers really make a difference? Can this next generation repair the world?

With their five dollars, my students reassured me. The world is in good hands.

~Lorne A. Bell

54

The Walk Home

When I look out at the people and they look at me and
they're smiling, then I know that I'm loved. That is
the time when I have no worries, no problems.
~Etta James

I slumped on my couch, weary from the stressful workday. My singular goal for the night was to stuff my face with chocolate ice cream.

Then my phone buzzed. I picked it up and read a text from my friend Sylvia: "Are you going to the high school reunion?"

Oh my god, had it really been twenty years already?

I realized that attending the reunion could be awkward since I had not kept in touch with anyone except Sylvia. I was about to text Sylvia that I was going to pass when I thought about Kyle. I had not thought of him in years, but he had changed my life.

It was 1979. To say that I was a nine-year-old outcast was not an exaggeration. I was the only Vietnamese kid in the school. In 1975, my family had landed in California as the result of a very unpopular war, speaking a weird sounding language that no one had ever heard. On top of that, I was poor, painfully shy, and terribly unathletic. Being a fourth grader who could not kick a soccer ball to save her life was the grammar school kiss of death. And did I mention that I wore the most nerdy, thick eyeglasses ever? I was Ugly Betty's less attractive Asian sister.

I never felt like I fit in and I was always self-conscious. It seemed like everything I did or said was stupid, lame, or wrong. Some kids were indifferent to me, some pitied me, and others teased me.

In the fourth grade hierarchy, I was definitely the lowest girl on the totem pole.

On the other end of the totem pole was Kyle. He was unequivocally the most popular kid in the fourth grade. Kyle had a sun-kissed glow to him that screamed health and vitality. He was gifted athletically, so when it came time to make teams for soccer or dodge ball, he was always the first to be chosen. All the girls admired Kyle's boyish good looks, so he was the unknowing subject of many schoolgirl crushes.

One day, after school concluded, I was taking my usual walk home when Jake came walking alongside me. Jake was a scary, brash sixth grader who lived a few houses down from my home. We had never uttered a word to each other until that day.

For children with low self-esteem, the unwritten rules of conduct include never making eye contact with anyone and always walking with your head down. In order to combat the boredom, I made up a game where I counted the cracks on the sidewalk. Since I was busy counting cracks, I never realized the exact moment when Jake aimed his frightening smirk at me. But what I do remember vividly is what he said to me.

"You are the ugliest girl I have ever seen! Your ugly, dirty face makes me sick! Why don't you go back to where you came from you gross little… " He proceeded to barrage me with a slew of offensive racial slurs with a satisfied smile on his face. I could tell that he was enjoying this tirade immensely.

I was humiliated and frozen in silence. Even though Jake was only about six inches taller than me, at that moment he seemed like a powerful giant, and I felt like a tiny ant. Tears began to form under my eyeglasses as Jake laughed and walked across the street, leaving his powerful words reverberating in my head. I wanted to disappear from the face of the earth.

Suddenly, I heard "Hey, Mai. Can I walk with you?" I turned and saw Kyle standing there; his infectious smile comforted me in a way that I had never expected. Those seven magical words stopped the flow of my tears. Without another word, we began the walk together. For the first time in my life, I felt protected.

From that point on, Kyle became my frequent after-school walking companion. Many times I wondered why he was walking with me. I was truly puzzled. But I never asked, in case he came to his senses and realized that he was jeopardizing his rock star status by associating with me. So I remained silent and just enjoyed his companionship.

Kyle's friendship even extended itself during school hours. He would often turn around to talk to me during class, resulting in stern disapproval from our teacher. Being reprimanded by Mrs. Jones actually became fun!

Seasons passed. Falls turned into winters. Winters turned into summers. Before I knew it, I was in the sixth grade. One day, the teacher announced that a new student, Susan, had joined our class. Later, I approached Susan and said, "Hey. Aren't you the new girl?" She just laughed and said "Yeah." Looking back, I realized that I would have never had the confidence to approach Susan had it not been for Kyle and how he made me feel about myself.

Eventually Susan and I became immersed in a circle of girls and these girls became our constant companions. It finally came to pass that I no longer "needed" Kyle.

On the night of my high school reunion, I was brimming with excitement. I could not wait to find Kyle. I wanted to tell him that he had turned one of the worst days of my life into one of the best. I was going to tell him that he literally walked me through some of the most difficult years of my life. I had no idea if he would even remember me or understand the impact he had on me. But if he didn't, I was fully determined to explain every wonderful detail to him. And to thank him profusely.

Sadly, Kyle did not attend the reunion. Neither did his friends. I went home and Googled him. Hundreds of results surfaced but they weren't him. I asked around but no one seems to know how to get in contact with him.

Wherever Kyle is now, I hope that he is well, successful, and fulfilled. If I ever find him, I will tell him that his smile brightened my dark world. I am going to insist that he keep smiling because every smile is an act of kindness. For me, that moment of kindness lasted a lifetime.

As a result of his friendship, I no longer count the cracks on the sidewalk because now I walk with my head held high. And I smile.

~Kristen Mai Pham

Chapter 7

Random Acts of **Kindness**

It Takes a Village

*We cannot live only for ourselves. A thousand
fibers connect us with our fellow men; and
among those fibers, as sympathetic threads,
our actions run as causes, and they come
back to us as effects.*
~Herman Melville

55

Taking Action

It is literally true that you can succeed best and
quickest by helping others to succeed.
~Napoleon Hill

Oleg was five feet tall, balding, middle-aged, and spoke English with a thick Russian accent. "I used to teach in university," he'd declare on a daily basis as he delivered packages to our New York City office. "In Russia, I was teacher and have degree. I teach computer technology. Here, in United States… I just messenger!"

Life was not treating Oleg well.

"Here he comes," my co-worker would whisper as he walked through the door and over to our shared cubicle.

Listening to Oleg's complaints became just another part of our day. We surmised that he didn't know many people in New York and needed to vent. He complained about his boss, his co-workers, his job, the weather, but mostly about his frustration in being "just a messenger."

"I teach computer science in Russia," he would remind us as my co-worker Emma handed him a cold Coca-Cola, which we always offered him. My boss always offers cold drinks to messengers, FedEx employees, most anyone that walks through the door. It's a nice habit, one that rubbed off on all the employees. Offering a cold drink to someone on a hot day might be the only kind action they receive during the week.

Kind actions make a difference, no matter how small.

Emma and I would patiently listen to Oleg as we went about our duties, making conference reservations and scheduling meetings for our boss. Of course, we felt sorry for Oleg, but after a while (because of the relentless complaining), I suppose we just turned him off.

One night, I had to stay late at the office as the company was having some computer issues. The network had been crashing on and off during the day. Not a good thing for a hedge fund! Prices of stocks are updated second-by-second and broken computers could result in a financial disaster.

Boris, our IT guy from an outsourced company was sent in to fix the job himself. He happened to be Russian (just like Oleg) and arrived just after 5:00 p.m. I was surprised to see him (as he was the head of the company) and assumed he must have been shorthanded that week.

I made him some coffee and showed him to the computer room. While he went into action, I tied up some loose ends at my desk. Eventually Boris, looking tired and worn, emerged from the computer room with good news: the network was fixed.

We both left the office, tired but in good spirits and I thanked him for working so late into the night.

It wasn't until the next day, when Oleg stood over my cubicle (complaining as usual) that it dawned on me.

Oleg needed a job… and Boris needed help.

This time, instead of just listening to Oleg's complaints, I took action.

"Do you really know how to fix computers?" I asked.

"Of course," he answered.

"Then, wait here a minute," I said as I dialed Boris's number. I had his business card on my desk (just in case the network crashed again).

After a few minutes, Boris was on the line. I quickly assured him that the network was working fine. "I'm calling for another reason," I said.

After I explained Oleg's situation, I handed Oleg the receiver. They spoke in Russian for a few minutes, but from the expression on Oleg's face, things were not promising.

"I meet him later today," he said flatly, handing me back the phone.

I wondered why he didn't smile, but figured he was just a realist.

A couple of days later, as I set my coffee down on my desk and asked Emma about her plans for the weekend, the phone rang.

I didn't recognize the person's voice at first, then realized it was Oleg. Boris had hired him! "I am in New Jersey and work today on computers for IT company. I will not be messenger anymore," he said.

I looked at Emma and relayed the information.

"Oleg got the job?" she asked smiling from ear to ear.

When I hung up the phone she added, "Mary, you changed his life."

I remember those words as if it was yesterday.

I actually changed someone's life. And all it took was a phone call. All it took was a little action.

How I didn't put the pieces together earlier, I don't know. I just wasn't in the right frame of mind, I suppose. A little action on my part would have saved a year of Oleg's suffering.

Imagine if we all were action-oriented on a regular basis. Just think of the difference we could make in others' lives. What a different world it would be!

I happily remember Emma's words and although my action was slow, it was still action.

And I'll never forget Emma's words: "You changed his life."

I'll also never forget Oleg on the other end of the phone that morning, complaining about his long commute to New Jersey for his new job.

~Mary C. M. Phillips

56

Relay Race

*Never worry about numbers. Help one person at a
time, and always start with the person nearest you.*
~Mother Teresa

As I walk along the sidewalk in front of Surplus Unlimited, the car that is about to change my life has just turned onto Route 82 from the CVS parking lot. I look up and notice the elderly couple in the car heading toward me. As the car rolls past, the driver suddenly collapses against the steering wheel. Right in front of my eyes, he collapses. His wife, a pale woman in her mid-eighties, stares blankly out the passenger side window. With an oxygen tube in her nose, she seems relaxed, breathing calmly. She is unaware that her car is now rolling — without a conscious driver — down the center of a busy four-lane road.

Stepping off the curb, I instinctively begin to jog alongside the moving car. My mind methodically assesses the situation. *This is not good… the old lady doesn't even realize her husband just passed out… traffic is heavy… that car is about to crash… SOMEONE NEEDS TO STOP THAT CAR!*

I reach forward, but there is nothing to grab. I pound on her window.

"Your husband! Your husband!" I scream at her through the glass. First she looks startled, then confused.

"Roll down the window!" I yell, gesturing wildly. Bewildered, she seems happy to comply. With the window down, I am able to grab the doorframe. I pull hard against the force of the moving vehicle. On the far side of the car, the traffic streams by in the opposite direction. Cars pass one after another. Nobody stops. Nobody slows down. Nobody even seems to notice. By the time it registers that there is a crazy lady hanging on to the doorframe of a moving car in the middle of Route 82 they have already driven past. The whole scene is so unlikely. So impossible.

Doubts roll through my mind: *How exactly does one stop a moving vehicle without getting killed in the process? This is not working... But if I go in front of the car I'll get run over... This is crazy! I can't stop a car!* (Now, I'm reasonably fit for a forty-four-year old mother of two, but stopping moving cars is not part of my fitness routine. How could I possibly have that strength?)

Then I hear the WORDS. I don't hear them with my ears, and I'm not thinking them. They're coming from somewhere outside of me. Like I can feel them. The words direct me, clearly and calmly:

"Just. Keep. Pulling."

I keep pulling, and the car begins to slow. (Thankfully, the driver's foot must have slipped off the gas pedal when he lost consciousness.) But, I'm on the passenger side, so there's no way I can reach the shift lever or the brake.

Just then, a woman appears from behind me. She runs alongside the driver side door. She opens the door and, as the car is slowing, she manages to shift it out of "Drive." I don't know what gear she shifts it into, but the engine makes a horrible crunching noise. A joyful "We did it!" feeling sweeps over me.

Next problem: the car is now stopped in the center lane with traffic still moving in both directions around us and we need to help this man. Quickly! The woman calls 9-1-1 while I check his vital signs. He's not breathing. He has no pulse. He has about five minutes until he's dead.

Thoughts start running through my mind: *I need to start CPR... You can't do CPR on a person sitting in a car... Do I remember how to do CPR?... There's no way I can lift this guy and carry him through this traffic to the side of the road… By the time an ambulance arrives, he'll be dead.*

Over my shoulder, I notice a black SUV has pulled up behind us. A man is standing beside me and says, "I'm a paramedic." I step back. He confirms that the man indeed has no pulse. He quickly unbuckles the man's seat belt, and he and the woman carry the unconscious driver to the sidewalk. Over his shoulder, the paramedic yells back to me, "Watch my kids!" Looking into his SUV, I see two toddlers strapped in car seats.

I walk around to the passenger window to check on the elderly lady. Soft gray curls frame her fragile face. There are tears in her eyes. Her hands shake in her lap. She can only manage to whisper, "Will he be okay?"

"I hope so," I tell her softly, as the paramedic begins CPR.

And he was.

Passing residents help save man's life – Strangers stop car, give man CPR (Norwich's *The Bulletin*, 9/27/09)

~Jacqueline Kremer

57

The Neighbors

We're here for a reason. I believe a bit of the
reason is to throw little torches out to lead
people through the dark.
~Whoopi Goldberg

As my husband muttered the words, "I don't love you anymore" he stared at the floor. Out the window. Up at the ceiling fan. Anywhere but in my eyes. "I've found someone else," he said, "and I want a divorce." Thus my thirty-five-year marriage came to an end. Angry, sad, stunned, hurt and filled with unspeakable anxiety, I rented a small house and moved to a neighborhood where I didn't know a soul.

The day after I moved in came proof that at least one of my new neighbors was friendly. I found a gift bag beside my back door. Inside were a square wire basket and three cakes of berries-and-nut suet. The note that accompanied it said:

I'm Julie. I live in the house right behind yours. I don't know if you're a birdwatcher, but we have lots of them in this neighborhood. Enjoy!

I hung the feeder on a tree branch outside my kitchen window, where the cardinals and chickadees and downy woodpeckers found it within minutes. Suddenly, I felt a little less lost and lonely.

That is, until the very next day, when an unexpected winter storm came barreling in. Ice and snow covered my driveway and the steep road in front of my house. Tree limbs bent under the weight of the ice, threatening power lines. Temperatures dipped into the single digits. Though I knew that pacing the floor and wringing my hands wouldn't change anything, I paced and wrung anyway. Even if county work crews plowed the roads, they wouldn't plow my driveway. How would I get to the grocery store? And if the electricity went out, how would I stay warm? I had a fireplace but not a stick of firewood.

The snow finally stopped falling but the thermometer didn't budge. Nothing melted. While shivering in my front yard one afternoon while my dogs did their business, I noticed my across-the-street neighbor shoveling his driveway. I introduced myself and learned that his name was Jerry. "I don't have a snow shovel," I said. "May I borrow yours when you're finished?"

"Of course," he told me. "I'll leave it beside your front door when I'm done."

Jerry was true to his word. Several hours later, when I again went outside with the dogs, I found a snow shovel leaning next to my door. A snow shovel I didn't need. Because someone had already cleared my driveway. And left several armloads of dry firewood on the porch.

But that's not where the winter storm story ends. Just about dusk that same evening, my doorbell rang. There stood a burly, bearded man holding a plastic grocery bag. "I'm Chuck," he said. "I live at the top of the hill." He pointed to a house about a hundred yards away, where a bright red pick-up truck with gigantic knobby tires was parked in the driveway. "I know it's hard for you folks down at the bottom of this road to get your cars out in this weather. So I brought you these." Inside the bag were milk, bread, eggs and several cans of soup. Before I could thank him or offer to pay, he turned and was gone.

On his way, no doubt, to another neighbor's house.

Spring arrived at last. And with it, my chance to pay back the kindnesses my neighbors had shown me during the long lonely winter. While planting zinnia seeds I'd harvested from the flowerbed at my old house, I set aside a handful for Julie. Anyone who loved birds was bound to love zinnias. When Jerry mentioned that he and his wife would be out of town for several days, I offered to feed their cat and collect the mail. For Chuck, I baked the most delicious item in my repertoire — a lemon meringue pie.

But I didn't stop with just paying back those who'd done good deeds for me. I began looking for ways to pay those neighbors' kindnesses forward by helping other neighbors.

The elderly man who struggled to make it to the end of his driveway to get the newspaper? I tossed it onto his front porch every afternoon. The young woman with twin toddlers who lived next door? I offered to watch them on Monday mornings so she could go to the grocery store alone. The little girl who just couldn't get the hang of riding a two-wheeler? I held on to the back of her bike seat while I jogged down the street and hollered "Keep peddling!" until she finally figured it out.

Perhaps I'll never know how those neighbors will choose to pay my good deeds forward. But I have no doubt that they will. Kindness begets kindness begets kindness. And the chain of love grows ever longer.

~Jennie Ivey

58

The Secret Gardener

Kindness is the golden chain by which
society is bound together.
~Johann Wolfgang von Goethe

After cleaning and organizing our basement Joe and I were looking forward to steaks cooked on the grill, a freshly tossed salad, some crusty bread and a glass of Cabernet Sauvignon to celebrate a job well done. We almost made it too, but just as I was pouring the wine Joe spread the slats of the kitchen blinds and peeked out at the hill of weeds we sarcastically referred to as Yellowstone.

"Annie, I just can't put it off any longer. First thing tomorrow I have to climb that hill and whack those weeds."

When we had bought this house twenty-five years ago, that embankment wasn't even a blip on our radar. Joe had said, "Oh it's no big deal, Annie. I can jump up there once a week and clean it up with a weed whacker in less than an hour."

Of course we were in our mid-thirties then. Now, Joe is sixty and I'm getting close. Even as a young man Joe needed to wear his golf shoes with metal spikes to get the job done. One false step early on ended up in a "sit n' slide" of epic proportion. And we'd gotten in the bad habit of letting that hill go untended for weeks, resulting in an ugly mess of tall weeds.

That evening we ate our steak with crusty bread and salad, but the wine was more for drowning our sorrows than toasting the fact that we finally had a clean and organized basement.

"We'd better turn in early, Annie. Tomorrow I declare war on the weeds; war is never easy."

And so we did, but Mother Nature had other plans. At about 1:00 a.m. we woke to a huge thunder clap and the skies opened up. It rained all night and throughout the next day.

"I guess we'll have to take care of the hill after work tomorrow," I said. I didn't hear any cheering so I figured that didn't go over very well.

I'd been suggesting that we hire a landscaping service to do it for us, but Joe was insulted by that idea. "Why would I do that? I can still climb that hill. I'm not too old. I'm still in pretty good shape."

"I wasn't suggesting you weren't able bodied, Joe. I was suggesting you hate it and why bother? You can now afford to pay a lawn service to take care of it for you."

"No, not until I absolutely can't do it anymore."

Really? It wasn't like we were talking about surrendering your driver's license.

The next night, Joe wasn't particularly eager to deal with the hill. After dinner, Joe mumbled, "I'm going upstairs to check out something on my computer." Translation: "I'm not firing up that weed whacker tonight and you can't make me."

As the sun set on another day in the war on weeds, I looked out the window to see how much ground they'd gained after all that rain. Wait, what? Someone had manicured the entire incline as if it was the South Lawn of the White House. It hadn't looked that good since… since ever.

"Joe!" I yelled up the living room steps. "Hurry up! You're not going to believe this!"

"What is it, Annie? Are you okay?"

Joe bounded down the steps two at a time.

"Someone weed-whacked the hill. It looks better right now than it has in the last twenty-five years. I'm not kidding, you've got to see it to believe it."

We stood on the back patio hand in hand gazing in wonder at the meticulously manicured mound of earth.

Every day for a week we came out and admired our beautiful hill. Then it started to get messy again.

"Okay, Annie. This coming Saturday I'm going to take care of it so it doesn't get out of hand."

"Now there's a good idea, Joe."

That's what I said but not what I thought. It still meant climbing that hill in the sweltering heat. But guess what? The day before we planned to clean it up, someone came in and did it again for us! And they did it again and again and again every two weeks until the first frost in November.

To this day we still don't know who is responsible and we're halfway through the second summer of not having to take our own weed-whacker out of the shed. We've interrogated neighbors, friends, family, and workmates with intent to pay whoever is taking care of us but we haven't come up with a single lead. The magic always takes place during the day when we are both at work and we've never seen one clue left behind.

Every evening as I clean up the dinner dishes I look out the window at our well-groomed hill of weeds and I pray… "Dear God, thank you for the gift of our secret gardener. Bless whoever it is with a long and happy life. And if it's not too much trouble, Lord, save this soul from the pains of hay fever and the aches of muscle strain. For we have grown accustomed to this kindness and are greatly entertained by watching our own garden tools collect dust."

~Annmarie B. Tait

59

The Kind Blacksmith

*Too often we underestimate the power of a touch,
a smile, a kind word, a listening ear, an honest
compliment, or the smallest act of caring.*
~Leo Buscaglia

have been blessed by many acts of kindness throughout my life. There was a childhood gift of clothing purchased by a family friend so that I could have a new first-day-of-school outfit after my dad lost his job, a new computer given to me so that I could return to college as an adult, and money given to me anonymously right after I lost my job so that I could heat my house.

There have been so many acts of kindness that have touched me deeply. But the one that stands out the most was the one that happened, of all places, at the blacksmith shop at Old Sturbridge Village in Sturbridge, Massachusetts.

I had visited the village that day with my two children and my mother, who came along to enjoy this living museum, but also to assist me. While my daughter, age eleven, did not need the additional oversight, my son, at age seven, most certainly did.

When my son was a toddler, it was very clear to me that there was something different about him. After countless trips to different specialists and the completion of extensive testing, a diagnosis of a particular chromosomal disorder was made, whose symptoms were also consistent with autism and ADHD. My son was constantly in motion and had no sense of danger, requiring that his caregivers watch his every move to prevent him from running away or heading into traffic. He also loved strangers, thinking that everyone was his potential best friend. He greeted everyone with a hug.

The fact that he looked much older than his actual age, and he acted much younger, made it even harder for strangers to accept him. Although my son was still too young to recognize when he was being rejected, every harsh word, rebuff, or look of pity broke my heart. I had started to dread taking him out in public.

That day, at the village, I had walked around clutching my son's hand, ready to protect him from being hurt by anyone. For some reason, my son had perseverated on the idea of visiting the blacksmith building. He nattered away about the shop for the entire day, constantly asking if it was time yet to visit the blacksmith. Knowing that rejection in any form at that place would cause my son to experience a huge meltdown, I saved that building for the end of the day.

Finally, I could avoid it no longer. With great trepidation, I allowed my son, his body quivering with eagerness, to pull me into the black-smith's building. Although I had thought that I was holding his hand firmly, my grasp was not firm enough.

My son pulled his hand out of mine, ran over to the blacksmith, wrapped his arms around the man's legs, and asked if he would be his friend.

My heart stopped at that moment.

I expected that he, like almost everyone else that we had encountered, would extricate himself from my son's clutches and push him away, muttering something about this not being possible.

What he did next, though, caused me to burst into tears.

The blacksmith knelt down so that he was at my son's level, gently moved my son back so that he could look him in the eye, and then held out his hand for my son to shake.

He said that he would be honored to be the friend of such a fine young man.

That sweet man then looked at me with a kind expression, and asked me if it would be okay for my son to help him with his work.

I nodded through my tears, and the blacksmith spent the next hour allowing my son to "help" him as he worked the forge. I was in awe of the way that man remained patient, answering my son's incessant questions and also managing to keep him safe despite the fact that he was always in motion.

When that hour was up, my son proudly walked away, with the piece of metal that he had helped the blacksmith forge clutched tightly in his fist, and his head held high.

For the first time, someone had actually seen my son as a person of value.

The blacksmith not only gave my son an experience that was a dream come true, but gifted my son with things of more intrinsic value: Kindness. Acceptance. Value.

I will be forever grateful to that blacksmith for spending an hour of his day with a boy with special needs.

~Marybeth Mitcham

Faith Restored

Never doubt that a small group of thoughtful,
committed citizens can change the world.
Indeed, it is the only thing that ever has.
~Margaret Mead

What does a Peace Corps volunteer do after teaching science to elementary students for two steamy, wet years on the tropical Polynesian island of Samoa?

If he can, he trots off to nearby westernized New Zealand.

And what first act does he commit to integrate himself back into Western European culture? Does he search for museums? Does he ferret out the library on the hallowed grounds of a university? Does he see a Shakespearian play? Or does he seek out the largest and most gaudy movie theater in the North Island of New Zealand?

The answer is none of the above.

Two years of boiled fish, coconut cream, rice, and questionably-cooked pork left a food craving hard to satisfy. So this ex-Peace Corps volunteer made a beeline for a McDonald's, although I did it at the slower pace I had become accustomed to in the tropics.

As I scanned both sides of Queen Street, looking for the McDonald's I had heard of even in far-off Samoa, people rushed past me in their business suits, ties, and time-sensitive schedules. "Civilization," I thought, with a smile. The paved streets and noises of the city left my mouth agape. Quaint do-it-tomorrow Samoan village life and get-it-done-now city life clashed within me. I turned and faced the clean windows of an apothecary shop. My Anglo reflection stopped me. A sea of white people rushed by. I hadn't had a moment of anonymity for two years among a sea of lovely bronze-hued skin. Being stared at and the object of harmless, but unasked touching, had been my norm in Samoa.

Finally, here in New Zealand, I could pace a street and not be noticed. I could speak English, even if I had an American accent, with native speakers. But one question lingered for a returning Peace Corps teacher. Would I be re-accepted? Would I be able to re-adapt? Would modern western societies like New Zealand or America have a place for me? I didn't feel like I fit in anymore. Two years ago, my twelve-week training course had ended with a casual remark by one of our trainers: "The toughest part will be coming back. Being re-accepted will be the challenge."

Although no jarring golden arch spanned the front of the building, the bold McDonald's sign did make it easy to locate. The refurbished classic Victorian building with a cathedral ceiling impressed me, but then again, I had squatted in thatched huts for more than 730 days. At the moment, it didn't take much to impress me.

I ordered my food, enjoyed the smell wafting through the warm paper bag, clutched my sweating drink, and secured a solo seat on the second-floor terrace. There, I slowly and with much satisfaction dug into my order of French fries and a Big Mac. The rain outside encouraged me to take my time and peruse my fellow humans down on the first floor from my perch.

A young overweight man with Down syndrome ordered or at least attempted to order lunch. Confused, and perhaps a little nervous, he changed his order once, twice, and then again. Soon, a line formed behind him as things slowed down. I stopped chewing and leaned forward to watch.

The scene at the counter seemed destined for disaster. The young man dug into his pockets, pulled out some change, slapped it on the counter and faced the manager.

"Here's my money," he stated loudly and with unrestrained joy written all over him.

"Sorry, lad," said the manager, "But that's not enough."

Oh no. If Western society couldn't help this boy, maybe I really *didn't* fit in anymore. I felt even more isolated.

The people behind the boy pressed closer, anxious to be on their way. Then, a thin, young girl with yellow ribbons in her hair, perhaps twelve years old, wormed her way to the boy's side.

"Here." She opened her small child's purse and placed a folded bill on the counter. "I'll pay for him."

There was an uncomfortable silence. Then an elderly man in the crowd called out, "I'll pay for the boy."

Another person made a similar offer and then another did the same. The manager held up his arms.

"No, no," he said. "This one is on me."

The manager bagged what the young man had ordered and then added some more. He passed the full bag over. The young man beamed. "Thanks! Thanks heaps!" and he hurried out into the rain wearing a beatific smile.

From my perch up on the second floor I bit into my burger, listened to the rain continue and closed my eyes. I smiled and the words echoed in my mind...

"I'll pay for him."

"No, I'll pay for the boy."

"No, no, this one is on me."

The young man wasn't alone, and neither was I.

~Paul H. Karrer

61

Unrequested and Unexpected

He who sows courtesy reaps friendship, and
he who plants kindness gathers love.
~Saint Basil

Once upon a time, before six-lane highways and face-less, voiceless, text messages — you know, in the Good Old Days when our parents were asking what the world was coming to — it seemed like we were more connected as people. At least that's what I thought.

Then, in early winter of last year, I underwent surgery to have my left foot re-constructed. I was discharged from hospital on a blustering snowy afternoon. We turned the corner and… "Look at the driveway! Our walk! Who could have? Who would have?" It was fully shoveled. Our twenty-foot long, double width driveway and our walk had been cleared of snow by our elderly neighbor, who, himself, was awaiting a hip operation.

Within the next few days, the phone began to ring and e-mails to arrive — inquiries about my wellbeing. Flowers arrived. Friends dropped by to chat or play *Scrabble* but mainly to ease my serious case of Sititis — no, not an infection, just plain, old too much sitting. I was confined to my chair on wheels for six inching-along, very tedious weeks.

Rides to the hospital were provided when needed and a large, substantial vehicle was loaned to us when we had to make our way to the outpatient clinic on yet another snowy day. All this was offered — not asked for.

And then, two months later and just three days before I was to collect my new orthotics, my partner, going down our back steps to the beach, slipped and broke her ankle. It was a clearly audible snap — a very bad break in five places. There was surgery and a cast and crutches and, again, the chair on wheels.

Once more, when we returned from hospital, when Cecily took her turn at invalidism, our friends and neighbors were immediately on the scene to assist wherever possible. Again, flowers and phone calls and offers of help arrived.

"Would you like us to come by and make dinner?"

"We're going into town. Do you have a grocery list?"

"Shall we come over with a bottle of wine?"

"We'll do the daily dog walks. We love Farlie." And, without fail, they took her for far longer and far better walks than she had previously enjoyed.

And then there was a knock on the door. "We've been away for several weeks, visiting our grandchildren, and just heard Cecily's bad news." In a thermal case, a neighbor was carrying a casserole large enough to feed us several times, a Caesar salad, homemade cheese scones ready for the oven, and freshly baked cookies for dessert.

This outpouring left us staggering with surprise and gratitude. To our neighbors and friends we could not say thank you loudly or often enough.

And as to my concerns about living in a time of faceless disconnection? It took almost a year of the unexpected and the unfortunate; but that year, and the people who stepped in to assist and to encourage, their simple acts of caring and kindness, unrequested and unexpected, made me realize my good fortune in having a home in a small-town community which still inspired such random acts of humanity.

~Robyn Gerland

62

A Busload of Kindness

If you want to be a rebel, be kind.
~Pancho Ramos Stierle

The Greyhound bus has never failed to be anything less than interesting every time I have taken a ride. The bus is always full of characters — a real hodgepodge of cultures and backgrounds. The stops are never ending, the people are never shy, and the atmosphere is never dull.

One ride in particular stands out. Salt Lake City was my departure and Tacoma was my destination. It was New Year's Eve and I had just celebrated my birthday the day before, in bed with the flu. My body still ached and the medicine I was taking was making me woozy. I was hoping to get a nice, quiet seat next to an empty one so that I could sleep through most of the twenty-four-hour trip.

That was my plan at least, but when I boarded the bus it was loud, crowded, and the last place on earth I wanted to be. I looked for a seat that wasn't next to someone, but as I reached the back of the bus I realized my hopes of sleep and solitude were unrealistic.

I was reminded of my days in elementary school, riding the bus home with the bad kids sitting in the back of the bus. Apparently, this was still the scenario for adults riding the Greyhound.

I found my seat in the second to last row of the bus. It was an aisle seat squeezed in between a bald, fidgety man in his late twenties and a narrow aisle that led to the bathroom, which was conveniently located right behind me. Also right behind me were two boisterous, intoxicated older men who were losing no time getting to know their neighbors. Across the aisle from them sat a quiet older lady who didn't seem to appreciate their interest in their fellow bus riders.

When the bus started and we slowly exited the parking lot the gentlemen behind me announced to the entire bus that just because we were on a bus on New Year's Eve, that didn't mean we couldn't celebrate the joyous occasion. I sank in my seat and closed my eyes, hoping the sleeping pill I took before boarding would have a more powerful effect than normal.

I couldn't have been asleep for more than thirty minutes when I heard the guys behind me counting. Being medicated and half asleep I was trying to figure out what they were counting and why they were counting backwards. Then I remembered — oh yeah, New Year's. The bus was dark and quiet, with most of the riders trying to sleep. Except, that is, for my neighbors, Opie and Carl, who made it a point to let every man, woman and sleeping child on the bus know that it was midnight and time to celebrate.

Opie and Carl's behavior caught the attention of the bus driver, who pulled over and headed back to us. It didn't take him long to notice the illegal drinking that was taking place in the back of the bus. The guys were not harming anyone, but they were, according to the bus driver, causing a scene and were to be kicked off the bus at the next stop. By this time everyone on the bus was awake and watching the events unfold in the back of the bus.

Opie started to panic. Wherever he was going, someone was going to pick him up at the bus terminal for a job, and if he missed his ride he wouldn't get the job. The bus driver paid no mind to Opie's story and apology and headed back to the driver's seat, his mind made up. Opie went down front and begged the bus driver not to kick him off. He needed this job. The bus driver then angrily warned him if he said another word he was going to leave Opie and Carl outside in the freezing cold right on the side of the road. Opie walked back to his seat at the back and everyone he passed saw his defeated face and felt for him.

All of a sudden I heard a yell. It was the quiet older lady who sat across the aisle from me. She stood up from her seat and loudly proclaimed that if Opie and Carl were getting kicked off, the driver would have to kick her off, too. Then another man, a couple of rows ahead, stood up and also stated that he would have to be kicked off. It was the middle of the night, on a desolate mountain road, the temperature dropping by the hour and none of those people cared. All they cared about was the possible dire fate that awaited Opie. After the fifth person stood up for Opie, it seemed like the whole bus was ready to depart, right then and there. The bus driver caved. He managed to calm the protesters by stating Opie and Carl could stay on the bus after all.

As the bus pulled back onto the dark, narrow road I felt something new and miraculous. I had witnessed something that I had never seen before — the power of a group of people to be kind and understanding and make something good happen. I couldn't see him in the dark, but I heard Opie's voice and I knew how grateful he was; he was moved and his hope in humanity had been restored. It was a touching experience that I will never forget, and every time I think of Opie I am reminded that we are all human, we all make mistakes, and we all deserve a second chance.

~Jennie Wyatt

63

Charles's Garden

Kind hearts are the gardens. Kind thoughts are
the roots. Kind words are the blossoms.
Kind deeds are the fruits.
~Kirpal Singh

We moved to southern Minnesota about a year ago, and in that time I've learned a lot about small town living. I've learned that even before the librarian meets you, she knows exactly who you are and where you live. The postman knows you, too, because he played cards with your husband once. The waitress at the local bar welcomes you with a hug, and neighbors bring you cookies. Folks stop by for a quick chat when passing your house, so it's best not to make a habit out of walking around the house in your underwear.

Then there are the gardens. In this farming community, nearly everyone has one. And one of the first things I was asked when we moved in was, "So, are you planning to have a garden?"

Charles asked me this. A retired farmer, he often shared with me the fruit of his labors: beautiful butternut and acorn squash, red potatoes, and buckets of ripe tomatoes, cucumbers, onions, peppers and beans.

There was no way Charles could've known the dread I felt when he asked that simple question. I had tried, and failed, so many times to grow my own flowers or food that I'd pretty much given up. Aside from a bumper crop of patio tomatoes, my attempts at gardening had always failed. And as much as I want to be that woman who enjoys romping barefoot in the soil, I'm just not. I don't like the gritty feel of dirt under my nails, the surprise contact with earthworms, or the massive amount of sweat involved.

Of course, I didn't say any of this to Charles, who had spent a lifetime gardening. I just smiled brightly and said, "Oh yes, I would love to have my own garden!" Technically, this wasn't a lie. I did want a garden, I just didn't want to try and fail, yet again. Besides, it was the end of August and much too late for planting. I figured by the time spring rolled around Charles would have more important things on his mind.

But I was forgetting another characteristic of small towns: Word spreads fast. I found myself fielding questions about which fruits and vegetables I planned to plant, where I would put my garden, and what size it would be. I got the distinct feeling this was going to happen, with or without me.

One cold day in late fall a friend arrived with a tractor and plow. "How big do ya want it?" he asked.

"Well, let's start small," I said, trying not to sound too pathetic. "How about a twelve by twelve square?"

He went straight to work. When he finished, my garden was easily four times that size.

All winter long, that patch of dirt in the back yard stared at me. I stared back. Some days it seemed as big as a football field. Still, I had to admit, the rows of black dirt had a certain beauty about them. As winter thawed into spring, I felt flickers of excitement when I thought of my garden. I knew I wanted tomatoes, peppers, and onions for salsa, cucumbers for pickles, and beans for canning. Never mind that I didn't know how to do any of this. Charles had planted an idea in me, and it was growing, spreading roots in my heart. I began to think this whole garden thing might actually work.

In late April, Charles stopped by to check on my garden. "We need to get this dirt turned over," he said. "Work the soil up a bit. I've got someone I can call who'll come and do it for you."

The next morning when I went to check my garden, Charles was there with a bag of fertilizer, working it through the newly tilled dirt. His heavy work boots sunk into the rich black soil, and for the first time I wondered how it would feel against my bare feet.

A few days later he showed up with a bag of potatoes. We dumped them out on the kitchen counter and cut them into little chunks. In his unpretentious way, Charles told me how to cut each chunk so it had an "eye" in the center. This is how I learned where a potato seed comes from.

After that, Charles taught me how to use string to make my rows neat and even, then winked and said, "Now I'll know what happened if your rows aren't straight."

By the middle of June, my garden was planted with tomatoes, peppers, watermelon, beans, potatoes, onions and squash. Just when I thought the hard part was over, Charles asked me yet another question. "How are you planning to cultivate it?" he asked.

"What do you mean?" I asked, thinking we had already done that.

"I mean, what are you going to do about weeds?" Charles said with a smile.

"Oh, that! I'll just have my kids do it," I said, with a wave of my hand.

Charles looked somewhat doubtful, but he nodded anyway. It was almost as if he knew how my summer would unfold, and how busy I would be with church activities, summer camps for the kids, and visits to and from family.

Before I knew it, it was the night before we were to leave on a two-week mission trip. Amid all the packing and planning in the days before, I had completely neglected my garden. So that night, I ran out to assess the damage.

My heart sank. The garden was a mess, running wild with weeds where the vegetables were supposed to be. After everything Charles had done, I should've at least stayed on top of weeding it. I felt like a complete failure, but there was nothing I could do about it until we got back from our trip. I could only hope for two things: that Charles would not see it until I had a chance to fix it, and that there would still be something left to fix when I got back.

Two weeks later, we returned from our trip late at night. I was weary and exhausted, and had a sleepy toddler in my arms, but I went straight to my garden. What I saw by moonlight made me gasp.

Clearly, Charles had been there. Every row was neat as a pin. Every plant stood proudly in place, surrounded only by dirt. Not a weed could be seen anywhere. My hand flew to my mouth and I began to cry, big tears that splashed the watermelon patch.

I vowed from that moment on to make time for my garden; to weed and water it, to harvest and preserve its fruit, to nourish my family and bless my friends with it.

And that's exactly what I did, with one exception. I no longer thought of it as "my garden." It is, and always has been, Charles's Garden.

~Debra Mayhew

64

A Perfect Day

*If there be any truer measure of a man than by what
he does, it must be by what he gives.*
~Robert South

"There's No Such Thing As A Small Kindness"
read a bumper sticker I recently saw and I was
reminded of one of my favorite maxims from
Coach John Wooden — "Wooden-isms," I like
to call them: "You can't live a perfect day without doing something for
someone who will never be able to repay you."

What I love about these kind acts is that they are often contagious.
Here is a sampling of two recent back-to-back days made more perfect
by kind acts:

My wife and I, and our daughter and son who were both home
for a visit from San Francisco and New York City, had just crammed
together around a table for two in the self-seating bar area of a local
Irish pub when a young couple seated at a bigger table across the
room waved us over.

They kindly insisted we switch with them and proceeded to move
their plates of food and drinks to our table.

I was so engrossed in my family's reunion celebration that the
couple left before I thought to buy them a round of drinks. Instead, I
"paid it forward" and when I paid my bill I asked our waitress to put two
drinks on my tab for the next couple that sat at the two-person table.

While I was on my daily run — and I do mean "daily" as I have run at least three miles every day since July 3, 2003 — at my favorite local park, a driver pulled alongside me at the soccer fields and rolled down his window. Instead of asking for directions somewhere, he asked if I like avocados.

"Avocados?" I asked.

He explained he always saw me running and just wanted to give me a token of thanks for inspiring him. He then handed me a beautiful avocado, with a sticker on it from the grocery so it wasn't even a freebie from his own back yard.

A woman who was in the audience when I gave a recent talk at a service group about my book *Wooden & Me: Life Lessons from My Two-Decade Friendship with the Legendary Coach and Humanitarian to Help "Make Each Day Your Masterpiece"* mailed me the book *Life Wisdom from Coach Wooden* that she came across at a local library fundraising sale.

She included this kind note: "I thought you might enjoy this if you do not already have a copy."

I enjoyed it, and again "paid it forward" by mailing a small check to the library.

Speaking of books, and Coach Wooden, another person at one of my talks bought four copies of *Wooden & Me* and instead of taking them he requested I donate them to disadvantaged youth on his behalf.

I donated eight instead of four.

At the park where I run, there is a farmers market every week. And oh, boy, did I get out-haggled on this day while buying a bouquet of gorgeous sunflowers for my lovely wife.

I gave the lady a twenty-dollar bill and she gave me back fifteen. However, I really did not think five dollars was a very fair price so I handed her a five-dollar bill back. She looked confused. I smiled and said, "Keep it."

She shook her head no: "They only cost five dollars."

"Yes, but they're so beautiful I want you to keep it," I explained.

"That's too much," she replied and pushed the five dollars back at me.

"Okay," I finally relented, but requested five singles as change.

This she did and I handed four of them back to her.

She smiled, kept one, and gave three of them back to me.

I gave her two back and tried to leave, but she forced one more back. And then, for my meager two-dollar tip, she gave me a ten-dollar hug.

Thinking about it as I write this, even after those sunflowers have lost their bloom, still brings a smile to my face.

My friend Scott had a similar tipping experience after taking a shuttle from long-term parking to Los Angeles International Airport. Upon being dropped off at his terminal, he realized his smallest bill was a $20.

Scott asked the driver if he could make change, but was told: "Don't worry, you can get me next time."

Getting this same driver ever again was, of course, a long shot. But a bigger long shot is for Scott to stiff someone of a tip, so he handed over the $20 bill.

Remarkably, the driver refused it.

Scott insisted, and persisted, until the driver accepted.

However, the driver then dug deep into his pocket and insisted, and persisted, until Scott accepted a wad of uncounted one-dollar-bill tips — thirteen it turned out — as change.

"I was struck by how hard he pushed to not take a tip that he obviously thought was too much," Scott told me. "There was no doubt he was sincere. The dignity with which he handled this small exchange was inspiring."

Inspiring. That's a good word to describe the countless people who incorporate the words on that bumper sticker — "There's No Such Thing As A Small Kindness" — as a routine part of living a perfect day.

~Woody Woodburn

Chapter 8

Random Acts of Kindness

The Joy of Giving

*What counts in life is not the mere fact that we
have lived. It is what difference we have made
to the lives of others that will determine the
significance of the life we lead.*
~Nelson Mandela

The Power of Yes

If you are really thankful, what do you do? You share.
~W. Clement Stone

t's always surprising what can happen when someone says "Yes."
Like the day my wife, Audra, asked me to run errands with her.

Shortly after we arrived at our first stop, an office supply
store, I heard God say, "There's someone here you need to do
something for." It was near the start of the school year, and I felt it
should be a teacher.

There was no question about whether or not I would do it. The
sensation was just too powerful not to be real, and God had blessed
us and put us in a position to be able to help others.

I just couldn't find a teacher.

For forty-five minutes, as Audra shopped and checked items off
her list, I strolled around and inconspicuously glanced in people's
shopping carts to see what was there.

As discreetly as possible for a 225-pound amateur bodybuilder
and former Mr. Florida titleholder, that is. I'm sure people thought I
was crazy!

No one's selections seemed like things a teacher would buy, but
the feeling of needing to help somebody intensified. I was convinced
it would happen.

Audra finished her shopping and we got in the checkout line.
Maybe we'd find a teacher there.

I peeked around the woman in front of us and thought, "There's my sign, right there!" Her basket was filled with notebooks, folders, crayons, markers, colored pencils, scissors and rulers.

"Are you a teacher?" I asked.

"Yes, I am."

I smiled and said, "Today's your lucky day. I'm going to buy what's in your cart."

"Seriously?" she asked. She started to cry.

I took out my credit card and paid for everything, making sure it was credited to her rewards account.

But that wasn't the end of it. The teacher, Sharon Leto, shared her excitement about her "classroom angels," as she called us, with a local reporter. The story was picked up by other papers, television stations and the Associated Press. It was shared more than 6,800 times on Facebook.

Now it was my turn to be shocked as dozens of people — teachers, spouses of teachers, school parents and others — left comments about being grateful for and inspired by our action. It was as if educators felt that by our doing this for one teacher, we had shown gratitude for all of them.

A year later, I called Sharon and invited her to go school shopping. She declined, saying she had already received her incomparable, one-time, random act of kindness. However, she said she was conducting an orientation for new teachers, and new teachers need stuff. Could we help them?

Sharon's selflessness allowed us to assist another fifty educators — and we convinced her to let us get her supplies, too. At the orientation, I thanked the crowd for impacting their students' lives in so many ways, not only in their subject areas. They mentor, serve as role models and provide classroom materials bought with their own money. For everything they do for our youth, they deserve much more recognition than they get.

The teachers seemed to be touched more by our thankfulness than by the gifts they received. People appreciate being appreciated.

In my business as a nutrition coach and personal trainer, I've found that if I can encourage people and teach them how to take more control over how they look and feel, hope returns. The discipline they develop makes their lives simpler. It becomes much easier for them to do things and they feel better about themselves.

I think that's what I inadvertently did for teachers — helped them feel better about themselves and lifted them up — when I said, "Yes," and did what God asked me to do in that store.

~Rodney Burton

66

Gifts to Give Away

*An effort made for the happiness of others
lifts us above ourselves.*
~Lydia M. Child

As principal of an elementary school of about 350 students, I spent a considerable amount of time encouraging teachers and students to model acts of kindness. Our school improvement team created a system whereby recipients of an act of kindness would write about it on a card and submit it to the office to be read aloud over the intercom during the next morning's announcements. The cards were then taped around the building, creating an amazing schoolwide chain of acts of kindness.

The cooks wrote cards to acknowledge kind acts happening in the cafeteria. The custodians wrote kindness cards for students who went out of their way to be respectful of our school property. The playground aides wrote cards for students who they noticed being kind to others. Teachers and students wrote cards for each other when an act of kindness was observed.

Our school began shifting its culture. We focused on these acts of kindness rather than disobedience and broken rules.

This kindness program led to the best retirement gift ever for me. At my party, I was given two presents from each of my colleagues. One was for me and one was for me to give away! Some were simple, like gift cards to a coffee shop or a restaurant. Others were more complex, such as gift bags to take to a cancer center. I got packages of thank-you cards so that I could write encouraging notes to others, thanking them for the difference they made in my life. I was even given beautiful books for my grandchildren and additional books, beautifully wrapped, to give away to someone else's grandchildren.

I kept the gifts to give away in my car so that I would have them wherever I went. I was always on the lookout for just the right person to bless. For example, one time when I was helping in a homeless shelter, I saw a student from my school. I ran to my car and brought him back a book to share with his sister. The delight on their faces was priceless!

I had so much fun giving away these wonderful gifts. Once, while at Olive Garden, I took my four-year-old granddaughter to help me pick out just the right person to receive an Olive Garden gift card. I'm not sure if she really understood why we were handing a total stranger a present, but when I asked her if it felt good to be a blessing, the smile on her face told me that she was beginning to understand. I had gone full circle, from helping a building full of little ones start a life of kindness, to educating my young granddaughter in the joy that giving can bring to us.

~Linda S. Locke

67

Playing Nice

*Kindness is the language which the deaf can
hear and the blind can see.*
~Mark Twain

was waiting in an airport terminal for the first of two connecting flights that would take me from Newark, New Jersey to a business conference in Palm Springs, California. Across from my seat, a young couple were examining their boarding passes. The woman looked nervous. The man was sighing in resignation. To my right, a tattooed man in glasses was wringing his hands.

"Newspapers aren't in yet," the tattooed man suddenly said. "I wanted to get the *Post*, but the lady said they're late today."

I looked over to confirm he was talking to me. One of the tattoos was a python. He was definitely not the type to get by with Sudoku on the plane.

"I don't see how we're getting out of here on time," he then said, even though we were still forty minutes from departure. To him, the glass wasn't just half empty; it was bone dry. I politely excused myself "to stretch my legs."

As I passed by the closest gift store, I saw a lady stacking newspapers, including the *Post*.

I picked one up for myself… then impulsively bought another.

Mr. Moody Snakeskin was no longer in the terminal when I got back, but when I boarded the plane, I saw him in the first class cabin flipping through a month-old SkyMall catalog. Clearly, I'd gotten there just in time.

"Your *Post*," I said. He looked up in confusion, then saw the paper. His eyes widened.

"Uhh… thanks," he said awkwardly, fishing into his pocket. I waved him off and strode happily to my window seat in coach.

Some feed the hungry. Some comfort the afflicted. I relieve the bored.

As I settled in my seat, the young man who had been sighing in the waiting area sat down next to me.

"Weren't you traveling with someone?" I asked him, remembering the nervous woman he was with at the gate.

"We booked late, so my wife's in the back of the plane. She hasn't flown before."

"Why don't I switch with her so you guys can sit together?"

"She's in a middle seat," he said, as if revealing a terminal condition. "I don't mind."

Reliever of the Bored, Uniter of the Separated.

As the plane lifted off, I offered my newspaper to my new row-mate, an empty-handed business traveler. He politely refused, but an hour into the flight, thumbing through the SkyMall catalog, he asked me if the offer was still good.

For someone without reading material in the middle seat of Row 23 on a crowded flight, I suddenly found myself in a really good mood. I was definitely getting high off being nice. All the SkyMall's ceramic critters, inflatable stereos, and Harry Potter wands couldn't make me feel any more content.

On the second leg of my flight, a teenager and I were fortunate enough to have an empty seat between us. "Sweet," he said, plugging in headphones.

The extra elbowroom may have been some kind of karmic reward, but I wasn't looking for a medal. The pleasure of being generous was reward enough… and addictive. I even considered hanging around the luggage carousel extra long just to see if I could lift a heavy suitcase for someone!

No one spends time in an airport terminal for fun, but if you find yourself there battling boredom, give being nice a try. You might even get some extra elbowroom for your effort.

~Joel Schwartzberg

68

A Well Kept Secret

I am only one; but still I am one. I cannot do
everything, but still I can do something. I will
not refuse to do the something I can do.
~Helen Keller

My friend's daughter works at a minimum wage job in a nursing home in Iowa. She takes any shift offered, but she's fifty and the extra hours and heavy lifting of patients are taking a toll. Her husband of twenty-five years has had a sketchy employment record due to a medical issue and a recent car accident.

When I learned five years ago that their home of fourteen years was listed for sale by the sheriff due to unpaid taxes I felt drawn to help. I came up with a fun way to help anonymously.

My husband and I live in a retirement community in South Carolina. Our friends here travel all over to visit their families and for vacations. I decided to have them assist me.

After I heard about my friend's daughter, I decided that I would send her money anonymously. One of my neighbors happened to be on her way to Vermont to visit her grandchildren. I gave her an envelope addressed to the daughter of my friend. It contained a crisp new one-hundred-dollar bill along with an unsigned note suggesting that it would be nice if she could do a small act of kindness for someone every day. Something as insignificant as giving a compliment, a smile or holding a door for someone would be enough. My neighbor promised to drop the envelope in the mail in Vermont.

I have repeated the same act many times over the past five years. Each time the gift has been mailed from a different state or country. With every gift there is a short note stating my hope that the kindness will be passed on.

I hear stories from my friend about the mysterious envelopes that arrive at her daughter's home from all over the country. She said they have given up guessing who is sending them. They just remember the mysterious giver in their prayers.

The family continues to struggle but I like to think that each time an envelope arrives in the mail their day is just a bit brighter.

~Mary Grant

69

A Be-the-Gift Birthday

Happiness is a perfume you cannot pour on others
without getting a few drops on yourself.
~Ralph Waldo Emerson

On October 16, 2014, I turned forty years old. I wasn't entirely certain how to feel about this milestone — empowered or depressed, invigorated or old. But, after reading a blog post entitled "How to Have the Best Birthday, the Best Today, the Best Anyday..." several months earlier by Ann Voskamp, author of *One Thousand Gifts*, I was determined to celebrate my birthday differently. In preparation, I printed out her "Be the GIFT" tags which I would attach to the flowers I purchased and the cookies I planned to bake on my birthday morning.

I would make my birthday about blessing others instead of expecting something for myself. In doing so, I discovered an unprecedented joy on what could have been a difficult birthday.

The day began when I woke up for an early visit to the gym. In the 5:30 a.m. darkness, I approached my van, startled to see something large looming in the driver's seat. My heart skipped a beat as my eyes adjusted, and then I laughed with relief as I realized it was a gigantic birthday balloon. I climbed in with my oversized companion and drove to the gym, my first venue for the "Be the GIFT" experiment.

Along with my gym shoes, phone and ear buds, I also carried a little flower tube stuffed with vibrant pink, blue and yellow daisies with a "Be the GIFT" tag attached. I hung it on the personal trainers' door file holder and stepped onto the treadmill.

Scott, my personal trainer, arrived shortly thereafter. I watched him in the window's reflection as he headed to the door and stopped to examine the strange item before him. He looked at it, then opened the door, then came back to look at it again, removing it from the file holder. I later found that he had put the flowers on one of the meeting tables and taped the gift tag to his desk facing anyone who might come in for consultation, thereby sharing my joyful message with countless others.

After returning home and getting everyone fed and lunches made, I dropped off the boys and another flower bouquet for a surprised and smiling secretary at school. Then, I returned home to bake cookies and assemble more bunches of flowers. I finished baking just in time to place a package of cookies and flowers out for the mail carrier.

Shortly after, I began to notice that for every good deed I did, another came my way.

My first visitor arrived as I was stepping out of the shower. My friend Sarah had shown up unexpectedly, gift in hand, and we sat and enjoyed a visit together while my children snuck away to the basement to play. I unwrapped the beautiful wrapping paper, which contained a lovely relaxation package of lavender-scented oil, Earl Grey chocolate, and a bag of herbal tea.

As Sarah rose to leave, my friend Kristina and her children arrived. We also had a pleasant visit, and she presented me with a peace lily plant to add to my budding indoor plant collection. It was planted in a hand-painted pot that says, "Your Friendship is a Blessing." I sent both friends home with flowers.

When the mail carrier had taken her gift and turned the corner, I retrieved the mail for the day. My mailbox was full of birthday cards, the most I'd ever received. I have a sneaking suspicion that a dear friend of mine recruited a bunch of sweet women from church to bless me with birthday cards, and they did. I was nearly in tears looking through the stack filled with such beautiful sentiments.

After lunch, the kids and I were on our way to deliver our surprise gifts for my birthday. We trooped into the small bank lobby, where we shared our birthday joy with our favorite bank teller, who always gives my five children the same flavor suckers so they don't fight over them. Next, we stopped with flowers and cookies to cheer up our unemployed neighbor. Then, we headed across the street to bless our pediatrician and his wonderful assistant with flowers, a plate of cookies, and a thank-you card.

Another special stop was our home away from home, the library, where our gifts were met with genuine gratitude. I think they even fast-tracked a book request I made; it arrived the next day. After school, I caught up with a few random parent friends and surprised them with flowers, too. One mom said that she was going to pass hers on to a friend who was having an especially difficult time. Another mom sent me a card a few weeks later to thank me for my little gift of encouragement on a stressful day.

From there, the kids got to be more directly involved. I took my five children to the park, where they sprinkled quarters on the playground equipment for unsuspecting children to find. Then, we headed to ShopKo, where they filled all of the 25-cent candy machines with quarters. Finally, we stopped at Goodwill, where I gave each of the children one dollar to hide in a piece of merchandise. We had attached our "Be the GIFT" tags to the dollar bills.

For the first time since I was a teenager, I bought my birthday cake instead of making it. When we returned home, another friend arrived unexpectedly, bringing me a personal birthday cupcake! Of course, I sent her off with a little bouquet of flowers.

Dear friends watched our children so that my husband and I could go out for dinner. When we returned, all of my children shared their sweet cards and gifts with me, and we sang and enjoyed the store-bought cake.

As the day came to a close, I reflected that, unlike so many birthday celebrations in my life, on this day, I made a point of being joyful and relaxed about the schedule. I chose not to live with expectation but to embrace with gratitude whatever came my way. In the process, I was able to do all of my favorite things: bless others and make them feel special, spend spontaneous time with friends, and celebrate with my family.

Giving to others and being the gift, especially on my fortieth birthday, helped me to avoid any tendency to focus on myself. Seeing the surprised and thankful looks on others' faces and sharing the fun of giving anonymously with my children made my day better than I could have hoped for.

~Aimee Mae Wiley

70

Why Stop?

There is a sort of gratification in doing good
which makes us rejoice in ourselves.
~Michel de Montaigne

M y husband's eyes crinkled at the corners, his smile hidden behind a steaming mug of coffee. "What's on your mind?" he asked.

I hesitated for a few moments, measuring my response. "Just remembering, I guess. This project has been so fun."

He nodded, his focus on a half-empty bowl of cereal.

I sipped my coffee, staring through the picture window as I reviewed the previous month's events. During the past four weeks I'd committed to doing one kind act daily. I wanted to re-learn spontaneous generosity.

Several special memories came to mind.

There was the simple happiness on the service station attendant's face when I presented her with a frozen drink during a heat wave. "Thanks. I really needed a pick-me-up." She accepted the plastic cup with one hand as she swiped perspiration from her brow with the other and waved like an old friend as we drove away. From her I learned to give people what they need even before they know they need it.

There was the bank teller's squeal when I handed her a new copy of a popular author's latest book, its pages begging to be savored over a summer weekend. "I've been looking for something to read!" She taught me the pleasure of sharing small luxuries whenever I could.

I'd also driven all over town, delivering countless cookies, cupcakes and miniature Bundt cakes to neighbors, friends and co-workers. An elderly friend promised she'd bake for me the next week. I didn't argue. Through her, I discovered the true gift I offered wasn't sweet treats, but friendship. The best cure for loneliness is someone who cares.

Then there was the day my husband and I visited a bicycle shop, and the wide grin on a young clerk's face as I pressed a pink cardboard box from the French patisserie into his hands. "Really?" His brows rose higher, matching the octaves of his voice. "No, really? You're giving me this?"

I nodded, wishing I could make the moment last longer.

"You don't have to." He clutched the box a tiny bit closer to his chest. "It's not necessary." And then, the clincher. "What is it?"

The gift he gave me in return was laughter.

One day I visited my preferred coffee shop, and pulled around to the window. Glancing in the rearview mirror, I saw a dilapidated car behind me. The young woman in the driver seat's face looked exhausted. An unexpected thrill tripped up my spine as I covered the cost of my drink and paid forward for hers as well. I traveled quite a distance down the highway before I realized my lips were still turned up in a grin.

What could be better than receiving an anonymous gesture of grace?

Offering it. There is something pure and good in helping someone who can't possibly repay you. And who knows? Maybe he or she will feel compelled to pass it on.

My husband stood beside me, coffee pot in hand. "Would you like a warm-up?"

"Yes. No. Wait." I rose. This isn't over. I didn't have to stop just because the month was up. This was just the beginning. "I'm going out. Want to come along?"

"Sure. I'll drive." He returned the pot to the coffeemaker and followed me to the car. Steering into traffic, we started down the road.

"Where are we heading?" he asked, as we zipped past buildings.

"I'm not sure, exactly. But I think we're almost there."

"Another kind act?"

Smiling, I navigated as my husband maneuvered the car through heavy traffic. Finally slowing beneath a highway overpass, we rolled to a stop a few yards past a flimsy cardboard sign. Stark concrete provided shade for a homeless gentleman who didn't even turn to see we'd approached.

Taking a deep breath, I rolled down the window. "Hello."

His shoulders jerked as he pivoted, both eyes open wide. He moved toward the car like a soldier worn from battle. Perhaps he was. His threadbare clothes covered lined and weathered skin, but his eyes shone clear and bright.

"This is for you." I placed one dollar in his palm, instinctively recoiling as his grimy hand touched mine. Lowering my gaze, I fought the desire to pull back, instead willing my fingers to rest in his a few seconds longer. I didn't feel filth, or disease, or desperation. The only thing I sensed was the gentle touch of one human reaching out for another — one giving, one receiving.

As I exchanged glances with this man, my equal except for a series of unknown circumstances, I recognized something in his eyes. Compassion, pride — maybe even hope. He "got it." At last, I did, too.

Ducking his chin, he stepped back from the curb. "Thank you."

With those simple words, I understood spontaneous acts of kindness and the grace accompanying them. Nothing is as random as it seems — and blessings spread in all directions.

I leaned my head out the window and my husband prepared to merge into a lane. "No, I need to thank you." And I meant it.

A second later as we rejoined the stream of cars driving past, I heard him call out, his voice sounding above the town's bustle. "God bless you."

~Heidi Gaul

71

The Right Ending

I wondered why somebody didn't do something.
Then I realized, I am somebody.
~Author Unknown

was skimming through my mail, assuming it was all junk, when I saw my name and address handwritten on an envelope. The return address indicated it was from a prison in Ohio. Why was I getting a letter from a prison?

It turned out to be a letter from a twenty-one-year-old inmate named Mike who had just read my story in *A 6th Bowl of Chicken Soup for the Soul* about thank-you letters my brothers and I had written to my mom. Although I had received correspondence about my stories in the past, I had never gotten one from an inmate.

I have always considered fan mail my real trophies in life and the true benefits of being a writer. But I'd be lying if I said I wasn't a little freaked out before I began to read Mike's life story.

It started out by explaining how, at three years old, his mother left town forever, leaving him with her ex-boyfriend. After only a few days, the ex-boyfriend found the task of raising a boy a little too tedious for his lifestyle and unloaded him on his mother instead.

With all Mike's early childhood heartache, the dysfunction of not having a biological mother and father in his life, he grew to love this care-taking woman and the support that only she managed to find for him. Although she had already raised five children by herself, she treated Mike like her own son and was a constant comfort when his first girlfriend dumped him, when he wrecked his first car, and during all the other times when he needed her support.

He said that she continued to be loyal to him in prison, writing to him every day to tell him how much she believed in him and how she knew he would make it through this painful stage of his life.

As I finished reading Mike's letter, I was sad. Because, unlike me, he didn't think he'd ever be able to express how much his "mom" meant to him. He ended his letter by saying that he didn't think he could tell his honorary mother how much she meant to him. But he wanted to tell someone, so he told me.

No sooner did I read his last line than I knew I had to write back and plead that he reconsider. I mentioned how she deserved to hear the words that I had read in his letter. Although I was a little nervous to continue to correspond, I found it cathartic to think that my words could help. Maybe I could help Mike write a new ending for that letter. This was several years ago, and regrettably, I never heard back from him.

A few weeks ago I was straightening out my spare bedroom and came upon the letter. I wondered whether Mike ever followed through. And then I had an idea. I would go online and see if I could track down this woman, who had to be in her eighties by now. After all, he told me her full name, so maybe there was a chance she could be located. Maybe he even *wanted* me to look her up and pass on his message. It only took a few moments to find her and I dialed her number.

After she said "hello" and confirmed that she did indeed have a son named Mike in prison I told her about the letter. She said, "He never was the type of person to share his feelings, but I knew he cared." I asked her if she'd like me to read what he wrote from Cell Block D at 5:30 a.m. that reflective night and she said, "Yes, please!" As I paused between paragraphs, I could hear her happy sighs. A few times she mumbled, "Isn't that wonderful."

Before I hung up I asked her, "Would you like me to send you his letter along with my story that he read in jail?"

She said yes, and I mailed her present a few days later. I was overwhelmed with emotion and so glad that I had taken the risk and followed through on my impulse to help Mike, who couldn't bring himself to finish his story himself. I was so proud to share my trophy with its rightful owner. After all, what good are trophies without the stories that go with them?

~Jim Schneegold

72

Put-Pockets

Go into the world and do well. But more importantly,
go into the world and do good.
~Minor Myers

When I was twenty-nine years old, I saved every penny for a year, sold my car and everything else I owned, and bought a one-way ticket to Europe. I wanted to see the world while I was still in my twenties. I had waited for years to take this trip with friends, but there was always something that prevented them from going—a job, a new girlfriend, money problems. Finally, I made it happen and I went by myself. I landed in Copenhagen, Denmark, and traveled through Europe for six months. It was the grand adventure I always dreamed it would be, and though it was twenty years ago, I still remember some of the friends I made so clearly, it's as if I just came home yesterday.

While in the historic city of Brugge in Belgium, I became friends with two happy-go-lucky guys from Tel Aviv. Their names were Avi and Shlomo. At the time, these names were unfamiliar to me, but I was to learn that they were as common in Israel as the names Mike and Dave are in America. Avi was small, wiry, and fast-talking. Shlomo was huge, heavily-muscled and quiet. Avi said he was Shlomo's boxing manager back in Israel. Shlomo might have been intimidating if he wasn't so friendly and good-natured. The three of us hit it off immediately.

We were having dinner one night in an outdoor café and

people-watching when Avi said, "Watch this." He waited for an elderly man to pass by, pulled a few Belgian francs from his pocket, jumped up and followed him, then furtively slipped the money into his coat pocket, unnoticed. He came back to our table laughing. Shlomo also laughed, indicating to me that they had done this before.

"What are you doing?" I asked.

Avi said, "You've heard of pickpockets, right? Well, we're put-pockets! We give people money. Imagine their surprise when they get home and find money in their pocket they were sure they didn't have before."

They laughed again. I laughed, too, but couldn't help being concerned about them.

"Aren't you worried they're going to catch you and think you're trying to rob them?" I asked.

"A few people have," Avi replied. "They were pretty mad, but then they looked at Shlomo and calmed down real quick." He laughed again.

"You're both nuts," I said, laughing with them.

They put money in a few more pockets and I was amazed at how talented they were at not getting caught. A woman turned and looked at Shlomo once but he quickly smiled and said, "Do you know where the bus stop is?" As she answered, she looked away and pointed toward the bus stop, and he put more money into her purse and winked at us! His brazenness was unbelievable.

They dared me to try it but I was terrified of being caught, accused of thievery, arrested, and rotting in a Belgian prison for decades. But they finally wore me down and I gave it a shot. Perhaps by accident, perhaps not, I chose a young man about nineteen years old who looked very worried. He looked so worried, in fact, I instinctively knew he was troubled about money, a woman, or both. I fell in behind him and tried to put the equivalent of about twenty dollars in his pocket. But just as I let go of the money, he grabbed my wrist, turned around and yelled at me. I didn't understand his language but assumed he said, "Hey! What are you doing?"

My eyes opened wide and I said, "I'm not stealing from you. I'm giving you money!"

Fortunately, he knew how to speak English. In disbelief, he said, "You're what?"

"I put money in your pocket," I said again.

"You're a liar!" he yelled. He started looking around, I assumed, for the police. Avi and Shlomo walked over and stood behind me silently. His anger turned to fear.

"Check it and see," I said, motioning to his pocket. He reached in, pulled out the bills, and looked at me with a confused expression.

"Why would you put money in my pocket?" he asked.

"Just because," I said. I motioned to Avi and Shlomo. "These are my friends. We're giving people money tonight. It was just your turn."

There was a moment of silent confusion as he processed this. He looked at Avi and Shlomo again. They smiled their big, open-hearted smiles and his anger and confusion dissolved like fog in sunlight. He smiled, chuckled, and said, "You're all crazy."

"I tried to tell them that, too," I replied, relieved that he was calming down. "You're actually the first and probably last person I will ever try this with. Apparently, I'm a terrible put-pocket."

We all laughed.

"Anyway, keep it," I said. "Take your girlfriend out for a nice dinner tonight."

He thanked us and started to walk away, then turned and said, "Can I tell you something?"

"Sure," I replied.

Avi and Shlomo came closer.

The man looked down, as if ashamed, and said, "I just gave the last of my money to my landlord. I was late with the rent and he was threatening to evict my wife and me. We had a baby a few months ago but I'm not making enough money. At the end of the month, I'm always broke. I get paid in a few days but I was wondering how we were going to eat tonight and tomorrow. This money will make that possible. So, thank you."

He shook my hand and began to walk away. Avi, Shlomo and I looked at each other. Avi said, "Wait." The man stopped. Avi whispered to Shlomo and they both took out their wallets and handed most of their money to him. I did the same. I'm not sure how much money it was exactly, but it was a lot.

"No," he said. "I can't take this. I didn't tell you that because I wanted more."

He tried to hand us the money back but Avi said, "Take it. We're on vacation. We can afford it."

The man shook his head in disbelief, impulsively hugged us all, then abruptly left, probably because he didn't want to cry in front of us.

My choosing someone who was in such desperate need of money can be seen as nothing but coincidence. After all, the world is full of people with money problems. Or it can be seen as divine providence. Maybe the purpose of my entire trip was to make sure my generous friends and I would be there at the exact moment that a young man wondering how he was going to feed his wife and child was walking by. Maybe the very thought of committing an act of kindness attracts the attention of God, or the universe, whichever you prefer, and sets in motion a chain of events between total strangers that could never have been planned.

~Mark Rickerby

73

A Family Survival Story

Being deeply loved by someone gives you strength,
while loving someone deeply gives you courage.
~Lao Tzu

My husband and I were fighting too frequently. I was almost always short of breath. I checked the description of panic disorder and panic attacks on WebMD. My self-diagnosis was questionable, maybe these symptoms just boiled down to lack of sleep. Meanwhile, my husband was becoming more and more forgetful. Bills past due, dentist appointments missed, anniversaries and birthdays unnoticed.

Because our three-year old daughter had been diagnosed with cancer.

It was the unthinkable. We had sailed through three pregnancies in under four years, and we had been gaining momentum as a young family of five. Our routines were firmly established, we had schools figured out in the complicated urban jungle of New York City, and we were accumulating meaningful family bonding that we had imagined before children.

We didn't realize how carefree our life was… how simple… how luxuriously healthy.

One warm September evening we were thrown overnight into a brutal hospital stay that lasted more than a month. We found ourselves alternating between grueling days and nights at our daughter's bedside as she endured a merciless regimen of chemo, with time back home with her two brothers, who could not comprehend why our family was suddenly so fragmented. We tried our best to navigate the uncharted seas ahead and not completely rock our children's previously secure worlds.

We became accustomed to witnessing our daughter's pain, to the rigid vinyl hospital chair serving as a bed, to delivering seemingly end-less amounts of oral medication on an hourly basis, to administering shots, to falling asleep on command, to waking abruptly to weeping.

Ultimately we logged over 100 overnight stays on the stiff con-vertible chair that served as the caregiver's accommodation next to our daughter's hospital bed. And between two healthy children, one ill child, a brand new full-time job (oh, life's timing!), and a tenuous freelance job, we were spread so severely thin, that the bond that still tethered my husband and me was nearly sheer. We had become no more than grim soldiers occasionally passing each other by with tense faces and terse words that exchanged some small bit of information about one of the children.

When we finally came up for air, in the midst of our daughter's two-year treatment — one that thankfully was expected to lead to her full remission from cancer — I realized that the cracks in our marriage needed serious patching.

That is when I pledged the following five random acts of kindness to my partner, who had certainly been the person most relied upon during the cancer diagnosis, but perhaps also the one most neglected.

I decided not to openly tell my husband that he would be the recipient of these kind acts. And while it took some time to gain momentum, the positive outcomes resulting from offering random acts to a member of my own family was remarkable. Every day for one month I offered him one of the following:

> My Full Attention: Days passed by when I never paused to look into my partner's beautiful blue eyes. We were going through such a profound event in our family. Yet there were very few moments of reflection when we gave each other

our full attention or even had a full conversation. When I started to really look and listen again, the connection began to return and we had more sincere moments together. It was nourishing.

My Thanks: My husband deserved to be thanked for all the tasks he performed on a daily basis for our family. And so I began to express gratitude for all of the very smallest tasks my husband wordlessly finished as well as the biggest ones. I decided to thank him silently instead of out loud. Doing this helped me notice how many things he did automatically and how often he contributed selflessly. It deepened my appreciation to thank him for all of his efforts. It magnified my gratefulness.

Not Engaging: As the stress continued to multiply, criticism and small arguments were common. The warmth between us was cooling. I decided to take things less personally and I decided not to engage. It takes two to bicker. Instead, I actively listened. Gradually we were on the same side again. Our home was more peaceful and it certainly helped our children's spirits to see us united and communicating well again.

Vacation (from the daily routine): While a real vacation was impossible at the time, given the daily hospital schedule and potential threat of germs to my daughter's unstable immune system, I realized I could easily give my husband time off from the daily monotony. One morning I offered him a vacation from household duties and caring for the children. I left him alone to rest in bed and took on all of the morning duties, which we typically divided. I offered the option of breakfast in bed or breakfast to go. I put out the garbage. This loving care offered a much needed mental vacation and was rejuvenating to him.

Physical Connection: I took my husband's hand and held it as we walked into the hospital one day. What a difference it made. We had not been physically close since the diagnosis. I was exhausted; he was exhausted. But the simple act of holding hands was so reassuring. I committed to a good old-fashioned foot rub later that evening. And as we began to reconnect on a physical level, my husband's outlook seemed improved. We also felt emotionally closer. I realized we didn't need to have long, deep discussions. Just being present and holding his hand gave him much needed emotional support.

It was difficult at first, but I made this silent commitment and as the month went on, it became easier, because these acts of kindness toward my husband worked. They had a steady, positive impact on our family. They not only strengthened our bond as parents but also gave our children their security back and showed them concrete examples of love and devotion.

Through my deliberate acts of kindness, my husband and I and our family emerged stronger, more vividly alive, electric. And then we began to pass along sparks of inspiration to the others around us.

~Sky Khan

Random
Acts of
Kindness

Above and Beyond

*Doing what's expected of you can make you good,
but it's the time you spend going above and beyond
what's required that makes you great!*
~Josh S. Hinds

74

California Dreaming

No one who achieves success does so without
the help of others. The wise and confident
acknowledge this help with gratitude.
~Alfred North Whitehead

stand in front of the world famous Improv box office, with its marquee detailing the names of comedy superstars making appearances tonight. This club is in Ontario, California, but the Improv brand is known all over. It's the dream of thousands of struggling comedians to be performing even one unpaid eight-minute set at any of these clubs. Tonight I stand staring into the lights and think back ten years ago to one terrified, crying boy.

In 2005, I graduated from Edinboro University of Pennsylvania with a bachelor's degree in Speech Communications and no idea what to do professionally with my life. I knew that I loved theater and performing, whether it be in my improvisational comedy troupe, bantering on the public radio station, or writing silly articles in the campus paper; but I had no idea how any of this connected to paying real bills in the adult world, something with which I had no experience.

I had been raised on welfare and my parents were convicted felons. It was hard enough graduating from high school, let alone going on to higher education. There were times during college when students were told to go "home" for spring break or the Christmas holiday; how could I explain that outside of this dorm room I had no home, that my mother was living out of a car?

Two acquaintances I barely knew from college had moved to California before me and agreed to let me stay with them just to get started.

Their names are Andrew Croulet and Rhett Scott, and they together were everything that I was not: both were popular, good-looking and social. Andrew had no problem getting the cutest girlfriends; he even ran for college homecoming king and started his own fraternity. Rhett was the lovable goof who could liven up any social gathering, all the while never meeting a beer pong table he didn't like. If I was Screech, they were two Ferris Buellers. After thinking it over and knowing I had no other options anyway, I took the $1,000 that I had and boarded a plane to pursue my Hollywood dreams.

I'm not above admitting I openly wept on that flight. I cried to the point of choking as I watched everything I knew get smaller in the window as I crept higher in the sky. All I had seen growing up in Linesville, Pennsylvania was that you got married to your high school sweetheart, got a job at the local tool and die factory, and started a family. They grew up and did the same thing again and again. Also you went hunting — a lot.

I never really fit in. My dreams were bigger than buck season and yard sales on Sunday. I belonged someplace where it was okay to dream big, where ridiculous ideas were not shunned, but embraced. I needed a land of movie magic: flying saucers, giant lizards, and talking monkeys. I needed Hollywood.

Shortly after landing, Rhett got me my first day job, working in real estate sales. He lent me his car until I was able to buy my own. The townhouse we lived in had two bedrooms and Rhett slept on the couch so that I could have my own bedroom. Let me say that again: he gave me his room in his own house. Yeah — that's the kind of guy Rhett is. I believe he saw how fragile I was and that I needed space to write and cry.

Rhett co-wrote the first screenplay that I ever optioned. Andrew won stand-up comedy tickets off the radio and gave them to me for my first time networking in California. That led to my being in a stand-up comedy class taught by veteran comedian Gary Cannon, who is currently the warm-up act for Conan O'Brien's television show *Conan*. Gary was the first to suggest my name to a general manager to produce my own night of live comedy. One night turned into more nights and before long I had a career. I owe that career to Andrew Croulet.

My friends helped me in more ways than simply housing, transportation, and financial. They taught me about family. Rhett adopted a white Siberian Husky puppy while I was staying with them, and named him Hosehead. When I was growing up my mother would have pets, but as soon as they did anything remotely "wrong" she would give them away. I got used to that and when I saw that Hosehead was allowed to occasionally screw up and that we weren't going to toss him away, I understood that he was family. We were a small family. I can't put into words the effect that had on me.

Hosehead was a good dog. One night, as I climbed the steps to my bedroom, we had another guest staying in Andrew's room and so the two people whose names were actually on the lease were sleeping in the living room, one on the floor and the other on the couch. I overhead Andrew talking with Rhett, asking how they ended up like this. After all it was their house. Andrew patted Hosehead and asked him, "Why are we sleeping down here? Why did your master let this happen to us?" I had to laugh. You'd have to get to know them. That was just them; they always gave up so much.

Eventually I moved out. The comedy scene embraced me and before long I was getting bit parts in film and television. Most recently my killer clown comedy *Killjoy's Psycho Circus* was produced by Full Moon Entertainment and premiered on Robert Rodriguez's El Rey Network in prime time.

And now I stand in front of a glowing marquee at the Ontario Improv where I received my very first comedy paycheck almost ten years ago. Tonight, I'm the headliner; this is *my* show and *my* fans. So much has changed for me. Rhett Scott went to work for his family business in Virginia. He's a homeowner now, with real world problems like heaters and roofing. Andrew Croulet is the Director of Admissions for a chain of colleges in the Fresno area; he married the love of his life and has two kids. My party buddies have all grown up. We still talk, just not as frequently. Life does that to people.

As I watch the club begin to let in *my* audience for the night I think back to how I never would have survived without Andrew and Rhett. Their guidance and kindness changed me forever. Together their two giant hearts will forever influence my life and the choices I make. I flew to California a scared little boy and ten years later I'm a self-confident headliner thanks to my best friends Andrew and Rhett.

~Tim Chizmar

75

Security Matters

From caring comes courage.
~Lao Tzu

"Thank you for the opportunity to serve you," the security guy, Matt, says as soon as I open my front door. As I live alone with my son, and my car has been broken into for the third time right in our driveway, I started feeling vulnerable and hired his company, ICU, to install security cameras.

Not only is Matt's strict professionalism unexpected, his appearance is startling. This man has ice blue eyes, delicate features, pale skin, closely shorn salt and pepper hair, and an otherworldly aura.

If I didn't know better, I'd think he's an angel who's come to save me. But I do know better — life is good and I don't need saving. I'd like to believe my only problem is people breaking into my car.

"I should be thanking you for coming here on such short notice," I say, as I launch into a description of the shattered driver's window and my resultant frayed nerves. I then hear myself admitting that my twenty-one-year-old son Zach's friends regularly climb over the side gate late at night. "My dog starts growling and barking and I hear the kids making noise in the yard." I'm ashamed of my boy's obvious disregard for my feelings and my failure in taking control of the situation. Matt nods and seems to understand.

While we walk the property, he both thinks out loud and educates me: "The primary objective of camera deployment is to provide

360-degree coverage. Points of ingress and egress must be visible from all angles. Placement is critical for optimal results."

What is this guy's story? Definitely military. I think to myself.

My ordinarily fierce "guard dog," Leo, charges out of the kitchen and welcomes Matt into the back yard like a long lost pack member — licking him, loving him, and leaning into his leg.

"I'm sorry about the dog, he's usually vicious. Leo! Give the man some space." And I stand and watch this torrent of affection in awe. I'm now amazed and want to know more. "Since Leo already considers you family, do you mind my asking a personal question?"

"Not at all."

"What kind of accent is that?" It sounds German, or Danish, or even Russian.

"It's not really an accent; it's cultural." And with that non-response he walks off and resumes his measuring, Leo close on his heels.

"Cultural?"

The next morning at 8:00 a.m. sharp he arrives to install the cameras. I'm astounded at his speed of "deployment" and by day's end, I just log onto my iPhone or iPad in order to see what's happening outside. I do feel more secure, and the cameras are a welcome deterrent to both break-ins and midnight visitors.

Matt telephones every so often inquiring whether I'm satisfied with the system and whether it's performing as it should. He always concludes our brief conversations with the reminder, "I'm here if you need me. Don't hesitate to call." I don't know what to do with that kind offer but I do know it feels good to hear. Yet I convince myself his thoughtfulness is nothing more than business protocol; strangers neither say, nor mean, those things.

One morning, after enduring the longest night of my life wherein — dog barking led to — camera checking, which led to — seeing — and watching — my son smoking and drinking — alone — till dawn, Matt happens to call. Words rush out of me like water from a burst pipe: "I thought he didn't drink alcohol… or do drugs… his father's a recovering addict… I thought he knew better…" and I don't stop until my distress and our family's tragic addiction history have been told and re-told from beginning to end.

Matt listens and doesn't interrupt as I rant about trust and betrayal and genetics. He says he's "truly sorry that the cameras yielded these disturbing results." He can tell from my concern that I'm a "good mom," much like his own.

"I appreciate your faith in me," I say, nearly at a loss for words. And then as usual, he asks if there's anything more he can do. I hesitate and think *Can you come over and talk to Zach?* But, I say no and thank him for listening.

With each passing night, more is revealed. The shocking truth that my son smokes and drinks alcohol after I've gone to bed is plain to see, and my disbelief gives way to a sense of urgency. This can't continue. This isn't allowed. I must confront him. But what if he becomes enraged, runs away, hates me?

When Matt calls next, my nerves are frayed and I'm relieved to hear his voice. My words tangle into sobs. "My boy… has a problem… like his dad… and I'm scared." I confess, hoping that in my telling these truths, he and his cameras will magically protect us.

"I have to talk to Zach tonight and tell him he can't live with me unless he gets help."

Matt asks me what time the conversation will take place.

"6:00 p.m."

Then he assures me, as if he really truly knows: "Everything will be okay. You're a good mother. You're doing your job. You'll give him what he needs to make the right choice." And I cry tears of relief just from hearing those precious words.

"With your permission, I'll park outside your house at 6:00 p.m. and hold the perimeter. If he runs, I'll follow him to make sure he's safe."

I impulsively reject his kind offer. "No, I couldn't ask you to do that." I am an island. I take care of things myself.

"Barbara, it seems that you need help. I want to be there for you. I'll be in my car, right outside, if you need me."

What does he have to gain? I almost believe he'll be there.

So my boy and I meet in the den at 6:00 p.m. and a silver Honda pulls up and parks right outside. I see the outline of Matt's head in the driver's seat. My body relaxes.

"Sit down, Zach… I have something to show you," I say, and I play the videos, fearing both his reaction and my own. Whenever I start shaking, I look out the window and see the car — and its driver — right outside. I'm not alone. My backup helps me sit straighter in my chair and speak from a place of quiet strength and compassion.

"It looks like you need help, Zach."

He stares at his hands. I check on the Honda.

"You can't continue this self-destructive behavior and live here. There's an outpatient rehab I'd like you to see."

I check on the Honda and wait for Zach's response. After a long pause, he says, "Okay, Mom, okay. I'll go."

We hug in a way that feels like a beginning.

"He agreed to go!" I text Matt. "I'm taking him in the morning."

"Roger that. Well done. I'll be leaving now. Don't hesitate to call if you need me."

And with those parting words, the enigmatic security man who provided me with hope, confidence, and a reminder that I am not alone, drives off into the night.

~Barbara Lodge

Erie, Pennsylvania

If you can't reward then you should thank.
~Arabic Proverb

On a wintry Sunday afternoon, my husband and I were driving home to Fairborn, Ohio after spending the Thanksgiving holiday with my parents just outside Buffalo, New York. In addition to our suitcases, I had two boxes filled with things from my old bedroom — high school yearbooks and various awards — as well as the leftovers from Thanksgiving dinner.

I had had a wonderful time and my parents had welcomed my husband with open arms. We were in our mid-twenties and had only been married for two and a half years. We were still in that delicate phase of negotiating with whom to spend which holiday. Since his parents lived in Virginia, we could only be with one set of parents at each.

We had purchased a slightly used, yellow 1976 Subaru in August 1977. Subaru was an exotic foreign car brand at that time, and my dad was into cars. Discussing its idiosyncrasies helped my dad and my husband bond.

Snow started falling soon after we began our drive back, but neither of us thought it was a big deal. I learned to drive in Buffalo, and we had both gone to college in northern New York State, where everyone had a double major in snow and cold. We switched driving every hour or so at any opportune rest stop.

And then, all of a sudden, it *was* a big deal.

We were near Erie, Pennsylvania and on what we later learned was an infamous part of Interstate 90 — infamous for whiteouts. My husband was driving when suddenly the world went white.

Visibility had dropped to zero. He could not see to pull over or stop. Then we hit a car. Then a car hit us. And another car hit us. And another, and another, and yet more sounds of crumpled metal. After what seemed like forever, the whiteout lifted, the crashes stopped, and the pile came to rest. The world paused.

It went quiet, too quiet.

Then everything went into double time, and the screams and sirens started.

I do not remember the ambulance ride to the hospital. I do not remember the emergency room. I do remember being told that I had bumps, bruises, contusions, and lacerations but nothing broken. Basically, I should take two aspirin and get some sleep.

For my husband, it was a different story. A leg fracture was suspected, but, since it was not a compound fracture, he had to wait until the orthopedic specialist would be available. That would not be until the next day, so he was admitted to the hospital.

I took a taxi to a nearby motel and got a room. The next morning, I again called a taxi to go to the police impound lot and salvage what I could from what had been our new car. As the taxi pulled into the lot, the driver looked at a crumpled pile of metal that still showed some yellow paint and said, "It looks like a Volkswagen was part of that big pileup yesterday. They must have been crazy to drive that in the snow."

"No. That was my car, and it was a Subaru station wagon, not a VW bug. I am here to collect what I can from it. My husband is in the hospital with a fractured leg, but I am okay... I guess."

After the appropriate paperwork was completed, I returned to what was left of my car. To my amazement, the taxi driver had pulled open the tailgate and was transferring suitcases and boxes to the trunk of his car. He let me point out the items to rescue, but he wouldn't let me lift a thing. After he drove me back to the motel, he unloaded the salvaged items into my room, and then he took me back to the hospital. He would not accept payment for any of the rides or a tip for all the extra work.

I hugged him, and said, "Thank you. Thank you. Thank you."

He replied, "I have a daughter about your age. I'm just doing what I hope someone would do for her."

My tears flowed. All I could do was continue to thank him. I was still in shock. I watched him drive away and then went to see what the hospital had done with my husband. I must have seen his name on the taxi license, but I did not remember it. This story of an act of kindness is the only "Thank You" I can offer him.

~Jean Delaney

Once Upon a Rocky Beach

Among the things you can give and still keep are
your word, a smile, and a grateful heart.
~Zig Ziglar

Some years ago, I was doing a summer internship in Newport, Oregon, and decided that for the Fourth of July weekend, I would rent a car and head down the coast to see the redwoods. The first day, shortly after leaving Newport, I stopped at a rocky beach to walk a bit.

The day was quite warm and sunny, but the breeze coming off the ocean was cool and smelled of the sea. It evoked stories about oceangoing vessels and creatures hidden in the deep places, of the great singers and the tiny bright creatures that glow upon the shore at night, and I walked for some time across rocks the size of baseballs and along the narrow strip of sand next to the water. I waded into the shockingly cold water, and felt myself sinking down into the sand as the waves moved in and out around me. I listened to the soothing sound of the waves and to the cries of the gulls. I was at peace in that place.

After a time, I returned to my car to go on my way. It was only then that I discovered that I had dropped my keys somewhere on that beach. My heart sank; I knew that the odds of finding them amongst all those rocks were slim to none. Nevertheless, I searched for them for the next couple of hours.

Eventually, I went back to the car to think (as if thinking about it could possibly do any good). The car, however, was locked. I sat on the hood feeling miserable and hopeless, close to tears, for what must been almost an hour.

There were a few other people on the beach and at the picnic tables set on grassy islands in the parking lot, but I was shy and afraid to ask strangers for anything. At the time, I did not have a cell phone. And so I sat.

As the shadows lengthened and the breeze began to pick up a bit, a woman approached me. She asked if anything was wrong and if there was anything she could do to help. I told her what had happened. She looked at the beach and shook her head.

"You could look for a thousand years and never find them," she said.

"I know," I replied. "I gave up after a couple of hours. I don't think I'd last a thousand years."

"What can we do to help?" she asked.

It was only then that I noticed a man sitting a short distance away, who must have been with her. I asked her if they had a cell phone, and she said they did.

"But there's no signal here," she said.

They were clearly getting ready to leave, so I asked if she might call the car rental agency when they got to where there was a signal. She agreed, walked over to the man, and they got in their car and left.

A couple more hours went by. I walked on the beach a little more as the sun went down, still looking without much hope for the keys, and wondering how long it might be before help arrived. The sun set, and it grew quite chilly. Still nothing, no sign of rescue.

After what seemed like an eternity, and about the time I had given up all hope and was considering trying to sleep on one of the tables, the same couple reappeared. Rather than making the requested call, they told me that they had driven all the way back to Newport and stopped at the car rental agency, but were unable to get a new key without my presence.

"Get in," the woman said. "Let's go get the key."

I was completely floored. I had no idea what their plans for the evening might have been, but I was certain of this: they had nothing to do with running a total stranger back and forth to Newport from that beach. In any case, I got in the car. It was warm, and the atmosphere was close and friendly. After sitting in that parking lot alone for hours, getting progressively colder, it was pure delight. We talked on the long way there, and they turned out to be wonderful people.

We arrived back at the rental agency, then had to call and wait for somebody to show up. A man eventually came, looked up the information for the car in question, and cut a new key. The whole process probably took another forty-five minutes. He was kind about it, although it had obviously dragged him away from his evening plans, too.

Then we drove back to the beach, talking along the way. I thanked them profusely (which seemed to embarrass them) and asked if I might do something for them: buy them dinner, or a glass of wine, or anything at all. They politely refused, telling me only that someday I could do the same for someone else.

Ever since that night, I have made a point of trying to do more random acts of kindness. And whenever I do, I think of those people. Whoever you are (I have virtually no memory for names), and wherever you may be, thank you, and know that I'm still passing your kindness along at every opportunity.

~Lynn Goodman

78

The Skirt

*Let us be grateful to people who make us
happy; they are the charming gardeners
who make our souls blossom.*
~Marcel Proust

"Excuse me, would you please tell me where you got your pretty striped skirt?" I was addressing that question to an attractive young woman I had spotted standing eight people away in our cruise dinner line. For months, I had searched for a long skirt with the stripes correctly sewn together to create perfect chevron points, but all the ones I had found were mismatched in the sewing. The stripes on her skirt had perfect chevron points... so, I had to ask.

"Why, yes, of course. I bought it two weeks ago at Kohl's near Santa Clarita."

I thanked her and returned to my place in line.

Two nights later I spotted her again. She was a karaoke contestant on the ship. And, she was wearing the same skirt.

With a voice like a professional, she sang "Memories" from *Cats*. After the contest, I rushed over to compliment her, and also handed her a little note:

*When you remove your skirt tonight, will you please call my stateroom
and give me the SKU number on it, so I can easily find it when I shop?
I'm in Caribe 245. Thanks...*

She read it, smiled, and said, "Sure, I will."

For several more hours, my roommate Marilyn and I roamed the ship enjoying the variety of shows.

It was getting late so we headed toward our stateroom. "Don't forget to get tomorrow's news out of the rack by our door," I reminded Marilyn.

At our door, she reached toward the rack. Suddenly, her hand paused, frozen in mid-air. An amazed look spread across her face. Reaching into the rack, she removed an object, and handed it to me. It was the skirt!

I was stunned! A woman I had just met on the cruise had given me her new skirt, and I had no way to find her! Then it dawned on me. She said she'd leave the SKU number on my phone. I rushed into our stateroom, but the phone was not blinking. There was no call…

Now, I had a true dilemma. We were on board with over 3,000 other passengers. How would I ever locate her aboard such a large ship? During that sleepless night, I came up with a plan.

In the morning, Marilyn and I went to the main desk. "Excuse me, young man, will you please help me locate a passenger on the ship? It's very important that I thank her; she gave me her brand-new skirt."

I seemed to remember her name announced as Meredith. But his search found no passenger aboard with that name. So, I tried another tactic. "The woman who introduced the karaoke contestants called herself Carla. Will you please look up your employee named Carla?"

After searching through 2,100 employees, he found a name with Carla in the middle. "That's the only Carla we have on board," he said.

"Please tell me where I can find her."

"She's introducing another act in the Explorer's Lounge tonight at 9:30. You should find her there."

"Thank you so very much. You have been a tremendous help."

At 9:15 p.m., Marilyn and I entered the lounge. Carla was there.

"Carla, please help me find karaoke contestant #8, who sang "Memories" the other night. She gave me her brand-new skirt, and it's urgent that I thank her."

Carla smiled. "Yes, I remember her."

Now, at least, I had a contact. "Please contact her and ask her to come to my stateroom so I can get her address, and send her a gift."

"I'll do that," she said, hastily scribbling down my name and stateroom number.

A full day passed. It was now Friday. Had Carla been able to pass on my message?

We'd be back into the home port on Saturday, and I still had not found my benefactor. I was becoming worried that I'd never be able to thank this benevolent stranger.

That evening, we were ready to leave for dinner. There was a sudden knock on our door. I opened it and there stood the subject of my search!

With a hug, I swept her into our room, thanked her profusely for the skirt, and asked for her full name and address. She demurred, saying she wanted nothing in return, but I insisted. Under my continued urging, she finally wrote it down. Her name was Jennifer. And there was a big howl of laughter when she told us her stateroom number. She had been only two doors away from us the entire time! And the missing phone call? She had called and left her message, she said, but perhaps she had misdialed.

"I'm in the karaoke finals tonight," she added. "Will you come down and vote for me?"

Again she sang "Memories" in the contest, even more beautifully than the first time. Despite strong competition from a talented tenor, Jennifer won. We were thrilled, and rushed up to give her hearty congratulations.

After she left, Marilyn and I were finishing our drinks. A waitress came over carrying a large bottle of champagne, with only one drink already poured out.

"Here," she said, "we won't use this anymore tonight. Take it back to your stateroom, and enjoy."

We accepted it, with the perfect plan as to where it should go. Approaching Jennifer's stateroom, we tapped on her door. When it opened, we handed her the bottle.

"We brought you some champagne. Now you can toast your

karaoke victory!"

She laughed in surprise, and gratefully accepted it.

Once I returned home, I shopped for that just-perfect necklace and matching earrings — sparkly turquoise — to coordinate with the dress Jennifer wore in the karaoke finals.

A week later, she called thanking me for my gift; we chatted at length, really got to know each other, and have planned to stay in touch.

So now I not only have a lovely striped skirt to wear and enjoy, but I also have a wonderful new friend — all brought about by her remarkable, and totally unexpected kindness.

~Kay Presto

79

The Totaled Car and the Total Stranger

*Reflect upon your present blessings — of which every
man has many — not on your past misfortunes, of
which all men have some.*
~Charles Dickens

We were on our way! In Wyoming we would have a new home, a new job, and a new adventure. It was 1980 and my husband Gary and I were driving from Houston, Texas to Gillette, Wyoming with our three young boys, who were ages five, three, and one. Since we had a few extra days before we had to arrive at our final destination, we first drove to my husband's childhood home in Minnesota.

After a few days of rest and relaxation, we were back on the road. We drove due west toward Wyoming. It was October; the roads were clear, and the fall weather was fantastic.

We had been driving all day and we were all hungry. We stopped at a restaurant to eat dinner and when we came out I put all three boys in the back of our station wagon so they could sleep. There were no strict laws about seatbelts then. It was nine o'clock in the evening.

Gary got into the driver's seat, set the cruise control, and was planning to drive the last few hundred miles that night. Then our vehicle hit ice on a bridge about thirty miles east of Rapid City, South

Dakota. As soon as the car started to slide my husband touched the brakes to turn off the cruise control and this sent our vehicle into a spin. Our car immediately careened from one side of the bridge to the other. After the initial impact we lost our power steering. Gary was not able to control the car at all. We were thrown back and forth against the guardrail like a bruised and beaten fighter in a boxing ring.

We slid to a stop on the median between the eastbound and westbound lanes. It appeared that everyone was okay, although quite shaken and scared. We climbed out of our car to survey the damage and discovered that we would need to be towed.

Only minutes later, a car pulled up and a man climbed out to ask how he might help. It was cold now, and he suggested that I get in his car with the children. He had a little snack for the boys.

With the help of our Good Samaritan, my husband was able to get a tow truck to come and take our car to Rapid City. After it was gone, this compassionate man drove us to a hotel in the city. On the drive we discovered that he was a salesman, and on the road a great deal. He had been traveling east, but turned around to help us. He took us thirty minutes out of his way, and made sure we were safely deposited in a hotel room before he said goodnight and left.

The next morning Gary and I woke up wondering how we were going to get breakfast and more importantly, a rental car to get us to Gillette. Then there was a knock at our door, and we discovered the salesman had returned to make sure we got breakfast and had a way to get around town. He drove Gary to find our totaled car so that he could remove our valuables. Then he took him to rent a car.

Once we had a rental car our family was ready to finish our journey. Our bighearted benefactor wished us well, said goodbye, and was on his way east again. He had lost at least half a day of work and put some extra miles on his car, all for a family he had never met and would never see again.

Our bedraggled family arrived in Gillette with no car and none of our household goods. We were in a new, strange area where we had no family or friends. We were feeling a little forlorn, but I immediately bowed my head to thank heaven from my heart for the guardrail on that bridge and for the amazing stranger whose sacrifice and service made such a difference to our family.

~Gail H. Johnsen

80

Touched by an Angel

Angels can fly directly into the heart of the matter.
~Author Unknown

When my husband's car wouldn't start one morning, he came into the house and gave me the unwelcome news. I drove him to work and my youngest to school, and then I went off to my ladies Bible class. A man who happened to be at the building offered to follow me home and jump Don's car for me, so that I could take it to the mechanic.

That worked and I was on my way to the mechanic, when I realized I had a problem. The turn signals refused to operate and the dashboard clock kept fading out. Even though it was a warm day in south central Florida I turned off the air conditioning and prayed the battery would last until I got to the mechanic, or at least within walking distance.

I drove down the highway and got into the left-turn lane for the road that would take me to my destination. At that point, the car quit.

"NO!" I shouted at it. The car, of course, ignored me and sat there, so dead that even the hazard lights refused to work. There I was, stuck in the left-turn lane of the town's main drag, and there was nothing I could do about it.

I carefully got out of the car and popped the hood, hoping that would signal to other motorists I wasn't going anywhere anytime soon. Since I couldn't hurt the battery any further I kept my door open so I wouldn't bake in the car while I began the process of getting the motor club to send a tow truck.

While I was on hold, a car pulled up behind me and a dark-haired woman got out. I got out of my vehicle, motioning to it in an attempt to explain I wasn't going anywhere.

She opened the conversation by saying, "I was going to let you use my cell phone, but I see you have one."

How nice, I thought.

She reached into her car and pulled out an icy drink from a fast food restaurant. "It looks like you might be here a while… I brought you something to drink. I hope you like Dr. Pepper."

What? First off, I *was* thirsty. Secondly, I adore Dr. Pepper, though I usually limit myself to the diet kind. I gratefully accepted the soda.

Then the woman reached into her car again. "I'm on my lunch break… I brought you a sandwich." She handed me a sack with a chicken sandwich and fries and smiled.

My mouth fell open. This woman, who didn't know me at all, had gone out of her way to bring me lunch and a drink… just because.

A person with a fully functioning brain would've asked this angel her name, or at least offered to pay for the meal. But at that moment my brain had short-circuited. If this gal had reached into her car and pulled out a mechanic, I don't think I would've been surprised.

I did manage to stammer out a thank-you to her. She got back into her car and drove out of my life. I never saw her again.

This happened over fourteen years ago, and I still think about it. In a world where we hear about people treating others badly, this stands out to me like a beacon. It's something worth copying.

I haven't yet bought a meal for someone stuck on the road. But I have given rides to stranded strangers. I've offered to call for help for others in a similar situation. I try to lend a helping hand when I can to people who are in need, remembering the hand held out to me when I needed it.

I don't know who that woman was, but to me, she was an angel. And I'm grateful for the way she touched my life.

~Laura Ware

81

Restored Faith

> *Wherever we travel to, the wonderful people*
> *we meet become our family.*
> ~Lailah Gifty Akita, Think Great: Be Great!

Returning from a family holiday to England, we had a twenty-hour layover in Paris. Determined to make the most of our short stay, we decided to see the Eiffel Tower. Armed with only a map and a few phrases of high school French, we left the airport by train, heading to our first stop, Notre Dame.

We were to switch to a different line of the Metro once we reached the cathedral stop, but instead, we exited through the turnstiles. Once we realized that we made a mistake and that we would have to pay again to get back on the subway, we decided to find our way above ground. Standing in a huddle, we opened our map to figure out where we needed to go.

"Excuse me, but do you require assistance?" I turned to see a fashionably dressed man, perhaps in his mid-forties. His English was excellent but spoken with the most exquisite French accent I'd ever heard.

I answered for the family. "Well, we were trying to take the train to the Eiffel Tower but we left the station by accident.

"Oh, it is no problem. If you like, I can show you the way."

We eagerly accepted his gracious offer, anticipating that he would lead us to the top of the stairs and then simply point us in the correct direction. Wrong.

When we reached the street above, our guide, who introduced himself simply as Thierry, said, "Come, it is this way."

I looked at my husband and my daughter and shrugged. They shrugged back. Surprised, but grateful, I said, "Thank you," and we introduced ourselves. I asked, "Are you sure you have the time to do this? You don't have any other commitments?"

He responded, "Oh, no. I have the afternoon free. It is a beautiful day and it would be my pleasure to show you my city."

Thierry crossed the street and we followed along like ducklings. We walked down alleyways sprinkled with adorable cafés, by patisseries, whose luscious pastries sent the smells of heaven wafting through the air, and into cathedrals and courtyards that were so far off the beaten track we would never have otherwise found them. In one such church, Thierry told us. "There are more kings and queens buried here than in all of Notre Dame. But Notre Dame has Napoléon and therefore the fame and the money. Also, all the tourists."

The entire time we walked, our impromptu guide gave us the history of his beautiful city. It was a spectacular day in Paris. The sun was shining, the sky a saturated cerulean. The sights and sounds and scents of that day are indelibly etched in all of our memories.

In total, Thierry spent three hours walking with us through the streets of Paris. We found out he was married with two girls, one in her second year of medical school, and the other still in high school. He was a businessman but also a published author.

When we reached the tower, he said, "Well, I must leave you now. I hope that you will return to our city when you have more time. There is much to see here in Paris."

We thanked him profusely but he brushed aside our gratitude, saying only, "It was my pleasure. It is good for the universe to give back."

After a picture, hugs, and kisses on both cheeks for all of us, this gracious stranger walked out of our lives — but never out of our memories.

I truly thought this was to be a once in a lifetime experience, but this May I was proven wrong.

We were headed to Halifax to visit my husband's family, in particular his ailing mother who was dying of cancer. We wanted our girls to have one last visit with their nana.

My older daughter, Sarah, had ankle surgery two weeks prior to our flight. She was unable to bear weight and required crutches.

I booked a seat with extra legroom for Sarah so that she could keep her foot up during the flight. On the flight to Halifax we were all sitting close enough together for me to help her with her crutches, and to provide assistance as needed. Our return flight, however, proved to be more challenging.

Sarah was sitting at the front of the plane, in the premium seats. The rest of us were in the back of the plane, in the squished seats. I boarded early, with Sarah, to help her store her crutches and get settled. I struggled to stuff the crutches into the overhead bin, but they were too long. A voice spoke from my right. I turned to see a man, possibly in his mid-forties, who said, "Here, let me help you. There is more room back here."

He took the crutches from me and easily stored them away. I offered my thanks and turned to Sarah. "Okay, sweetie. You should be fine. I'll come back and check on you once we're underway."

The gracious stranger asked, "Oh, where are you sitting?"

I pointed to the back of the plane. Laughing, I said, "Oh, way back there, in the bowels of the plane."

"What is your seat number?"

Curious as to why he wanted to know, I said, "56B."

He smiled and stood to pull his briefcase from the overhead bin. "Fine. I will sit there and you take my seat so you can help your girl."

I tried to refuse. After all, he had paid extra for his lovely, roomy seat, but he refused to take no for an answer. "Please, I insist. It would be my pleasure."

Somewhat bemused, I watched him walk to the back of the plane where he would sit next to my husband. I wondered how we could be so fortunate as to meet another incredibly kind and gracious stranger.

He wasn't finished with us yet, though.

We landed in Montreal only to discover our flight to Vancouver was delayed by an hour. During the trip to Montreal, my husband and our kind stranger had chatted. He was a businessman who lived in North Vancouver and would be on the same flight as us. As we exited the plane, he said, "It seems we are stuck here for a while. If you like, I would be honored to have you as my guests in the Air Canada lounge." None of us had ever been in the lounge before.

Concerned, I asked, "Are you sure that's allowed?"

He replied, "Please, don't worry. It is fine." He led the three of us, all obviously Caucasian, to the lounge and when asked who we were, this dark-skinned man with a lovely Middle-Eastern accent replied without hesitation, "They are my family."

It's unlikely we will get the chance to enjoy such luxury again, but thanks to this stranger's generosity, we certainly enjoyed the experience.

These two different men, complete strangers from two different continents, have restored my faith in the innate goodness of humanity.

~Leslie Anne Wibberley

82

A Tankful of Hope

Kindness is gladdening the hearts of those who are
traveling the dark journey with us.
~Henri-Frédéric Amiel

t was 1990, and I had just graduated from college. It wasn't the graduation of which greeting cards are made, though, full of excitement, smiles, caps in the air and hope for the future. Instead it involved having a nervous breakdown two weeks before I was scheduled to begin my student teaching, crying in my faculty advisor's office and telling him that I didn't want to teach, I just wanted to be done, and could I please drop the education aspect of my degree and be finished immediately?

I wonder if he knew as deeply as I did that I was never meant to be a teacher, and if that is why he didn't spend more time trying to talk me out of such a rash decision. After all, I was literally two months away from the career for which I had just spent the past four years preparing.

When all was settled with the billing and financial aid offices I found myself with a few hundred dollars to my name, a 1985 Dodge Omni, and not much else in the way of worldly possessions. I rented a room from the friend of a friend, slept on a mattress on the floor, and stored my clothing in a blue cardboard storage box with drawers. I very quickly discovered that having a degree in English was not very useful in the job market. I circled ads and sent out résumés, netting only the occasional interview, most of which ended with either the words "Overqualified" or "Not enough experience." No, this was not a greeting-card graduation scenario at all.

My savings trickled slowly away, spent on rent, gas for my car, and the basic necessities. By December I had reached the point of crisis. After paying rent I was down to the last seven dollars in my bank account. But I finally found at least temporary success in my job search when I walked into the chain bookstore at a local mall and walked out with a job as a seasonal employee. Oh, how I stretched those last seven dollars over the next few weeks, living off of saltines and tuna. I watched the gas gauge on my little gray Dodge dipping lower and lower toward empty as I waited for that first paycheck to come in.

It was a cold and gray day barely a week before Christmas when my paycheck finally arrived. When my shift at the bookstore ended I trudged out to the edge of the mall parking lot. First on my list, stop at the gas station to put gas in the car. Second, deposit paycheck. I pulled out of the parking lot and onto the loop road surrounding the mall. And there, at the very first stop sign, I ran out of gas.

I don't know how many irritated drivers pulled out to go around me as I sat there. I'm sure there were quite a few. It was, after all, Christmas at the mall. But there I sat, tears slowly rolling down my cheeks, having no idea what to do. In a season that celebrates family, friends, and the comforts of home, I felt alone and unprepared.

And then... a knock on the window. "Are you all right?" the well-dressed woman asked. "Can I help with anything? I wasn't going to stop, but I thought I saw tears."

I don't remember all the details of what happened next. Somehow we got my car moved off the loop road and back into a parking space. Then she invited me into her station wagon, and drove me the few minutes to the nearest gas station. Along the way she talked to me, listened to me tell about being on my own, experiencing my first Christmas away from home, my worries and my hopes. She filled a gas can, paid for it, and drove me back to my car.

She wouldn't accept anything for her help; she just smiled and said "Do something for someone else some day when you are able." And I've tried. I've tried to live my life with eyes wide open for the tears around me. I won't say that I've done anything spectacular for anyone; I doubt I've changed any lives. But then, I doubt she would think that she had, either. But she did. She planted a seed of hope when I most desperately needed it.

~Loretta Tschetter

Kindness in Chaos

September 11 is one of our worst days but it brought
out the best in us. It unified us as a country and
showed our charitable instincts and reminded
us of what we stood for and stand for.
~Senator Lamar Alexander

I was ready for my first day of college. It had been a long process to get into my school of choice and now I was making the trek for the first time from The Bronx, where I lived, to faraway Long Island.

It was such a sunny beautiful day as I nervously made my way to the train station at the Castle Hill stop on the 6 line. I was underground when the first plane hit, so I was oblivious to what was happening above. As I strode into Grand Central to catch the train to Long Island I noticed how panicked people seemed. I shrugged it off as the normal hectic pace of the city and just moved on in line.

I reached the ticket window only to find that I had left all my money at home. I couldn't buy a ticket — I was going to miss school.

As I made my way back to the local train again, to go home, I noticed something odd. A woman was crying to her friend about something. Then I saw another. And then a man crying. I had no idea what was going on.

The next thing I heard was, "Everyone must exit the train immediately." I still had no idea what was going on.

As I made my way up the escalator I saw police rushing into the station and when I emerged on the street, the entire city seemed to have lost its mind. People fought for pay phones because their cell phones no longer worked. Grim-faced police tried to keep everyone from going back into the station. I quietly asked an officer, "What is going on, sir?"

He simply said, "Just stay out of the subway." Then I heard a shoeshine man telling people around him, "They brought them down!"

What was he talking about? Then I finally heard the news on a radio. I walked to the end of the block and looked south and saw the clouds of smoke.

I walked toward Times Square. I had never seen or heard this place more quiet and subdued. Hundreds of people all stood silently watching the big screens. Some were crying; others were angry. The world had changed right then and there for all of us.

I needed to find my way home, but I had no money and the subways had shut down. I made my way to an office building I interned at while in high school. No one was there. I called a friend who offered to pay for my cab if I just made it back to The Bronx. Bad news, no cabs were allowed to leave the island of Manhattan.

All around me I saw frantic, scared people who had no idea what to do. Then I heard a voice. A stranger said, "You need to find a way home. They are letting us walk the Queensborough Bridge." He saw that I was lost and took me under his wing. As we walked he told me that he had moved here from South America, and he had witnessed things like this all the time.

"I came here to avoid this kind of thing," he said with a disturbing amount of calm. He spoke as someone who had witnessed terror on a regular basis. The stranger and I walked the Queensborough Bridge with thousands of other New Yorkers. We could see the smoke plumes billowing from the wreckage of the World Trade Center. Everyone looked to the sky with fear as fighter jets flew overhead. The stranger calmly said, "Don't worry," and I felt better.

We walked into a part of the city I never ventured into before. He made a phone call, trying to find someone who could give me a ride home. I could hear the argument from the other end of the line.

Someone was telling him that I was not his problem. He argued back in Spanish, telling the other person that I had no way to get home. How it was the least he could do on a day like today. How he could not just leave me.

I told him it was fine, I could figure out a way from here on. He insisted on helping and tried to give me money to get on the subway that was still running in Queens. I told him my metro card was still good for one more ride. He wrote directions for which trains would lead me back to The Bronx. I will never forget this kind man. On the worst day our country had ever seen small acts of kindness like this one made a big difference for many. It certainly did for me.

~Freddy Nunez

Random Acts of Kindness

Eye Opening Kindness

One who is kind is sympathetic and gentle with others.
He is considerate of others' feelings and courteous
in his behavior. He has a helpful nature. Kindness
pardons others' weaknesses and faults. Kindness
is extended to all—to the aged and the young,
to animals, to those low of station as
well as the high.
~Ezra Taft Benson

84

The Hoodlums Across the Street

Judging is acting on a limited knowledge. Learn the
art of observing without evaluating.
~Pushpa Rana

Sara, my neighbor from two doors down, and I were sitting on the front porch enjoying a cup of coffee and a little gossip. She frowned at the bungalow across the street. "Have you met them yet?"

I shook my head. "Nobody has. They keep to themselves. When they come outside they never make eye contact with anyone."

"They sure don't fit into the neighborhood," Sara said, the corners of her mouth turning down as she stared at the bungalow. "I wonder why the Wests rented their place to those two when they moved to Florida."

I shrugged. "I think they are letting a property management company handle it for them. I suppose they can't discriminate."

"This cul-de-sac was so close-knit before they moved in," Sara complained. "It won't be the same again. What about our street parties? We've always included everybody. Should we invite them?"

I sighed. "I don't know. At this point nobody has even met them. I doubt they would come anyway. Like you said, they don't fit in."

For a few seconds we were silent as we thought about the two young men across the street. They had long hair, beards, pierced ears and tattoos. And if that wasn't enough, one of them had several piercings in his face.

Sara sat up straight and her eyes grew wide with curiosity when a car with the city emblem pulled up in front of Mrs. Swain's house next door. We glanced at each other and hurried over. Mrs. Swain had been a widow for several years and was recovering from breast cancer. She didn't have any relatives in the area and Sara and I tried to keep an eye on her.

We were a few steps behind a man with a clipboard when he knocked on Mrs. Swain's door. She looked very old, very thin, and very tired when she opened the door.

Sara gasped and grabbed my arm when we heard the man speak. "I'm sorry ma'am, but someone has complained about the length of your grass and I was sent out to investigate." He swallowed as he looked at the frail little woman who gazed back at him with troubled eyes. "It does appear that your grass is in violation of city code. If you don't have it cut in five days the city will send someone out to cut it and you will receive a bill for the service."

Mrs. Swain blinked at him in confusion. "Who would complain? Everyone knows that my old lawn mower is broken. And I've been sick too."

"I can't reveal the name of the person who complained," he said. "But you will have to comply." He cleared his throat. "In five days, ma'am."

"I know who would complain," Sara hissed. "It has to be those two hoodlums across the street." She glanced over her shoulder toward the bungalow, gave a start, and whispered hoarsely. "And look who is coming over to gloat."

Just then a voice that seemed too gentle to be coming from the scraggly young man behind me said, "What is going on? Is she alright?" He nodded toward Mrs. Swain, who stood in the doorway wringing her hands.

Sara looked at him coldly. Her eyes raked over him disapprovingly but he didn't seem to notice. "Some jerk reported her because her grass is too high."

The young man and his friend exchanged glances and nodded solemnly. Then without another word they turned and walked back toward the bungalow.

Sara snorted. "What nerve."

I sighed. Mrs. Swain was a sweet soul and she didn't deserve this aggravation. It was a shame that nobody had cut her grass for her but it just hadn't been convenient. My husband, Joe, was in the Army doing a stint in Germany, and I was seven months pregnant. I had to rely on my brother to get my own grass cut. Sara and her husband, as well as two other families on the cul-de-sac hired a landscaping service to do their lawn work. One family was on vacation and the only other person who lived here was a disabled veteran who had a buddy cut his grass for him.

"I'll be back in five days." The man from the city said, handing Mrs. Swain a citation. "I'm sorry."

As the man walked away, Mrs. Swain's eyes widened in surprise and we followed her gaze. The two young men were hurrying across the street, one pushing an old lawn mower and the other carrying a weed eater. Without a word they got to work.

When they were finished Mrs. Swain walked onto the porch carrying a pitcher of lemonade and a plate of homemade cookies. The tired men gratefully sank down into chairs and took huge gulps of lemonade.

Mrs. Swain's eyes were bright with tears as she took a chair too. "I don't get my check until next week," she said meekly. "But I have five dollars I can give you today for the gas."

One of the young men smiled at her. "We might be a little ragged around the edges, but we were raised right. It would shame my mama if I took money from you."

Mrs. Swain laughed. "I happen to like ragged around the edges. My late husband Frank was in the Navy when I met him. He had tattoos and he rode a Harley. It took my mother almost a year to admit that he was a good man in spite of her first impression."

The other young man spoke up. "We'll make a bargain with you, ma'am. We'll keep your grass cut if you keep making lemonade and cookies for us."

Mrs. Swain was beaming as Sara and I slunk away guiltily. The hateful words we had said about the two young men spun through my head. I turned and sped back to Mrs. Swain's porch and Sara hurried beside me. I thrust out my hand. "Forgive me for being rude. My name is Elizabeth and I live next door to Mrs. Swain."

"I'm Sara. I live two doors below Elizabeth." From the sound of her voice I knew that Sara felt just as bad as I did.

"No wonder they kept to themselves and didn't look at anyone." Sara said humbly as we walked back to my house. "They probably noticed the stares and the frowns aimed at them."

We both learned a valuable lesson that day. Never pass judgment on people because they don't look, dress, or sound like you. Often they may be much better people than you are in all the ways that matter.

Did we invite the two young men to the next street party? You bet. And they were an immediate hit with everyone. They were soon loved by everyone on our little cul-de-sac. Especially by Mrs. Swain, who took on the role of doting grandmother.

~Elizabeth Atwater

85

Big City Crime... with a Twist

The ideals which have lighted my way, and time after
time have given me new courage to face life cheerfully,
have been Kindness, Beauty, and Truth.
~Albert Einstein

had just arrived in South Korea for a one-year teaching position. I was looking forward to exploring the ancient palaces and
temples in downtown Seoul, just a subway ride away from the
suburb I was calling home.

Aside from the basics in Korean, I had little ability to communi-
cate. I decided to bring my home address written in Korean with me,
although I doubted that anyone who lived outside my neighborhood
could find where I lived — even *with* the address.

There was no number on my building. In fact, there were no
street signs or street names written anywhere in the suburb. Even the
market beside where I lived had different names depending on whom
you asked.

I understood that my building was officially Building 325 in
Korean, but I was also told that we lived beside Building 27. Apparently
buildings had official numbers that were never posted on their exterior,
which had been assigned according to when they were built.

I was quite confident that the address the landlord had written on
my piece of paper read something to the effect of, "Old, grey building

beside a big willow tree, up the hill from the loud market area." As I walked down the steps into the subway tunnel, I could only think that if I got lost I might never return.

While the subway map was quite intimidating, with at least twelve separate lines, I was relieved to find that taking the subway was extremely easy. Each station was color-coded, and had its name written in English as well as Korean. The announcements calling out each stop were quite clear, and the subway cars even had an electronic board that listed the next stop in English and Korean.

Since all the seats were filled, I stood. Off in my own world, wondering if I would find my next stop to transfer subways, I felt someone tugging on my knapsack. Assuming I must be in someone's way, I moved over slightly. But suddenly in one quick motion, I felt my entire knapsack ripped off my back, and in a flash it was gone.

I whipped my head around to see who the thief was. The subway hadn't stopped, so it wasn't possible that someone had jumped off. I looked at the people standing behind me, but didn't see my bag or anyone suspicious. I tried to look beyond them, but I didn't see how anyone could have possibly moved though the densely packed car.

I began to panic. I wasn't as worried about losing my money and identification, but my travel book, directions and telephone numbers were gone, and I was lost. I couldn't even remember the name of the subway station beside where I lived.

The subway was slowing down to come to a stop. As people began getting off I could see across the car. Directly across from me was an elderly lady, with her white hair pulled back in a bun — and sitting on her lap was my knapsack.

She had no unusual expression on her face and wasn't even looking in my direction. I wondered if the thief had taken my money and dropped the knapsack on her lap. It seemed unlikely that I had been robbed by the grandmother who remained seated across from me.

I tried to retrieve my bag back from her lap. But as I began to pull it up, she quickly grabbed it back and held onto it.

I looked around at the people standing beside me, and those sitting beside her, but no one took any notice of the unfolding situation. After a few unsuccessful attempts to rescue my knapsack, I was beginning to feel a little agitated that no one around me cared that I was being robbed.

Trying not to cause a scene, I did my best to negotiate through gestures. But she ignored my requests for my bag and scowled, pointing to my back. She picked up my bag in slow motion, illustrating how heavy it was. I finally began to understand.

She was holding my knapsack to help me. As I would understand more clearly later, there was a sense of cultural responsibility toward those who had the burden of standing.

As the subway pulled into the next stop, I looked around and noticed a middle-aged woman get on the subway and take a spot standing. Another elderly woman sitting down tapped her to get her attention and then took her purse, setting it on her lap. They didn't know each other and didn't talk; yet this older woman was more than pleased to sit with this stranger's purse on her lap throughout her journey.

As the subway pulled into the main downtown station and I was getting ready to get off, the woman gently handed me back my knapsack. But before I had a chance to thank her, she had disappeared into the crowd.

Sadly, coming from a large city, this considerate custom was more surprising to me than if I had been robbed. Everyone back home had heard of being robbed — that was usual city behavior — but having a stranger hold onto someone's bag out of kindness, in a city of twelve million people — that was truly unusual.

~Melissa Valks

Flower Children

Life is what happens to you while you're
busy making other plans.
~John Lennon

The official "summer of love" happened in 1968, one year after the Woodstock Music Festival, but mine happened three years later when I was eight years old.

Our house was on the corner of 26th and Pearl Street in Santa Monica, California, twenty-six blocks from the Pacific Ocean, the pier, the midway games and rides, and one of the prettiest beaches in the state. My parents took my brother and me to the beach almost every weekend, but on long summer afternoons I toyed with the idea of making the journey alone.

Don't get me wrong — I loved my street, but something inside me — inside all boys — pulled me toward the horizon and new adventures. The problem was, to my eight-year-old mind, there was no difference between twenty-six blocks and twenty-six miles. The furthest I had ever walked alone at that point was the three blocks to my elementary school.

One day I sat on the sidewalk and stared down it as far as I could. The blue water of the Pacific Ocean sparkled in the distance like a magical mirage.

Twenty-six measly blocks? I thought, trying to build my confidence. *No problem!*

I stood up and started walking.

Adults had proven themselves to be mostly kind and trustworthy, but there was always that odd character, like the old man who sprang out at my friend Dana and me one day as we took our usual route home from school through the alleys. Always on the lookout for new additions to our tree house, we had stopped to look through his trashcan.

"What're you boys doin' back here?" he yelled.

We froze in horror.

"Uh… nothin'?" I said, holding his trashcan lid.

"Nothin', huh?" he bellowed, squinting at us with his one good eye. "You're sniffin' glue, that's what you're doin'!"

Dana and I looked at each other, wondering what he was talking about. Neither of us had ever heard of anyone intentionally sniffing glue, though we had, on occasion, rubbed Elmer's Glue all over our hands, let it dry, peeled it off partially, then chased the girls around, pretending our skin was coming off. While we pondered his remark, the old man snatched the metal trashcan lid out of my hand and let out a roar that would make Bigfoot envious. We ran for the hills.

"And stay away from that glue!" he screamed. "It'll rot your brain out."

"He sure hates glue," Dana said as he ran next to me.

As I walked to the beach alone with that memory still in my mind, I worried about how many other people like that old man there were in the world. I shook it off and forged ahead.

I had passed the elementary school and was in uncharted territory when I heard strange music coming from a house up ahead. Unlike the neighbors' well-manicured lawns, the garden at this house was bursting with the wildest assortment of flowers I had ever seen, spilling over and between the picket fence. The dozen or so adults in the yard looked like the kind of people my father called "damn hippies."

Giant sunflowers towered overhead and purple cosmos exploded like mini-supernovas. California poppies, kangaroo paws, black-eyed Susans and dozens of other flowers blended into one giant bouquet. The fence pickets had been painted with rainbows, flowers, cartoon insects and words like "peace" and "love." The music was very loud, but soothing. I know now that it was a sitar, but then I just thought it sounded magical, like a ride at Disneyland.

One of the hippies was reading on the porch. Another was in the garden blowing bubbles that caught the breeze and danced around the flowers before floating away. Someone else was sharing a "cigarette" with a girl who had flowers in her hair, and a man with no shirt sat in the shade playing a guitar. Three younger girls in colorful sundresses whispered and laughed together.

I was so transfixed by this spectacle that I forgot they could see me, too, until one of the three girls exclaimed, "Awww! Look at the cute little boy!"

I looked behind me but nobody was there.

"Yes, you!" she said. "Come here!"

My parents had always told me not to talk to strangers, so I hesitated.

"Aw, he's shy," she said. "That's okay. We'll come out there!" And they came flooding through the gate.

"He's adorable!" one of them cooed, kneeling and wrapping her arms around me. The other two also knelt, hugging and kissing me. I stood in the middle, rigid as a plank, swallowed up in a sea of bosoms, silky hair and heady perfume. I was used to the occasional hug and kiss from my mother's friends, but nothing like this. This was complete and total love bombardment, and I liked it.

One of the girls ran into the house and brought out a peanut butter and jelly sandwich with a frosty bottle of Coke for me and we sat on the grass. The guitar player showed me how to strum the strings while he held the chords, and we sang "Puff the Magic Dragon," which I knew because my mother often sang it to me while tucking me into bed at night. The girls asked me all kinds of questions and gave me advice about a bully who wouldn't leave me alone.

"Just keep being extra nice to him," one suggested. "Eventually, he'll feel like a jerk for being so mean to you." That advice differed greatly from my older brother's. He said I should kick him in the testicles. (He used a different term.)

I was having so much fun with my new friends, I forgot all about the beach. The late afternoon sunshine was slanting through the flowers and the shadows were getting longer, so I told them I had to get back home. They offered me a ride but I said I could make it myself, independent man that I had become. The three girls walked me to the sidewalk and swallowed me in their arms again, then waved goodbye as I staggered away, my young heart suffused with the peace and love they had sworn their lives to.

I visited their garden often in the months that followed, until one day at the end of summer when I went to the house and found it empty. The garden was dry, and the house, once so full of music and life, was dark. An elderly man who lived next door was raking leaves. He yelled to me, "Is your name Mark?"

I answered "yes."

He said, "They told me to tell you something."

He paused for a second, then said, "What was it? Oh, yeah. They said they had to move out suddenly, and they were hoping to see you so they could say goodbye, and they love you."

I thanked him and walked home. I cried all the way. Over the years, though, the memory of the happy hours spent in that garden feeling safe and loved has banished whatever sadness I felt that day.

Mother Teresa said very few of us can do great things, but we can do small things with great love. Whether or not the hippie movement was a success, or their ideas and protests stopped the Vietnam War, the flower children in that garden were the real article. They lived up to their philosophy. For a few happy afternoons in one blessed summer, they made a timid, little boy feel like a prince, like he mattered, like the world wasn't such a scary place after all. What greater thing can any of us do?

~Mark Rickerby

87

The Prince and the Pauper

*Judge tenderly, if you must. There is usually a side you
have not heard, a story you know nothing about, and
a battle waged that you are not having to fight.*
~Traci Lea LaRussa

There used to be a homeless man in New York City whom
I would see from time to time. He was an icon. Sooner
or later, if you were a New Yorker you'd run into him.
He was humongous and frightening, wearing a heavy
green, woolen blanket-like poncho, rain or shine. His long unkempt
hair covered his head and face. His dark deep-set eyes would peer
out from under his dense eyebrows.

He'd sit on various street corners in midtown Manhattan with a
cup for money in front of him and a box of pencils he'd hope to sell. I
was twenty-something, a fearless New York girl. Not much scared me
but the truth is, whenever I saw this man shivers ran up my spine. If I
turned the corner and there he unexpectedly appeared it was definitely
a shock to my system.

So when I almost ran into him in the subway station as I waited
for my train late one night, it gave my heart a start. I was used to riding
the subway, since I worked in New York City and lived in Queens,
but this night I had gone out with some friends and it was later than
usual — after midnight.

The station was deserted but for the two of us and another man.
The homeless man sat on one bench and I purposely sat down on

one some distance away, next to the other man, who was extremely attractive and immaculately dressed.

"Movie star quality," went through my mind.

At first we sat in silence. Then the handsome stranger turned to me and smiled. As appealing as he was I was not about to get friendly with someone in a subway so late at night. I stared ahead.

He was not to be deterred.

"What's a pretty girl like you doing in the subway so late, sweetie?"

Ugh. How I hated when someone called me that. Especially a man I didn't know. It was rude and demeaning. I mumbled something noncommittal and opened a book, pretending to read. But I was getting nervous. I noticed the homeless man moving closer to us.

Oh, great, I thought, sardonically. *I have the Prince and the Pauper to contend with.* My nicknames for them amused me.

The train pulled in at last, to my relief.

As luck would have it, all three of us headed for the closest door — the door of the second car. There was no one else in this car. I stood up against a window holding onto the strap. The so-called Prince Charming came and stood ominously close to me, staring, giving me a creepy feeling. The Pauper sat down opposite us, occupying two full seats with his enormous frame.

I would have left but the train had already started so I made the decision to change cars. Anything to get away from the uncomfortable situation.

The doors between the subways cars were heavy and extremely hard to open and to shut, but like I said, I was a New York girl and had done it countless times. Trying not to give my two bizarre companions any warning, I charged for the door and pulled it sharply open. Stepping through it, as I struggled to shut it behind me I felt a powerful shove. It was the good-looking one. I don't know if it was intentional or accidental but I thought he was attempting to push me off the moving train onto the tracks between the two cars as he pulled my purse off my shoulder. I gave a scream and held on to the door handle real tight, but one of my feet was already hanging in mid-air. One shoe dropped to the tracks and I was losing my balance. The Prince took off into the first car with my purse, leaving me dangling. The Pauper suddenly appeared, grabbing my arm and pulling me to safety. I regained my balance but not my composure. At least not right away.

I ran back to the second car and sat down gasping. The two men had run off into the first car. I watched through the doors as the homeless man fought the other man for my purse.

Let them have it, I thought, still shaken. *It's only a purse. At least I'm safe.*

Then the homeless man did something that surprised me. He opened the door to my car and threw the purse in my direction. Then he disappeared into the first car.

I had my purse but more importantly my life. And if I could get off this train I knew I would be fine.

It was an express train so there were no more stops before mine. I sat there trembling for a few more terrifying minutes, which seemed like hours. Then I noticed someone coming through the doors in my direction. I panicked when I saw it was the Prince. But he was accompanied by two men in police uniforms and he was handcuffed.

One of the policemen approached me. "Did this guy bother you? We've been tracking him for weeks. He's been bothering women and snatching purses. I see you have yours. We finally nabbed him."

The train came to a stop and we all got off. One of the policemen walked off with the handcuffed thief as I explained to the other officer what had occurred. I had my purse so I guess maybe a real crime had not been committed but he took some notes and I promised to come to the police station in the morning to file a report.

"Oh, by the way," I inquired. "What happened to the other man?"

"What other man?" The policeman looked puzzled. "There was no one else."

"But there *must* have been. The man who pulled me to safety. He saved me from falling off the train and then he returned my purse. He ran into the first car after the other guy."

"There was no one else in the first car except this loser," the policeman repeated.

Bewildered as I was, considering what had happened, I was grateful that this horrible night had ended safely.

In the coming years I would still see the homeless man dressed in the green blanket–like cape or poncho, sitting on various street corners in the city. I tried approaching him a couple of times to thank him for probably saving my life and for returning my purse. My attempts to talk to him were returned with a blank stare. I even dropped a note into his cup expressing my gratitude. And of course at any opportunity I would drop a few dollars into his cup. His intimidating appearance no longer frightened me. I learned not to make judgments based on people's looks. I also realized that angels came in many forms.

~Eva Carter

88

A Sobering Experience

Not for ourselves alone are we born.
~Marcus Tullius Cicero

The phantom-like figure materialized out of the darkened snowy night. I was tending the till on the closing shift at a local gas station. The snowstorm had grown in intensity since I had punched in at mid-afternoon, and had slowed business and traffic down to nothing. Only fools and those in great need ignored the storm warnings.

Just moments before the faceless shape appeared, the Greyhound bus had inched its way south on the highway, late for its scheduled stop. The passengers getting off fended for themselves two blocks away. A figure made its way toward the station out of the bus's wake of swirling snow.

"Could you tell me where I could find the Catholic church?" he asked once inside. He wore no hat and rubbed his bare hands together, shifting his weight from one foot to the other.

I directed the stranger to St. Alice Catholic Church four blocks away. Thanking me, he turned and re-entered the snowy night. I felt uneasy while I watched him disappear into the storm. He would freeze dressed like that.

What was my responsibility to the nameless stranger? I could have invited him to my house, but with a wife and small children, it seemed a risk. Surely God wouldn't expect me to put my family at risk?

Twenty minutes later he came back out of the storm's darkness just as he had the first time. My heart sank. Once indoors, he shook the snow off of his coat and kept moving around.

"No one home?" I asked, after a customer had left.

Melting snow had formed droplets of water on the top of his thick black hair. They ran down the sides of his face as he shivered. "Are there any other churches in town? I need to find a place to sleep for the night."

Avoiding the question, I made small talk, trying to find out a little more about him. He told me he went by the name Sammy, that he was on his way to the Twin Cities, and that he was looking for a place to wait out the storm. "We have a two-bedroom mobile home with three small kids, but if you don't mind sleeping on the couch, you are more than welcome to stay." The words were out of my mouth before I realized the implications of such an offer. To my chagrin he accepted. I suggested that he could wait for me in the small café that was connected to the station. He smiled and followed me to the café's back entry.

Now what was I going to do? How would my wife handle my impulsive invitation? I walked to the phone and called to inform her so she would not be caught off guard when we arrived home.

I chastised myself for putting my wife and children in harm's way by inviting a perfect stranger into our home. He didn't look like a murderer, but my prejudices and imagination haunted me. The radio had announced that even the plows had been pulled off the roads and everyone was to stay home. I had no other options.

We set out walking homeward the nine blocks. When we arrived, the kids were in bed and my wife had fixed something warm for us to eat. The three of us visited as we ate. He shared about family that he was going to visit and his hope that the priest could help him out with the bus fare. He had only enough money to get this far. He never asked us for help; instead, he thanked us for putting him up, feeding him, and giving him a warm place to sleep.

As my wife and I settled down for the night, we quietly talked about his situation and our responsibilities, deciding to trust God to help meet his and our needs. When morning came, the kids initiated him into the family by jumping up on his lap, sitting next to him and asking all kinds of questions. He seemed to enjoy the attention and their energy. We ate breakfast together, packed him a small lunch, gave him what little cash we had on hand, offered a short prayer of blessing, and sent him on his way.

A week or two later we answered a knock at our door. He was on his trip home and had stopped in for a visit. We invited him to stay, feeding him and putting him up for the night. The following morning, as we parted, we extended an open invitation to stop by whenever he was in the area.

As mysteriously and suddenly as he came into our lives, he now vanished the same way. It was years later when a gentleman we knew came up to us and said he had a message from Sammy. Seeing that we were drawing a blank, he told us of making Sammy's acquaintance at an AA meeting he was attending while doing prison ministry. Sammy had listened to his story and heard the town that he was from. He had approached him after the meeting asking him if he knew us. Finding that he did, Sammy proceeded to tell him the story of our helping him and asked if he would deliver a letter to us.

In his letter, Sammy shared how he had made some poor decisions and was serving time in prison. It was there, when he had reached rock bottom, that he remembered how we had helped him years earlier. Our act of kindness provided a "life changing" experience for him. Now sober and living a new life, he wanted to thank us for making a difference and inspiring him to turn his life around.

That letter has served as a great reminder to us of how little things done in love can make a huge difference. We were merely sharing with him who we were, what we had, and our home. That random act of kindness sown in a difficult time became the seeds of a new beginning.

Sammy helped us to go beyond ourselves to see the dignity of each person we encounter, despite appearances or circumstances. He taught us the importance of hospitality, generosity, and opening our home to others. It was a valuable lesson.

~Michael Knuth

Kimchi and Kindness

*The very nature of kindness is to spread. If you are
kind to others, today they will be kind to you,
and tomorrow to somebody else.*

~Sri Chinmoy

Our plane had left without us. Behind the counter, a harried airline agent was squinting at his computer screen. "I'm very sorry, but it looks like we won't be able to get you on another flight to the U.S. for at least three days."

I sagged with frustration. For hours now, we'd been mired in the confusion, red tape and bureaucracy of travel complications. It was nearing 11:00 p.m. and the Seoul Airport was closing for the night. We'd just been asked to leave the building. Steve and I had no Korean currency. We didn't speak the language.

And in a crushing injustice, it happened to be the last day of our honeymoon. Finally, I crumbled with the realization that we'd be going nowhere tonight — but worse, we had nowhere to go. I began to cry.

As I turned away from the counter in despair, I felt a gentle hand on my shoulder. "Are you okay?" I looked up to see a neatly dressed Korean woman, a little younger than we were. I had noticed her earlier, sitting by herself on the plastic benches of the emptying airport. "I heard a little bit of your conversation with the flight agent," she said. The lights were shutting off around us and the custodian was rolling a mop and bucket into a closet. "I heard you speaking in English and

I wondered if I could help you."

Her kindness almost triggered a fresh wave of tears, but I pulled myself together and Steve and I let her lead us onto the dark sidewalk outside the airport as the janitor locked the glass doors behind us. The last of the cabs had pulled away. In the stillness of the muggy night, there was only the security guard, the young woman, and us. She dug her phone out of her purse and made a quick call, speaking in rapid-fire Korean. As she hung up, a lonely bus approached and the young woman tugged us along. "Come to my parents' house," she said. "They are expecting us."

"We don't have any money. We can't even pay for this bus," we protested.

"Don't worry. Don't worry," she said as she gave some change to the driver.

She introduced herself as Myung-Soon.

"Where did you learn English?"

"I received a scholarship to study finance in New York." She had just returned that May, and already by September she'd landed a position as a bank manager. "That's why I was at the airport so late. I was waiting for a client who never arrived."

On the nearly empty bus, we rode along the outskirts of downtown Seoul, past the steel and glass buildings and the lit billboards. Eventually, the towering city gave way to the modest suburbs. As we drove through the dark neighborhoods, I told Myung-Soon how we had come to miss our flight.

That morning, we had arrived in Korea from Thailand for our connecting flight home, only to learn that our plane would be very delayed. With a seven-hour layover ahead of us, we figured we'd take advantage of it — extending our honeymoon by seeing the sights of downtown Seoul.

We took the train downtown, but after an hour of walking around our steps dragged from the heat, the sticky humidity, and the end of a three-week adventure. So, stepping into the lobby of a fancy hotel, we sat down on the plush couches in the welcome air-conditioning — and promptly fell asleep.

When we woke up hours later, a quick look at the clock filled us with panic. We rushed to the train station, arriving at the airport huffing with relief that we'd made it back half an hour before our flight. Unfortunately, we were supposed to have been there two hours ahead, and it was with great frustration that we heard that the airline had given away our seats to passengers on the extensive waitlist. My spirits were deflated. We'd specifically planned the date of our return flight so that we would arrive in Seattle the day before my cousin's wedding.

Myung-Soon nodded sympathetically. "Well then. You probably have not eaten anything today. My mother has prepared a snack."

Truth was, I was terribly hungry, but it was after midnight by the time we stepped off the bus and walked the few blocks to her family's home. I hoped her mother wasn't waiting up and hadn't gone to too much trouble.

Their modest, clean home was brightly lit and the door was wide open. Myung-Soon's parents were dressed and standing at the entrance to their house, greeting us in Korean and bidding us to step inside.

When we walked into the main room, my eyes widened in amazement. The floor of the small living room was set with a large tablecloth. On it was a feast. I'm still not sure how all of that food was prepared in such a short time. Perhaps she had a well-stocked pantry, or maybe she was a culinary savant, but Steve and I felt like visiting royalty as we sat cross-legged on the cement floor and dug into the astonishing bounty.

There was kimchi, spicy cabbage that burned my lips; rich, deep green, leafy vegetables fried up in a sweet sauce with greasy noodles; a savory meat soup with the bones stewing at the center of the bowl; steamed rice cakes in a salty, fishy sauce. Seriously, where did all this food come from? For dessert, we devoured sweet and tart persimmons, so juicy that we scooped the insides out with a spoon.

By 1 a.m., we were immensely gratefully and absolutely stuffed. Overwhelmed with appreciation and exhaustion, we crawled into a comfy bed and fell into the oblivion of sleep.

In the morning, we realized Myung-Soon and her parents had all slept in one room, giving the main bedroom to the two of us. Over a light breakfast (more food!) of chicken broth and rice, Steve and

I engaged in a hilarious conversation with Myung-Soon's mom. We tried to make arrangements to get back to the airport. She spoke only Korean, and we gesticulated wildly to supplement our English, but mainly, we communicated in mime.

Fortunately, Myung-Soon stepped into the kitchen to translate and share the logistics of our plan. On her way to work, Myung-Soon would travel with us on a bus and stop at a bank so we could exchange our Thai baht for some Korean money. Then we'd head to the airport and hope for a flight to the United States — standby or bust.

After the bank stop, we offered Myung-Soon money to pay back her family for the generous hospitality. She shook her head and waved the envelope away. We insisted more strongly, telling her that we really wanted to repay her. Firmly, she shook her head. "It was our pleasure," she said.

Luck was with us that day, and we managed to get seats on a flight to Los Angeles. We worked our way back to Seattle from there. We'd missed the wedding ceremony, but managed to catch the evening reception. My suitcase hadn't arrived, but my eighty-six-year-old grandmother lived near the party venue and offered to lend me her clothing. The only outfit I could fit into was a brown, polyester skirt and a jacket that she had embroidered with gold brocade in the 1970s. Nevertheless, we wouldn't have been there at all had it not been for the kindness of a stranger.

On the bus back to the airport, Myung-Soon shared her story of being the recipient of a random act of kindness. It turned out, Myung Soon had been happy to have the chance to repay the generosity of her own guardian angel.

When she'd first arrived in New York, she was on a public bus when she realized that her wallet had been either stolen or lost. She told us how helpless she had felt: in a new country on her own, without any resources, on a bus ride that she couldn't even pay for.

The woman sitting next to her had noticed her distress, and when she heard what had happened, without hesitation she handed her forty dollars. Myung-Soon told us that the woman would not give her address or any information that would allow our new friend to pay her back. Since that day, Myung-Soon said, she had been hoping to repay that kindness. "So, thank you," she said to us, "for giving me the opportunity."

Steve and I have been married for seventeen years now, and I'm always happy when I find small chances to make somebody's day. It was a lesson I will never forget, taught to me in the late hours of a hot night in the home of a generous friend in Seoul.

~Ilana Long

90

The Loneliest Number

*Let gratitude be the pillow upon which you kneel to say
your nightly prayer. And let faith be the bridge
you build to overcome evil and welcome good.*
~Maya Angelou

Two years after the death of my husband, I had adjusted to living alone. I had settled into a routine and I was confident that I could handle whatever came my way. Confident, that is, until one hot July night, when two men attempted to break into my home through the back door and an adjacent window.

It was going on 10:00 p.m. and I was sitting in my family room. There were lights on outside and inside. The television was loud enough to be heard from the patio, so it should have been obvious that someone was home.

As I heard a loud, quick tug on my back door, and then someone at the window, I went from a state of calm to one of heightened alert that started my heart pounding. Someone banged loudly on my window and another on my door.

I yelled "Get outta here!" with as much authority as I could muster, then cautiously peeked out through the blinds as I dialed 9-1-1 for help. They had retreated to the back of my yard, but were still brazen enough to stand there shining flashlights directly at me. I was shocked at this boldness. By the time the police arrived, they were gone.

Although I had a security system installed a few days after that

90

event, my peace of mind had been shattered. I became more guarded, more anxious at night, and more suspicious of people in general. *Three Dog Night's* "One is the Loneliest Number" could have been my personal theme song as I became increasingly aware of my vulnerability.

Another incident occurred seven months later. The weather was unseasonably mild for a Colorado winter. There was no snow on the ground and little wind. In fact, one could go outside comfortably in just a light jacket. That night I changed into my pajamas and robe about 9:00 p.m. and settled into my recliner in the family room to enjoy a few word games on my laptop. Lucita, my thirteen-year-old Chihuahua, was already asleep in her favorite spot in the kitchen. As usual, the sounds of a TV program provided a sense of comfort in an otherwise too quiet house.

It was 9:45 when I heard a noise in my back yard. Muting the TV with the remote, I listened carefully as I tried to convince myself that it was nothing at all. Lucita sat up, as if on alert, but she did not bark or growl. Suddenly, I heard a male voice outside my nook window next to the patio. My heart began to hammer as I recalled the attempted break-in the previous summer. *Not again,* I thought.

There was a commotion outside the window, then the telltale squeak of the outdoor spigot being turned on. I quickly turned off the lamp, walked quietly to the window and peeked through the blinds. I saw no one; however, I noticed the garden hose had been pulled out into the yard. What on earth was going on? Was it a ploy to get me outside? Were they going to damage my property by flooding it?

I quickly called 9-1-1. The dispatcher notified a patrol officer, then asked if I happened to live near Cherry Park. Yes, I said. My back yard bordered the park. She said a fire had been reported in that vicinity. I asked her to hold on while I retrieved a flashlight and shone it out my window. This time, two teenage boys ran into the light and frantically motioned for me to come out.

The dispatcher stayed on the phone with me while I ventured outside. To my shock, the yard was filled with smoke. The boys shouted that my bushes were on fire, pointing toward my garden shed in the corner of the yard. I saw a man I did not recognize using my hose to douse the area. There were no flames, just smoke. I was still suspicious, but as I approached him with my flashlight, I could see that my seven-foot juniper had burned to the ground, as had a large lilac bush and half of another one. The ground was scorched and the air was pungent from smoke, causing my eyes to water.

Sirens and flashing lights soon filled the street and the park behind me as police and firemen arrived on scene. I must have been quite a sight in my nightclothes, looking stunned and confused, surrounded by strangers.

As a fireman took control of my hose, the man turned to me to explain. He had been heading home in his vehicle on the street next to the park when he noticed flames shooting fifteen feet high into my ash tree. Thinking fast, he parked, ran to my back fence, climbed over it, found my spigot, hooked up the hose with help from the teens who had been walking through the park, and extinguished the fire!

One of the firemen informed me that this was the fifth fire started by an arsonist that night. Dried leaves and pine needles blown up against the fence and under my bushes made for perfect kindling.

As I began to comprehend the seriousness of what had happened and how much worse it could have been, I felt a wave of relief. All this time, I had been imagining the worst, fearful and suspicious of who was outside my house, and what harm they were planning. This man and the teens, strangers to me and to each other, prevented what could have been a devastating fire, yet they wanted no credit for their actions. If they had not stopped to help, the fire would have spread to my tree, shed, wooden fence, neighbor's yard, and several large pine trees a few feet away in the park. It could have been an inferno in a matter of minutes!

I have learned from this experience that while it's prudent to be cautious, I must never let it prevent me from seeing the good in those around me. I am not alone!

~Marti Robards

91

My Hero Helen

I think a hero is really any person intent on making
this a better place for all people.
~Maya Angelou

My family was very concerned for my sister... and understandably so. How many people in today's society would invite two complete strangers to stay in their home? Oh sure, these strangers seemed nice, and they looked normal, plus their situation sounded sincere. But the pair came with no references and no shared acquaintances, and yet my sister invited them to stay with her in her Montrose, California home.

"What? I can't believe what you're telling me," our mother said when Helen told her of the arrangement. "Do you realize that they can kill you in your sleep? There are two of them and only one of you! Why they might rob you blind while you're at work!"

Actually, our entire family had the same thoughts and tried to discourage Helen from this undertaking, but it was our mother who really laid things on the line. After all, this was her daughter, these were complete strangers, and this was Los Angeles. For Pete's sake — there was no one Helen could call for a quick rescue if she needed it! It's not that my mother or the rest of our family lacks compassion or that we didn't think Helen had good judgment. It's just that we are protective of our kin and these could be potential criminals!

Let me back up. This story began with Helen on a flight from Los

Angeles to Phoenix. Although the flight was short, it provided ample time for my sister to get to know the Morrisons, an Arizona couple seated in her row. The plane was only in the air for a couple of minutes when the wife, Marcie, fell asleep, leaving her husband Daniel and my sister sitting next to each other in silence. Maybe it was a feeling of awkwardness that sparked it, or maybe it was the need to unload. Whatever the case, within minutes Daniel began to relate the couple's story, one that would keep my sister riveted for the duration of the trip.

He told my sister how he and Marcie had flown to Los Angeles that morning to meet with a doctor of alternative medicine about treating Marcie for her stage 4 breast cancer. Since the prognosis of the doctors in Phoenix had been bleak (they had given Marcie only a few months to live) the couple had decided to pursue other forms of treatment. Although they both felt good about what had been described to them that day, they were also dismayed to learn that the alternative treatment carried a $34,000 price tag and would not be covered by insurance. Additionally, they'd have to pay for a place to stay while Marcie underwent treatment.

"The money's not even a consideration," Daniel explained. "What's debt compared to keeping my wife alive?" At this point tears coursed their way down Daniel's face and my sister joined right in. Marcie was only thirty-five years old and they had five children between ages two and twelve.

When it came time to deplane, Daniel woke Marcie, and since she was unable to walk, requested a wheelchair. It was while my sister was waiting with them for the chair that she made the decision that had our family so concerned. Helen gave the Morrisons her business card and explained that they could stay with her during their trips to Los Angeles. "It's not much, I know, but maybe it would help with your money situation."

Helen received a call from Daniel the following week saying that he and Marcie had talked it over and they would like to take her up on her generous offer. They arrived the following Wednesday and left on Sunday. Helen admitted that the first night was a sleepless one — alone in her house with two people she had only known for an hour or so.

The uneasy feelings continued the next morning as she left for work. What would the place look like when she returned? When Helen got home from work that night, she found that Daniel and Marcie had prepared dinner and were waiting to share the meal with her. Helen slept well that night and had no second thoughts as she left for work Friday morning. And so this arrangement continued for several months.

A PET scan showed that despite all efforts, the cancer had traveled to Marcie's spine, tailbone, and down both legs. The Morrisons' miracle cure was not to be. Helen kept in constant contact with them over the next difficult months. She was there to help with fundraising efforts and to offer a shoulder to cry on. She couldn't help but wonder at the course of events. What force — what plan — had brought the three of them together and then compelled her to invite them into her home? Whatever the case, she knew that she had done exactly as she was supposed to.

I guess it would be an understatement to say that my family's feelings of concern changed to feelings of admiration! We are all so proud of our Helen! Acts of kindness have a ripple effect. What would happen if everyone in this world treated people in need the way my sister did?

Helen's tale of compassion has been added to the roster of life lessons she's taught me through the years. I've adopted values like generosity and thoughtfulness from witnessing her actions. I've aspired to self-development through continued education and a strong work ethic from her mentorship. My sister was my hero way before she took the Morrisons under her wing. Yet with every good deed she continues to do, her "super powers" keep getting stronger!

~Nancy Noel Marra

92

Never Judge a Book by Its Cover

*Let's stop judging others, and relieve them of
the heavy burden they are carrying on
their shoulders because of us.*
~Saurabh Sharma

I was sitting at work when I noticed a very disheveled man standing in the lobby. He looked lost and possibly homeless, or maybe even under the influence because he was unsteady on his feet. He made his way over to me and I asked if I could help him. He stared at me like he was trying to focus and finally said yes as he thrust some tattered papers in my direction. He asked if I could make him a copy of his military paperwork. I took the papers very gingerly from him so as not to tear them anymore than they already were.

As I made the copies he gave me some specific instructions on the order they needed to be in because he was partially blind. He told me that he had been blinded by Agent Orange while serving in Vietnam.

I was shocked, but took a deep breath and simply replied, "Thank you for your service."

He told me how he despised going out in public because he knew people stared at him, thinking he must be some homeless drunk because of the way he looked and how unsteady he appeared. He explained he was unsteady because he didn't see well.

I felt terrible because I had indeed thought the very same thing.

The veteran went on to say that he was college educated and had many hopes and dreams that were shattered. But at least he had his own home.

Then I noticed he was clutching a small brown paper bag. The bag was wrinkled and dirty so I asked him if he would like a plastic bag for his paperwork. He nodded and then asked me to hold out my hand. As I held my hand open he carefully opened up his bag like it contained some rare treasure and then he placed two items in my palm.

My jaw dropped and my eyes filled with tears. This wonderful man had just placed his Purple Heart and a Silver Star into my hands.

I thanked him again for his service and for blessing me with the opportunity to hold history in the palm of my hand. He gathered his items and carefully placed them back in his bag and started to walk away. I saw him take a few crumpled dollars and some change from his pocket. He turned back and asked if we had a vending machine so he could get some crackers.

He explained he was diabetic and he was getting shaky because his blood sugar was getting low. I pointed him in the right direction, but after staring at his money he put it back in his pocket and started to walk off the wrong way. Being diabetic myself I couldn't let him do that.

I scrambled after him and asked him if I could buy him a pack of crackers. He declined, stating he didn't want a handout and that he would eat something when he got home. He told me he was on his way to wait for the city bus. I couldn't in good conscience let this hero go hungry, so I said, "Sir, I know you don't take handouts. But can I buy a distinguished veteran lunch for protecting my freedom?"

He was taken aback for a minute and then told me he supposed he could accept that. I walked outside with him and into the park adjacent to my office. He asked if he could just sit in the park while I got his lunch. He didn't want anyone making fun of him.

I ran to the local sub shop and purchased his lunch and a gift card that would feed him for the rest of the week until his pension came in. I rejoined him in the park and sat down with him for only a few minutes because I was supposed to be working. He thanked me over and over for my kindness and for not judging him like everyone else. I hugged him goodbye and then he stood up and gave me a very crisp salute.

Tears flowed freely down my face. I told him it had been an honor and a privilege to meet one our nation's heroes. I will never forget his gratitude or the lesson this total stranger taught me that day. I will never again judge a book by its cover.

~Peggy Sprunt

Random Acts of Kindness

Holiday Helpers

Christmas is a season for kindling the
fire for hospitality in the hall, the genial
flame of charity in the heart.
~Washington Irving

93

Chicken Soup for the Soul

No Random Act

Remember there's no such thing as a small act
of kindness. Every act creates a ripple
with no logical end.
~Scott Adams

peeked out from under the covers to check the time. The clock read 4:00. I rolled onto my back and stared at the ceiling. It was 4 p.m., not 4 a.m., and I had managed to waste away another entire day in bed.

It was a week and a half before Christmas and despite all the pep talks I had given myself I was having a really hard time staying positive. In a few days I would be facing the anniversary of my daughter Kyley's death, followed by her birthday on December 23rd. I had always looked forward to this time of year and now I just prayed for it to hurry up and be over.

I sat up and let my feet dangle over the edge of the bed. I had put off my Christmas shopping long enough. I decided to head to a neighboring town to find the perfect gift for my husband Joey. I wrapped my long hair up in a messy bun, skipped the make-up, and did nothing about the ratty old sweats I was wearing.

I made it into town and stopped by a few local boutiques, festive with holiday music and bright Christmas décor. Shoppers hurried from display to display, eagerly picking out the perfect gift for their loved ones. I left empty-handed but not completely discouraged. I still had two more stops and I was determined to find something, anything, before I headed home.

I suspected the local trading post would have a few good "guy gifts." I headed that way and arrived at 6:04 p.m. The sign on the locked gate showed I had missed them by four minutes! I took a deep breath. The thought of having to go out another day and do this all over again was overwhelming. I shook my head. It wouldn't come to that because my next stop was a huge, multi-level specialty store where I knew I would find the perfect gift for my husband.

I arrived and was pleasantly surprised that the parking lot wasn't all that crowded. Great! I started walking toward the front door when I noticed a lady who had come out of the building. She was looking at me with that "look." You know the one, the "I know something you don't know look." I recognized it and stopped. "Are they closed?" I asked her.

"Yes ma'am. We close at 6:00," she pleasantly replied.

My shoulders slumped as my head fell forward. I felt defeated. This was a huge store. It was the holidays. How could they be closed? I could sense that she was walking toward me. She stopped in front of me and asked that fateful question: "Are you okay?" Now, if you are a woman and you've ever had a really bad day, you know what happens when someone asks if you are okay. Yep, you cry… a lot, and you spill the beans about whatever it is that has got you down. And that's exactly what I did. I told her about Kyley, about the anniversary date, about her upcoming birthday, and how I just wanted to buy a present for my husband. I was pitiful.

The lady told me to wait there. I watched as she rushed back toward the building, knocked on the locked door, and disappeared inside. She reappeared a minute later and motioned for me to come to her. She was excited as she told me that the manager had agreed to open the store for me. I protested, now feeling rather embarrassed, but she set her purse and car keys on a nearby counter and asked what I was looking for. She led me to the back of the store and showed me where I could find the perfect gift for Joey.

"I don't want you to feel like I'm hovering over you, rushing you, so I'm going to go stand right over there." She pointed to a nearby display a couple of aisles over. "You take your time and if you need help, don't hesitate to ask." She smiled sweetly before walking away.

I stood there looking at the huge empty space that was normally filled with hundreds of people and I knew this woman had already helped me.

That night I had needed to be heard. I needed someone to know I was hurting and to acknowledge that pain, and although I didn't realize it at the time, I needed someone to unlock the doors of a major department store after hours and let me in. I walked to where she was standing and asked her what time the store opened the next morning. I thanked her and told her I would never dream of keeping her and the others who had volunteered to stay behind for me from their families. I would return the next day during their regular business hours. I hugged her goodbye and told her I would see her the next morning.

The following morning I woke up, got dressed, and made the drive back to the store. I walked down the main aisle and immediately recognized the woman coming toward me. I asked her name and told her I wanted to thank her again for what she had done for me the night before. She looked puzzled. I smiled and told her I was the crying lady in the parking lot.

"Oh, my! You look so different! I didn't even recognize you!" she said.

It is pretty amazing what sleep, a new day, hair and make-up, and just a little bit of kindness from a stranger will do for a girl.

I shared with her how much her act of kindness truly meant to me. I found my husband the perfect gift and I was on my way.

You hear lots about "random acts of kindness" but I got the distinct impression that this was no random act on this lady's part. I do believe that I captured a glimpse of how this woman, Carol Roberson, lives her life every single day. Wow, what a wonderful world it would be if it were filled with people like Carol.

~Melissa Wootan

94

A Perfectly Timed Gift

*Blessed is the season which engages the whole
world in a conspiracy of love!*
~Hamilton Wright Mabie

I t was two days before Christmas and I still felt numb. Steve had passed away in late September and I was doing the best I could to celebrate the season. My two adult sons wanted to carry on some of our family traditions like our Christmas Eve Open House, but I knew others would end.

Every year, Steve and I always put a special gift for each other under the tree. I made sure he had something fun, and he made sure I had something from Saffees, my favorite women's clothing store. No matter what other additional gifts we exchanged, these were the two that mattered most.

Although Steve was no longer here to celebrate, I kept wondering what I could give him. That probably seemed strange to everyone, but for thirty-seven years we had exchanged gifts, and I just wasn't ready to stop. I stubbornly asked my sons, "What should I buy for your dad?"

I finally settled on naming a star after Steve. Because he was an avid space enthusiast, I knew it was the perfect gift, and I could envision him having fun seeking it out just to see the heavenly orb that now bore his name. I didn't mind not having a gift from him, except that it was just another sign that he was no longer with us.

Later, as I was putting the finishing touches on wrapping presents, the phone rang. It was the manager of Saffees, whom we had gotten to know quite well over the years. "Vicki, could I stop by your house after work? I've got something I need to give you."

I couldn't imagine what Bonnie might have for me because I knew Steve was too ill to have pre-arranged something three months in advance. So I waited patiently until she arrived at the door, and to my surprise, she was holding a beautifully wrapped present to place under the tree.

She explained that the owner of the store had suddenly awoken in the middle of the night and thought, "What about Vicki?" He knew our tradition and he and Bonnie had selected something they knew I would like. They wanted to make sure that Steve's traditional gift for me continued on what they knew would be a very difficult Christmas Day.

As I accepted this special act of kindness, it was difficult not to cry. For one last time, our tradition was honored — I gave Steve a gift of fun, and my package from Saffees was under the tree.

~Vicki L. Julian

95

The Spirit of Giving

*Christmas is not a time or a season but a state of
mind. To cherish peace and good will, to be
plenteous in mercy, is to have the real
spirit of Christmas.*
~Calvin Coolidge

Christmas at the bookstore was a mixed bag. On the one
hand, the days flew by. It was busy all day, and I never
stopped. I arrived, started working, and then someone
told me it was time for my lunch break. I ate as fast as
possible, got back on the sales floor, and suddenly it was time to go
home. The list of things I'd wanted to accomplish was about as long
as when I got there; I'd just manage tomorrow.

On the other hand, that list was important. The stock barrelled
in. We could never quite get everything in its place fast enough. The
reality was someone was going to ask for that one item the computer
said we had — but was still in the back room, awaiting stocking.

Christmas was a balancing act of off-hours tasking, constant
shelving, and running all day. It was exhausting, but also exciting. It
also unfortunately robbed me of the joy of the season, even on some
of the best days. I'd go home, and all I wanted was to eat something,
take a bath, and sleep.

As a manager, I worked Christmas Eve and Boxing Day — December
26th. Often that meant staying until an hour after close on Christmas
Eve to make sure set-up for Boxing Day was ready, and arriving very

early on Boxing Day to get stickering and signage placed. It was not uncommon for me, since I take the bus, to get home as late as 8:00 p.m. on Christmas Eve, and rise at 5:30 a.m. on Boxing Day to make it back to the mall on time.

Thus, Christmas Day was a chore — a day off in the middle of a busy period. I didn't want to participate, but I forced myself to entertain family and be surrounded by loved ones when — honestly — I just wanted to wear my pyjamas and read a book on my one day off.

Customers, too, were a mixed bag. Regular customers I saw all year showed up in mid-December with Christmas cards, or — the ultimate good day — trays of coffee or tea they'd brought down from Tim Hortons as a treat for the staff.

Other customers weren't big readers, but instead were buying for readers. These customers we only saw once a year or so (maybe twice or three times if you include Mother's Day and Father's Day), and often they were frustrated. The bookstore wasn't a place they felt comfortable. They were unsure which book might be right in the vast sea of titles, and — given time was short until Christmas — they were in a rush. They said things I'm sure they didn't mean. Certainly, Christmas brought out some of the most impatient and sharp commentary from customers of any time of year.

But, sometimes, it also did the opposite.

One year, I found the kind of customer we often dreaded standing in the kids section. He was a man of about thirty-five, holding a piece of paper, and looking completely lost. He had only one bag in his hand from another store, and there wasn't much in it — just candy, I think. He looked tired, and it was just a couple of days until Christmas — he was definitely running out of time, and looked like he'd barely begun.

Bracing myself for "I don't really know what I'm looking for," I asked if I might help him.

When he turned to me, he looked like he was on the edge of tears. He didn't reply to my question, he just stared, and I did something I had never done before — I touched his shoulder.

"Are you okay?" I asked.

"Sorry," he said. He seemed to snap out of it, and took a deep breath. "I need presents for my nieces, my nephew, my brother-in-law, and my parents." He took another breath. "I don't really know what they like, but I know they all like to read. I just need…" He nearly lost his words again, and I could tell he was working hard not to cry. "I just want to make sure there's something to open."

He turned back to the shelves. I could tell he wasn't seeing anything.

It was controlled chaos all around me — people were shopping, I could hear the registers going non-stop, and I knew at any moment the phone could ring.

"Let me help," I said. "Is that your list? How old are your nieces and nephew?"

He handed me the list. I learned the twin nieces were eight, and the nephew was six. I asked him a few questions about what sorts of things they enjoyed, and was starting to get some ideas when his entire body shook.

"Are you okay?" I asked again.

"My sister just died," he said. He was barely holding himself together. "Cancer. She always did Christmas, you know? I figured…" He exhaled, slowly.

I have always kept a pre-loaded gift card for Tim Hortons in my pocket at Christmas. Sometimes, a staff member really needed a few seconds to calm down after a really bad moment with a customer who maybe had a terrible day and took it out on him or her.

"Here," I said, and gave him the gift card. "Go upstairs. Have a coffee, get a donut. Have you eaten today?"

He shook his head.

"I've been there," I said. "My father died around Christmas. It's awful. Tell me about your folks and your brother-in-law. Then go, take your time. We'll have something ready for you when you get back."

He told me about his family, and left.

I went to the cash desk, and while the staff rang through customers, we brainstormed. I explained the man's situation, and what we needed to gather. I asked the staff if they'd mind if I put the last of the "staff treats" budget into paying for some of the items. Everyone agreed.

While I was explaining the situation, some of the customers in line did something I'd never seen before. One by one, some offered up a little bit of money — five or ten dollars — one woman offered fifty.

We found books, toys, some mugs with hot chocolate and a few other small touches. We managed to find enough that everyone would have three items to open. Another staff member and I skipped our break to crouch low behind the cash desk and wrap the items, figuring any chore we could take off the man's plate would help. What wasn't covered by the unexpected donations from the other customers, we covered ourselves.

When the man returned, the gifts were wrapped and tagged. He stared at me when I said it was fine, that it had all been taken care of, gift receipts included, just in case. He gave me back my Tim Hortons gift card, and then gave me a hug.

That year, Christmas Day didn't seem like a burden at all. I was exhausted, and knew I had to get up before dawn the next morning, but I gathered with my friends and loved ones and felt incredibly lucky to spend the day with them.

~Nathan Burgoine

96

A Different
Kind of Christmas

*Christmas is most truly Christmas when we celebrate
it by giving the light of love to those who need it most.*
~Ruth Carter Stapleton

didn't have a plan. And that was painful. It was Christmas Day, our first in California after having moved from Austria due to my husband's work, and we had no family to share it with. We hadn't met enough people yet to invite them for dinner. We thought about Christmas back home in Austria, with the magical fragrance of fresh cookies in the air, snow blanketing everything outside in silence and the mysterious anticipation about what the Christkind (the Austrian version of Santa) would bring this year.

Typically there had always been lots of presents. Not because we parents overwhelmed the kids with them, but simply because many people came together that day and everybody wanted to give something. That certainly wouldn't be the case this year because we hadn't made enough contacts yet. Of course we had been exchanging good wishes in the days and weeks leading up to the big day, but on Christmas Day itself? That would surely be a family affair; a day when people would withdraw to enjoy privacy with their own loved ones!

But that is not what happened on this day! Somebody must have sensed our situation and thought about how they could put a smile on our faces that day. They must have wondered what the best time would be, how old each of our children was, and what would give them the most joy. And they had also decided that it would be a complete surprise and they would remain anonymous.

We were just about to open the presents when a loud whoop of excitement went through the house. Ten-year-old Esther had just opened the front door and couldn't believe what she was seeing. Right in front of her was a pile of presents as tall as she was! Every single one of them beautifully wrapped in green, red and gold! She looked at each of them from the bottom of the pile to the top and then, stretching up, she discovered a note way up on top. A Santa Claus was drawn on it along with a message: "For the three Austrian girls! Have a wonderful Christmas!"

The others ran quickly to see what was going on and couldn't believe their eyes. A small present would have been "realistic" but such a high pile? They had never seen anything like it in their entire lives! What a surprise!

The rest of the day was saved and not just that, the entire Christmas holiday was marvelous. It turned out that our three girls had received many, many board games. They were not new, as our experienced parents' eyes quickly detected. But somebody must have thought of us and knew how much joy these gifts would bring us. And this somebody took the effort to pick a special occasion, wrap each present individually, and add a personal note. The timing of the gift and the loving wrapping were worth so much more than money! A pure act of thinking about us without even expecting a thank-you.

Our kids tried of course to guess who the presents were from but they just could not work it out, so they drew a huge picture of Santa Claus with chalk in the middle of the street with the words "Thank you Santa!" As it doesn't rain very often in California the picture stayed there for a long time and I am wondering how often the picture must have put a smile on the face of our mysterious giver!

Later that day a neighbor dropped by and gave each of the girls a ten-dollar voucher for a local bookshop.

It wasn't the financial value that made that Christmas so special. In fact it was probably the lowest-cost Christmas that we had ever had as a family. And yet it was the most valuable in many ways, especially for me as a mother. I was given many presents that day that had nothing to do with money: There was the gift of not having to manage a beautiful feast and yet see a wonderful outcome. The gift of being given so much without the expectancy of having to give anything in return. The gift of getting a present totally unexpected, far away from home. The gift of being made part of a community. It was a real feast of love, of unearned love.

Did I ever find out who played Santa Claus for us that day? Maybe, but that is a different story…

~Sandra Wright

97

A New Tradition

Mankind is a great, an immense, family. This is proved
by what we feel in our hearts at Christmas.
~Pope John XXIII

As I walked into the Fifth Street Bar and Grill my aunt stood up from a table in the corner, beside a window that spilled winter sunlight.

As usual, it had taken weeks to agree on a time for our semi-annual lunch. She worked as a psychologist and ran her own bustling private practice, and she also owned a couple of vacation properties that she always seemed to be in the process of selling, renting or redecorating. I hadn't seen her in months.

"Hi," I exclaimed. "You look great." And she did: she wore her dark, straight hair down to her lower back in glimmering waves. An assortment of fashionable jewelry sparkled on her skin. While we hugged, I worried that I might wrinkle the fabric of her tailored white blouse, which smelled of Chanel No. 5.

"So it's been a while! How are you? You must be almost done with your classes," she said in a rush of enthusiasm as we sat down.

"Yes, this is my last semester."

We talked for a while about my imminent graduation from university, and then I asked her about her properties. Her eyes narrowed and she became even more animated, waving her hand through the air as she talked so her gold bracelet caught the light. Apparently, she had set her sights on a condo in an exclusive new development beside a golf course, where prices were sky-high. It was the epitome of luxury.

"We're just waiting to hear back about our offer," she said.

"Wow."

"Yes, fingers crossed."

My aunt loved everything about real estate and luxury living. She'd worked hard to earn her wealth, and I admired her cutthroat attitude to business. I felt as if some of her adrenaline rubbed off on me as she regaled me with stories about her investment successes. I'd even begun looking at condos for myself — albeit cheap ones — and she was the first person I wanted to tell if I ever bought my own place.

On that sparkling, winter day we had an even more successful lunch than usual. I measured success by whether or not she ordered tea or dessert so we could continue to chat. She ordered both, and we were on our second cup of Earl Grey when she proposed a new idea.

"I wonder if maybe... this has been so much fun, maybe you wanted to carry on and do something else together?" she asked.

"Sure, that'd be fun."

"Okay, great." She paused, tapped a French-tipped fingernail against her lips. "To tell the truth, I was thinking it might help us get into the holiday spirit and, well, I wonder if maybe we could start a new tradition."

"What?" I asked, suddenly full of anticipation. From her face, I could tell she felt excited — and if she was excited, it meant there must be at least some degree of risk involved in her plan.

"I have this one-hundred-dollar bill burning a hole in my pocket, and I was thinking maybe we could find a homeless person and give it to him or her."

I couldn't have been more shocked if she'd told me she wanted to go swimming in the restaurant's fish tank.

I swallowed down a gulp of tea and tried not to look as surprised as I felt. It's not that I'd thought she was uncharitable — although we'd never talked about charity before. Mostly I was surprised that she either didn't know, or didn't care, that giving money directly to a homeless person in our city was thought by some people to be less-than-ideal because the money, some said, could be swiftly exchanged for booze or drugs.

"Sure," I said. "I think that's a great idea. It's very generous of you."

"I was thinking that we could walk around until we find somebody who we really want to give it to. And say 'Happy Holidays.' What do you think?"

"Yes, that sounds good."

"Okay." She grinned. "And maybe we can do this again next year. It could be our holiday tradition."

"Absolutely."

Off we went, squinting in the harsh winter light on the main street of downtown and searching for someone who appeared most in need of my aunt's one hundred dollars. As we walked, she continued to talk in rushed, excited tones as she had done during lunch. Her boots made a staccato clicking sound along the sidewalk. I was becoming tired just trying to keep up with her: her quick, constantly churning mind and her fast walking were almost too much for me. Luckily she found her prospect almost immediately. The fabric of his coat had faded to a pale, greyish green. I saw dirt on his cheeks and vagueness in his eyes as we approached. He was slouched against a building, and parts of his scalp showed through his white hair.

I lingered a step behind my aunt as she neared him, strutting in the brisk no-nonsense way of hers and smiling widely.

"Hello." She rustled in her purse, producing the one-hundred-dollar bill. She held it out toward him. "Here, I want you to have this. Happy Holidays."

He extended a rough hand and hesitated, staring at the money. Then he raised his face to look at her. She nodded encouragingly.

Shaking, he folded his fingers around the bill. His gaze was steady as he looked at my aunt, eyes filling with a youthful kind of light.

"Miss, thank you." He took her hand in his, and kissed it once. I smiled at them both, but I wasn't involved in this interaction: it was private, and existed only for the two of them.

On the walk back to the car, my aunt remained silent for a while. Her steps were slower.

"He seemed happy, didn't he?" she said thoughtfully.

"Yes, he did," I agreed. "You made his day."

I felt that I'd just witnessed something spectacular, but I couldn't quite define why.

It wasn't until later that I realized: not only did the man look genuinely joyful when he accepted the money — which in my mind made the event worth it no matter how he invested that bill — but I had the impression he had given my aunt a gift as well.

And the fleeting, magical exchange they shared had an effect on me, too: I learned that the good energy of any gift can spread outward, touching those who are simply spectators and creating a memory that sticks and shines for years. Never again will I even consider believing that certain forms of giving are "lesser" than others.

~Jessica Lampard

98

From Gloomy to Grateful

This is the message of Christmas: We are never alone.
~Taylor Caldwell

A family of six living paycheck to paycheck usually means a pretty skimpy Christmas. But in 2014, it finally felt like we were going to have more than one or two presents under the tree. I had a list, a budget and a plan. It was going to work!

Then our dryer broke. A family of six creates a full load of laundry every day. Since it was the middle of winter, hanging laundry outside to dry wasn't an option. I had one dryer rack because that was all I had room for in my house. Going to a laundromat was out of the question — I would have to live there to get it done. Then the brakes on our van started squeaking, signaling that it was time to replace the brake pads. It was one thing after another. In one week, we went through nearly all the money we had set aside for Christmas.

The night I had planned on ordering the presents for the kids, I stared glumly at the lists I had made. I crossed off the most expensive gifts first, feeling a pang of sadness when the remote control tractor that scoops had to come off my older son's list. It was the one thing he had asked for over and over. I kept telling myself that Christmas isn't about the presents and that the kids were still young enough to not really care about how many presents they didn't get. It didn't work. All I felt was frustration that the same thing seemed to happen all the time, not just at Christmas. We would finally get just a little bit ahead and then something would happen.

I cried to God that night, telling Him how I was so tired of feeling so hopeless. I wailed that it wasn't fair — that I didn't want to be a millionaire, but I just wanted to know what it feels like not to worry about money. I just wanted to give my kids a nice Christmas, for crying out loud! What's so wrong about that?

The next day, I went to the gas station to fill up the car. I knew we only had twenty dollars to spend on fuel until my husband got paid the next day. There wasn't enough fuel in the car for him to get to work, so that was where our last twenty was going. I went to the cashier to pay and she said, "Someone just came and put twenty dollars on every pump, so go ahead and pick one!" I walked back to my car, stunned. I had heard of this kind of thing happening and thought it was awesome, but I never expected it to happen to me.

The day after that, there was a knock on our front door. It was the local leader of our church. He handed me an envelope, wished me a Merry Christmas, and walked away. Inside were gift cards worth 150 dollars.

A week later, my husband was at the store buying some diapers and other necessities. There was a lady in front of him and he noticed that before she left, she handed the cashier an envelope. The cashier rang up his purchases, he paid for them and then was handed the envelope the previous customer had left behind. Inside was a one-hundred-dollar bill. The stranger had told the cashier to give it to my husband as a Christmas gift. When he came home and handed me the money, I couldn't stop crying. I've been the receiver of kind deeds before and I had always been grateful for them — but these deeds were coming at a time when I really needed them.

I thought money towards gas, gift cards and a random one-hundred-dollar bill were more than enough to prove to me the generosity of people's hearts. I was to be proven wrong. The same night that we were anonymously given the one hundred dollars, there was a quiet knock on the door. I was in the middle of changing a diaper and it was so quiet that I wasn't even sure I heard it. I called out; "Just a second!"

in case there really was someone there, hurried with the diaper, and then went to the door. All four of my little ones were right at my heels. When I opened it, I discovered two big boxes full of wrapped presents. Tears began to sting at my eyes. Of course, there was no person standing there for me to thank. I yelled out, "Thank you!" and then brought the boxes inside.

The kids saw the packages and knew they were for them. I couldn't stop them from unwrapping them, even if I had wanted to. They were each labeled by name for the kids, so whoever our anonymous gift giver was, they knew us and we knew them. There was a sled and some books for our older son, a play doctor's kit and doctor's dress-up outfit and crayons for our older daughter. A baby and a stroller and dress-up dress for our younger daughter, some balls and puzzles for our baby boy. Presents that were immediately loved, hugged, and played with.

It wasn't until after I had gotten the wrapping paper cleared away that I saw the envelope. It was sitting at the bottom of one of the boxes with the names Josh and Nicole on it. I picked it up, hoping there would be a name of our gift giver. What I found inside left me in tears.

There was a note, but it wasn't signed. It said simply:

Joshua and Nicole
We were given a gift when our budget was tight. Now we are happy
to pay it forward. You are an inspiration!

Inside the envelope — not one, not two, not three — but TEN one-hundred-dollar bills — one thousand dollars. I think I quit breathing for a few seconds. When my husband got home from work and I showed him what had been given to us, I thought I was going to have to administer CPR. He too, was completely speechless.

We still didn't have a huge Christmas by any means. It was very tempting to go out on a major shopping spree, but I remembered my pleas to God just a few weeks before of wanting to know what it would feel like not to have to live paycheck to paycheck. This completely unexpected money was an answer to those pleas. It wasn't enough to meet all of our obligations—but it was enough that not every single cent from my husband's next paycheck would have to go to bills. It was just enough. It was exactly what I wanted for Christmas.

~Nicole Webster

99

Life Changes

I believe the world is one big family,
and we need to help each other.
~Jet Li

As my daughter Meg recovered from a corrective spinal surgery due to her cerebral palsy my thoughts were preoccupied. Her twenty-four-hour care had exhausted me. Unforeseen complications required additional nursing and our home had few quiet moments.

The holidays were here and I'd had little time to think about them. In fact, I only wanted to forget and have them pass by quickly. Difficult times make you wonder how soon they will evaporate and turn into hope again.

I sat in the rocking chair by the picture window one afternoon. An unexpected knock at the front door took me by surprise. There I found six friends with broad smiles on their faces.

"We hope you like turkey!" they chimed in together.

"It's so nice to see you!" I said, wondering what they were up to.

Across my kitchen counters they arranged a holiday feast. First, a covered roasting pan was set on my stove; it held a cooked turkey. A fabric-covered jar had been filled with brown gravy and placed next to some bread stuffing, mashed potatoes and butternut squash. A basket covered in white linen held the fresh aroma of homemade bread and cinnamon rolls.

Another countertop was covered with pecan, apple and pumpkin pies. I stood there, stunned by this kindness, as each person gave me a warm hug.

"We've been thinking of you and hope you like our little surprise."

I remember when I was young, my father stood at the head of our holiday dinner table. He would spread his arms open, palms up and say, "Eat well and give this house a good name."

I held back tears the following day before this bounty on our table, thankful for caring friends as I repeated my father's words. It was the only way I knew how to honor them and I vowed one day to repay this kindness.

Several years later our church had the opportunity to start a community food bank in our small town of 900 people. I volunteered to be the coordinator.

Our food bank was located in a small house beside our church. It had a large flagstone fireplace in the living room, with inviting comfortable stuffed chairs. The cozy atmosphere welcomed our guests to relax a moment and enjoy a cup of coffee and conversation as we prepared bags of food for them.

Every Saturday for ten years Meg and I greeted our neighbors, listened to their life stories and shared our family's heartaches, hopes and dreams.

The holiday season had once again become my favorite time of year. During one holiday rush, I found myself surrounded by fifty frozen turkeys. I broke out in laughter, as I sang "Fifty frozen turkeys finding families" and danced around the room to a musical beat.

Meg sat in her wheelchair wondering if I had gone insane. Non-verbal, she began pointing to one large bird on her chair tray. My new mantra, "fifty-*one* frozen turkeys finding families!"

Together Meg and I filled the empty boxes spread across the room with cans of food and packaged goods, enough for each family to cook and enjoy a full holiday feast.

As a special treat, Meg and I had baked one hundred applesauce cakes, cookies and pumpkin breads as our personal holiday gift to add to the boxes.

After volunteers had loaded their vehicles, they drove miles through our mountainous community to each home, delivering their delicious cargo. The sudden knock upon the door, just like the one on mine, came as welcome relief for many. My greatest joy is in playing a small role in replicating the gratitude and relief that I felt when my own turkey dinner showed up unexpectedly that long ago day.

~Debbie McNaughton

100

Two for One

One can pay back the loan of gold, but one dies
forever in debt to those who are kind.
~Malayan Proverb

How could I be so absentminded? It was two nights before Christmas and I had lost my purse. My license, my debit card, a handful of credit cards and over two hundred dollars in cash — all gone.

It had already been hard to generate enthusiasm for the holidays. Our Sheltie, Jacob, who was more like a child than a family dog, had recently been diagnosed with lymphoma and wasn't responding to treatment. I dreaded losing him and feared my husband's reaction to that loss. Jake was the first pet my husband had ever truly opened his heart to, and he refused to even think about what the chemo's ineffectiveness might mean. Though I had not given up hope, I knew that the prognosis wasn't good.

Nevertheless, it was a tradition that my sons, their wives, and our grandchildren would spend Christmas Day at our house. So we mustered what energy we could, loaded Jake in the back seat of my car, and set out to purchase the things that would hopefully make our hearts and our home more festive.

The weather matched our moods that evening. The icy fingers of a cold rain made it difficult to see past the headlights of the cars coming toward us.

While we traditionally listened to Christmas carols on the radio, tonight we drove in silence. As we did, I began to think of those we shared the road with that night. I wondered how many of them were feeling the spirit of Christmas. How many were stressed about finances? How many were alone? How many of them were grieving losses that had occurred over the year or were anticipating losses of their own? It struck me how little we ever know about those we interact with daily.

Our first stop was at the dollar store to pick up wrapping paper, stocking stuffers, and decorations for our buffet table. As we approached the register, my husband said, "I'll be out in the car with Jake." He returned a few minutes later. "Do you have the car keys?"

"No," I responded. "Did you check your pockets?"

"Twice." My husband sighed deeply. "I'll go back out. Maybe I dropped them when I got out of the car."

I scoured the aisles in futility before leaving the store as quickly as I could. When I got back to the car, my husband was inside with the motor running. "You found them. Thank God!" Jake wagged his tale and kissed my face as I hastily loaded the packages. "Where were they?"

"In a puddle next to the car, but you really need to get another set."

"Yeah, I know," I replied, guilty for not having replaced the set I'd lost months earlier.

We drove to the grocery store, again in silence. As we got out of the car, I reached down for my purse and fear gripped me in the gut as I realized it wasn't there. "Wait," I cried to my husband who was already walking toward the store.

"What now?" he moaned, sounding somewhat annoyed.

"My purse. I think I must have left it in the cart at the dollar store."

My husband didn't say anything as we both climbed back in the car.

Fifteen minutes later we returned to find that another car now occupied the spot where we had previously parked. The cart was still there, but it was empty. I jumped out of the car and began searching the bushes before my husband had a chance to park.

It didn't take long to realize my efforts were useless. My purse was gone. I started to cry. While the tears began over the current situation, it opened up a flood of emotion I had been holding at bay for the past few weeks. It was all just too much to handle. "Are you alright ma'am?" a blond woman about my age asked. I hadn't even noticed her approach me.

"I lost my purse. Left it in the cart," I stammered.

"Did you ask in any of the stores? I did the exact same thing one time and someone found it and turned it in." She motioned toward the row of stores in front of us.

"I was in the dollar store."

"Okay, you go there, but we should check them all. I'll check down here. Could you check down there?" she motioned to my husband, who had now joined us.

"I had over two hundred dollars in it. Even if we find it, it'll probably be empty," I said, as much to myself as to her. I was actually thinking back to a time when an opportunistic thief had stolen my purse from under my nose during another shopping trip years earlier.

"I wouldn't be so sure of that. There are still some good people in the world," she responded optimistically.

"Perhaps you're right," I agreed half-heartedly.

I was at the courtesy desk giving the manager my name and address when the woman reappeared. "Any luck?"

"Afraid not," I whispered.

"Me neither. You never know though, it still may show up. In the meantime…" The woman took my hand and pressed something into my palm before closing my hand into a fist. "Merry Christmas," she whispered in my ear, before disappearing out the door into the night.

I was so startled it took me a minute to open my hand, but when I did, I gasped. I couldn't believe it; the woman had given me two one-hundred-dollar bills. What really mattered the most to me wasn't the money, but that I had come across someone special, someone who really cared.

That was enough to bring me out of my funk, but the night held yet another random act of kindness for me. For when we arrived home there was a white station wagon I didn't recognize in front of our house. A stranger dressed in a black parka stood on our front porch ringing the doorbell. She had not only found my missing purse, but had taken the time to drive a half hour out of her way to return it to me, completely intact.

"God bless you," I exclaimed as I grabbed her and hugged her tight. "How can I ever thank you?"

"No need. It's what we do for each other," she said getting back into her car. "Merry Christmas."

Unfortunately, it was to be Jake's last Christmas, so its memory remains bittersweet. It was made a little more special, however, thanks to two angels, each offering kindness to a crazy woman with a sick dog and a husband with the patience of Job.

While I have no way of contacting them personally to thank them for their gifts and explain what their kindness meant to me, I've tried to follow their example and now pass their kindness forward whenever and wherever I can.

~Catherine Mayer Donges

Receiving

Kindness in words creates confidence.
Kindness in thinking creates profoundness.
Kindness in giving creates love.
~Lao Tzu

"Hello," I said into my phone as I hurriedly swallowed my cereal.

"Mrs. Grumbein, this is the Captain. Would it be convenient if we deliver today about 1:00 p.m.?"

"Yes, that would be fine." Both apprehension and excitement flooded my heart as I hung up the phone. Someone had given our name and phone number to a Marine squadron, and they were bringing us Christmas presents. I made sure the house was as spotless as it could be with four children living in it.

As 1:00 p.m. drew near, I perched on the edge of the couch. Each time I heard a car, I jumped up to see if they were here. Each time it wasn't them, I was relieved, yet disappointed.

Finally a huge SUV pulled into the driveway, and four Marines in Blue Dress uniforms got out. One glanced at the broken-down station wagon sitting beside our driveway. Now I was embarrassed as well as grateful and excited and nervous.

I greeted them with a smile. My heart was pounding so loudly I wondered if they could hear it.

"Mrs. Grumbein, we're here on behalf of a squadron on base.

The Marines have collected toys for families who might be having a difficult time this holiday season."

"Please come in." Two came in and two went back to the SUV. They made several trips and soon my living room was full of boxes and bags.

"We hope you have a blessed Christmas, Ma'am," the oldest Marine said.

I tried to say "Thank you," but my throat suddenly closed up and tears welled up in my eyes.

He looked uncomfortably at the floor, hat in hand, and turned toward the door.

"Thank you," I managed to squeak, when they were halfway down the porch steps.

"Yes, Ma'am," he said, putting on his hat and smiling at me.

"What squadron are you with, so I can send a thank-you card?"

"We can't tell you that, Ma'am. No thanks necessary."

I watched through the window as they drove away, wondering what they thought of me.

I had always donated, not received. We weren't always like this. My husband had been laid off, and we were struggling. I'd wanted to say this to them, but the words wouldn't come out. I felt ashamed and humiliated.

I quickly wrapped the gifts, so I'd be finished before the school-aged children came home. I stashed them in closets and under beds as quickly as I could.

On Christmas morning I felt a twinge of guilt as our four children tore open the gifts with gusto, thinking they were from us.

My nine-year-old son opened a game box and taped inside the lid was an envelope.

"What's this, Mom?" He handed it to me.

I opened it and read aloud:

May the joy of Christmas be with you all the year through.

All around the card were the signatures of all the men and women in the squadron, except instead of their real names, they'd signed nicknames, like Pug, Buck and Ace. They had done this kindness for us and we would never even know who these men and women were, or who had given them our name.

At the bottom of the card, written in small, neat letters, it said:

Although the sea gets rough, no storm lasts forever.

I was suddenly ashamed of being ashamed. I finally understood.

~Sharon Palmerton Grumbein

Meet Our Contributors

Amanda Adams is currently working on her B.A. degree in English. She raises and plays with her three sons and works with her husband who is a sculptor. She likes to hike, read, and travel with her family. She plans to be involved in professional publishing one day.

Devora Adams is a writer and life coach from New Jersey, where she lives with her husband and four girls. E-mail her at the_write_direction@yahoo.com.

Elizabeth Atwater and her husband Joe live in a small town in North Carolina on a horse ranch. She does volunteer work for senior services and hospice. In her free time she loves to write.

A former teacher, **Lorne Bell**, now writes business, travel, and lifestyle stories for *The Boston Globe* and several New England publications. He also owns Boston Editorial Consulting, a communications firm for progressive businesses. He lives in Massachusetts with his wife and Golden Retriever.

Juan Bendana is a youth motivational speaker and best-selling author. He has dedicated his life to helping young people find out what they want to do with their lives. He is also a snowboard instructor, sushi fanatic, and has a passion for travel.

Francine L. Billingslea has found a passion for writing in her later years. She was first published in 2007 and has had over forty-five publications since then. She loves traveling, writing and spending quality time with her loved ones.

Margaret E. Braun-Haley is a regular contributor to the *Chicken Soup for the Soul* series and has had her stories translated into a number of languages. She is frequently asked to write or speak about miracles. When not writing, she enjoys spending time with her children, grand-children and great-grandchildren.

David Brigham received his B.S. degree from State University of New York at Oneonta, his M.S. degree from Albany State University, and his Ph.D. from Syracuse University. After a forty-year career in higher education, he lives with his wife in a log house in Eastern Tennessee and is starting a career as a writer. E-mail him at davidebrigham@ gmail.com.

Nathan Burgoine grew up reading and studied literature in university while working at a bookstore. His first novel, *Light*, was a finalist for a Lambda Literary Award. His second novel, *Triad Blood*, is available now from Bold Strokes Books. He lives in Ottawa, Canada with his husband, Dan, and his Husky, Coach.

Personal trainer **Rodney Burton** is blessed to be able to help others every day. He shows people how to change their lives and reduce stress by making smarter diet and exercise choices under any circumstance, at any age. Learn more at resultsnutrition.net. He thanks writer Barbara Routen for telling his story.

Eva Carter has worked in telecommunications and is currently pursuing her creative side, with photography and writing. This is her eleventh story published in the *Chicken Soup for the Soul* series. Eva enjoys yoga and NIA, a dance class. She and her husband, Larry, live in Dallas, TX. E-mail her at evacarter@sbcglobal.net.

After graduating from Edinboro University with his B.A. degree **Tim**

Chizmar moved west in pursuit of his dreams. Since that time he's been on television, in films and toured all over the world headlining stand-up comedy shows. Tim is a lifelong dreamer but when times are tough he gets by with a little help from his friends.

Deb Cooperman got her first journal at twelve. She now teaches women journaling as a way to rediscover themselves and write through the ups and downs on this roller coaster called life. She believes in Yoda and The Force, Mr. Rogers… and that most things can be made better with bubbles, fairy lights, and glitter. Learn more at debcooperman.com.

Jean Delaney received a Bachelor of Science in Chemical Engineering from Clarkson College in 1974 and a Master of Science in Chemical Engineering from University of Dayton in 1982. In retirement, she enjoys writing, gardening, birding, tai chi and many other activities. To this day Jean remains married to the love of her life.

Piper Dellums is an author, public and inspirational speaker, international victims advocate, member of the United Nations delegate commission on the status of women, film producer, mother of two, environmentalist, international human rights and dignities activist, and survivor. She received degrees from UC Berkeley and New York University.

Catherine Mayer Donges holds an MFA degree in Creative Writing from Wilkes University, and her book, *Martyr's Redemption*, is due to be published in May of 2017. Her previous story, "The Reunion," appeared in *Chicken Soup for the Soul: Dreams and Premonitions*. She lives in Central Pennsylvania with her husband, seven dogs, and cat.

Alice Faye Duncan writes for children and adults. Her picture book, *Honey Baby Sugar Child*, is a mother's bouncing love song dedicated to children everywhere. Duncan's adult book, *Hello Sunshine*, is a handy guide to help workers de-stress on busy or cloudy days. Learn more at alicefayeduncan.com and read her blog at uncloudyday.com.

Melissa Edmondson is proud to have her fifth story published in the *Chicken Soup for the Soul* series. She is the author of a book of essays entitled *Lessons Abound* and a book of original poetry entitled *Searching for Home: The Poetic Musings of a Wanderer*. She lives in the North Carolina mountains with her husband and four teenage children.

Andrea Engel earned a culinary degree and worked as a chef and general manager for many years. She now focuses on her passion for writing. Her debut novel, *Ghost of a Shadow*, was written with her sister and is the first in a series. She continues to write short stories and work on additional collaborative projects.

Josephine Fitzpatrick loves to read, write, bird-watch, swim and knit. She has kept journals since she was a child. She co-facilitates a memoir-writing class for senior citizens at California State University, Long Beach. She and her husband have been married for over fifty-five years, and have three children and six grandchildren.

Michael Ford lives in Florida and is obtaining a bachelor's degree in Psychology. He plans on moving to California and becoming a teacher or guidance counselor.

Skye Galvas joined the Air Force from a homeless shelter in 2010. Now a civilian, she lives with her family in Salt Lake City and works as a business consultant, advocate and speaker. She plans to release her book *Alacrity* in 2017. E-mail her at skyegalvas@gmail.com and read her blog at skyegalvas.com.

Heidi Gaul lives in Oregon's Willamette Valley with her husband and furry family. She loves travel, be it around the block or the world. Her writing has been included in several *Chicken Soup for the Soul* books and *The Upper Room* devotionals.

Robyn Gerland is the author of *All These Long Years Later*, a book of short stories; the past editor of the internationally distributed glossy,

Hysteria; a frequent contributor to the *Chicken Soup for the Soul* series; and a contributor and columnist for several magazines and newspapers. She is also a member of The Federation of British Columbia Writers.

Lynn Goodman has a BFA in studio art and a B.S. degree in biology. She wants to be a research diver when she grows up, and is currently acquiring the necessary skills. She is also working on her first novel and a series of children's books about life in the oceans. She enjoys diving, sailing, beach bonfires, hiking and traveling.

Gloria Anderson Goss is a member of Gold Star Wives and a watercolor artist living in Central Pennsylvania with her husband Jeff. Her article, "Why Helicopters Don't Fly and Young Men Die" was published in the *Congressional Record* on June 20, 1984.

Carol Graham is an award-winning author of *Battered Hope*, talk show host for "Never Ever Give Up Hope," international keynote speaker, business owner, and certified health coach. Carol has five grandchildren and has rescued over thirty dogs. Her goal is to share hope and encouragement. E-mail her at batteredhope@gmail.com.

Mary Grant, a former teacher and bookstore owner, resides in Bluffton, SC. Her writing has appeared in newspapers, magazines, and six *Chicken Soup for the Soul* books. She is a freelance writer for a local newspaper and has recently published a book of short stories. Mary enjoys traveling and is an avid cycler.

Sharon Grumbein graduated from Craven Community College in 1986. She plays flute and volunteers at Two Rivers Healthcare. She lives in Havelock, NC, with her four youngest children and two beloved cats. Sharon has been previously published in several magazines and in the *Chicken Soup for the Soul* series.

Heather Harshman is an estate planning attorney, law professor, writer, and mother of two little ones. In between her jobs and being a mom, she posts short stories and stories about faith and traveling on her blog at HeatherHarshman.com. She enjoys bicycling, traveling, snowboarding, and camping with her family.

Jill Haymaker is a romance author and family law attorney in Fort Collins, CO. She is the author of the *Peakview* series of romance novels, featuring older characters, set in the beautiful Rocky Mountains of Colorado. When not writing, she enjoys hiking in the mountains with her dog, Laddie, sports and the great outdoors.

Stephanie Hunter studied abroad in Japan for a year while completing her degree in Global Studies. Upon graduation, she returned to Japan for three years to teach English. These days, she lives with her husband in Ohio where she teaches ESL and writes dystopian novels under the name S. Hunter Nisbet.

May Hutchings is a freelance copywriter, editor and blogger. May enjoys time with her son, writing, music, teaching and animals. This is her second story published in the *Chicken Soup for the Soul* series. She has won awards for her creative writing stories and is now writing young adult and children's fiction books.

Jennie Ivey lives and writes in Tennessee. She is the author of numerous works of fiction and nonfiction, including dozens of stories published in the *Chicken Soup for the Soul* series. Learn more at jennieivey.com.

Gail Johnsen has a B.A. degree in Speech and Drama from Brigham Young University. She enjoys writing and recently self-published her book called *My Miraculous Moments*. Gail is the mother of seven grown children. She loves to sing and act and she believes that service should be included in her plans every single day.

Vicki L. Julian, a University of Kansas graduate, is the author of four inspirational books, various newspaper and magazine articles, and a contributor to six anthologies. She also writes a faith-based blog and a Christmas-themed children's book is soon to be published. Learn more at vickijulian.com.

Paul Karrer taught in Korea, England, Western Samoa, Connecticut, and California. He's appeared on *Good Morning America*, *First Edition*, and *CNN*. He's been published in *The New York Post*, *Christian Science Monitor*, *San Francisco Chronicle*, *Teacher* magazine, *Educator Weekly*, and writes a column for *The Salinas Californian*.

Sky Khan is an author and educator. She is a passionate advocate for new parents and she also counsels parents of cancer survivors. Her life is guided by her work with the dying, her study of Buddhist principles, and her experience raising four children in New York City with her best friend Ben.

Michael John Kildare is an Australian dedicated to capturing those small special moments in life that make it all worth it. He is a father of three, world travelled and experienced.

Michael Ray Kingsbury is a stand-up comedian/storyteller and proud father of a child with autism. He has been featured at the Vermont Comedy Club and was a finalist in the WordXWord storytelling competition. This story was originally published on TheMighty.com.

Gwen Navarrete Klapperich is a training consultant who volunteers for the American Red Cross and other nonprofits dedicated to public health, environmental, and disability rights advocacy. She thanks her son Arthur for allowing her to share his story. Their family resides in the beautiful state of Hawai'i.

April Knight is an artist and author. Her latest novel, *Stars in the Desert*, is a romance story about people willing to sacrifice all they own for love. April is a member of the Kiowa Native American tribe and has a column in the newspaper *Indian Life*. Her favorite pastime is riding horses.

Michael Knuth lives in northern Minnesota with his wife Lori. He has been writing Christmas stories for his family for over thirty years. He enjoys road trips with his wife, visiting their five adult children and three grandchildren, camping, canoeing in the BWCA of Minnesota, and reading. He is a certified spiritual director.

Jacqueline Kremer, a teacher in Connecticut, is happiest when she is baking cookies, reading, skiing, running, walking, figure skating, laughing at the antics of her two (mostly grown-up) children, Sarah and Benjamin, and spending time with her wonderful husband, John. She walks through life with a joyful smile and a grateful heart.

Jessica Lampard studied writing at the University of Victoria, where she graduated with a Bachelor of Arts degree. She enjoys hiking with her dog, playing tennis, and inventing recipes. She is currently working on a novel.

Annette Langer has been published four times in the *Chicken Soup for the Soul* series. Her other published work includes: *Healing through Humor: Change Your Focus, Change Your Life!* and *A Funny Thing Happened on My Way to the World*. Learn more at AnnetteLanger.com.

Allison Wilson Lee is a home schooling mother of two. She enjoys blogging, volunteering, and baking sourdough bread. She edits stories for Cru, an interdenominational Christian ministry. Allison graduated with a degree in Environmental Biology but is more proud of having donated 286 ounces of breast milk.

Linda S. Locke retired after serving as a school principal for twenty-one years. The mother of three and the grandmother of two, Dr. Locke has published seven books, four of which are children's books on the topic of helping victims of bullying to find their voice. She has also published a Christian romance novel and a compilation of inspirational blogs.

Barbara Lodge has essays in *Parabola* magazine, *Literary Mama*, *The*

New York Times' Motherlode, the LA Affairs section of the *Los Angeles Times*, and the anthology *Blended*, and upcoming in *The Rumpus Voices of Addiction*. In 2016 she founded TruthTalks™ workshops to help parents talk, and listen, to their kids who abuse drugs.

Ilana Long is the author of *Ziggy's Big Idea* and is seeking representation for her new Young Adult science-fiction book. She enjoys watercolor painting, hiking, singing and performing improv and stand-up comedy. Ilana and her husband live and teach in Costa Rica with their twin teenagers. E-mail her at ilanalong@hotmail.com.

Paul Lyons, a former middle school teacher now travels the world as a stand-up comic and writer. He just published his first book called, *Carpe Diem, Mañana* a humorous account of his spiritual journey from insecurity to self-pity. The book shares his daily accounts of focusing on each moment to understand and discover its joy.

A Hope College graduate living in Cincinnati, OH, **Diane MacLachlan** is inspired by stories of challenge, joy and personal growth. Her family and her faith are her greatest joy. She gives special thanks to her daughter Katie, who reads every story and edits it to perfection, and to her best friend Jill, who encourages each endeavor.

Nancy Noel Marra has written four novel cookbooks: *The Gourmet Club: A Full Course Deal*; *The Book Club: Just Desserts*; *The Investment Club: An Appetizing Venture*; and *Sorority Sisters: Let's Do Lunch*. Her short story, "A Hug from a Teenage Boy," was included in *Chicken Soup for the Soul at Work*. Nancy lives in Boise, ID.

Debra Mayhew is a pastor's wife, mom to seven, part-time teacher, editor and writer. She loves small town living, stormy weather, good books and family time. Learn more at debramayhew.com.

Debbie McNaughton is a freelance writer, mother, and advocate for her daughter with special needs. Her short stories, drawn from journals of everyday life over the past thirty years, have appeared in local and national magazines and *Chicken Soup for the Soul: Find Your Inner Strength*. She is a wash-a-shore on Cape Cod.

Marybeth Mitcham holds an MPH in nutrition and works as a professor and a nutrition and healthy living educator. She is an Adirondack 46er, motorcycle rider, pianist, and published freelance author, who, when not working, can be found hiking, hovering by the wood stove, digging a pond, or via e-mail, at marybeth.mitcham@gmail.com.

Elizabeth Moursund received a Bachelor of Arts in Theatre from Providence College in 1998. She lives with her husband and three boys in Southern Oregon. She spends her time volunteering with the PTA as well as chauffeuring her kids to sports and music practices. She finds time to write while waiting in the school pick-up line.

Beki Muchow believes in magic and looks for it every day. A talented author who writes from the heart, her work is on UntiedShoelacesOfTheMind. com and FictionMagazine.com and in print in *Binnacle Ultra-Short*, *The Storyteller Magazine*, and *Writer's Mill Journal*. She lives in Sherwood, OR. E-mail her at BekiMuchow.writer@gmail.com.

Margaret Nava writes from her home in New Mexico where the skies are always blue and the chilis red hot. In addition to her stories in the *Chicken Soup for the Soul* series, she has authored six books and written numerous articles for inspirational and Christian living publications.

Freddy Nunez is a simple man living with his wife and three children in Virginia. He enjoys writing fiction but draws from his real life experience for all his characters.

Irene Onorato is a published author of several inspirational romance novels. She and her husband James, both radiation protection technicians, retired from the nuclear power industry in 2014 and now reside in Louisiana with their cats, George and Henry, and their dog, Deacon.

Kristen Mai Pham received her Bachelor of Arts degree, with honors, from California State University, Fullerton. She resides in California with her partner in writing and in life, Paul. Kristen loves *Star Wars* and food. She plans to write inspirational screenplays for TV and film. E-mail her at maidepp@yahoo.com.

Mary C. M. Phillips is a caffeinated wife, working mom, and writer of essays and short stories. Her work has appeared in numerous anthologies including *Chicken Soup for the Soul*, *Cup of Comfort*, and *Bad Austen: The Worst Stories Jane Never Wrote*. She blogs at CaffeineEpiphanies.com. Follow her on Twitter@MaryCMPhil.

Marsha Porter fell in love with writing in grade school when the punishment *du jour* was a 500-word essay. She's devoted her life to inspiring her teenage students to pick up a pen and change the world. She also rescues and rehabilitates injured, abused or ill animals, which has made her life complete.

Kay Presto has stories published in a variety of *Chicken Soup for the Soul* books. She's an award-winning television and radio broadcaster and photo-journalist, covering motorsports. She has recently completed a middle grade go-karting novel, and has written a variety of children's books. E-mail Kay at prestoprod6@yahoo.com.

Linda Holland Rathkopf is a playwright and fine artist. Her plays have been produced in six states, her writings have been published in anthologies, and her artwork has been displayed in galleries around the country. She is the proud grandmother of four boys whom she encourages to color outside of the lines.

Mark Rickerby has written stories and poems for over a dozen *Chicken Soup for the Soul* books. He is the head writer of *Big Sky*, an upcoming western TV show, co-author of his father's memoir, *The Other Belfast*, and a voice actor. He also wrote and sang fifteen songs on a CD for his greatest accomplishments, his daughters Marli and Emma.

Cara Rifkin is a born and raised Chicagoan who received her Bachelor of Science in Mathematics from DePaul University. She volunteers her free time promoting social justice and human welfare causes. A self-proclaimed "news junkie," she also researches and writes about a variety of business topics.

Marti Robards worked as a registered nurse for ten years, then as an administrative technician for twenty-five in municipal government. She is now retired and enjoys family, church, writing, reading, gardening, playing the folk harp, and trying her hand at many various crafts. She says, "Life is Good!"

Nan Rockey lives in Bloomington, IN, with her writer husband and her non-writer dog. They enjoy long walks in the woods and eating cheesecake when they aren't in the woods.

Heather Rae Rodin serves as Executive Director for Hope Grows Haiti. An award-winning writer and author of *Prince of Vodou: Breaking the Chains*, Heather has always had a passion for a story. Heather and her husband Gord live in Ontario, Canada. When not in Haiti, she enjoys time spent with their large and growing family.

Lisa Romeo lives in New Jersey. Her writing appears in *The New York Times, O, The Oprah Magazine*, many literary journals, anthologies, and websites, and is listed among Notables in Best American Essays 2016. She teaches writing at several universities and is at work on a memoir. E-mail her at LisaRomeoWriter@gmail.com.

When **Goldy Rosenberg** isn't volunteering and working, she likes to catch life's nuances and highlights in written form. She is currently working on a novel.

Jim Schneegold has been published in *A 6th Bowl of Chicken Soup for the Soul* and *Chicken Soup for the Grieving Soul*. It is his true pleasure in life to share his experiences with readers, and if his stories can move, touch, or affect them in any way, it's the sharing that makes it all worthwhile.

Lindy Schneider, author, playwright, and artist has been featured on the TV show *Inside Edition*. Her watercolors appear on Amazon's best-selling notecards. She is co-author and illustrator of the children's book *Starfish on the Beach*. See her artwork at peakspublishing.com or search her name on Amazon.com.

Pamela Schock has two children and four grandchildren. She loves to travel and garden. After working for almost a decade in the Napa Valley wine industry, Pam is writing *Tales From the Tasting Room*, a collection of heartwarming and humorous short stories about her encounters in the tasting room. E-mail her at pamelitatales@aol.com.

Steve Schultz is the head varsity boys' basketball coach and English teacher at Fountain Valley High School. Steve is also an internationally published writer, a speaker, writes a monthly magazine column, a former candidate for mayor, and the CEO and founder of a company called Elevate. E-mail him at personalbest22@gmail.com.

Joel Schwartzberg is a nationally published essayist, author, and speechwriter based in Chatham, NJ. When not writing, he loves horror films, cats, and mall-shopping with his three high school-age kids.

Thom Schwarz, RN spent most of his most formative years working in the emergency room and at the bedside of his hospice patients. He wants to be just like his kids when he grows up. E-mail him at thomapl@Yahoo.com.

Darlene Sneden is a writer and editor who currently divides her time between New Jersey and South Carolina. She finds great adventures wherever she is. It's all in the attitude! To follow along, check out her blog at adventuresofamiddleagemom.com.

Peggy Sprunt has been married to her high school sweetheart, James "Scott" Sprunt, since 1982. She has two adult children, ages thirty and twenty-seven, who are her entire world. Her favorite pastime is writing and creating stories. One day she hopes to write stories for children.

Avi Steinfeld, a Chicago native, received his Master of Science degree from Touro College in 2010. He currently lives in Brooklyn, NY, where he works as a school psychologist for children with special needs. Avi is also a freelance humor writer and has had a number of articles published online.

Joyce Sudbeck began writing short stories at retirement, six years ago, with some modest success. She has had a number of them published in *Chicken Soup for the Soul* books, *Thin Thread* books, and in magazines. She shares stories of memories taken from her life. She feels as though she is writing her memoir — one story at a time.

Polly Tafrate is an eclectic freelancer who's published articles on diverse topics — education and parenting (having taught first grade for twenty-five years), travel, health, volunteering, Saturday schools, cooking, op-eds, grandmotherhood, and whatever else piques her interest. She welcomes assignments. E-mail her at pollytafrate@hotmail.com.

Annmarie B. Tait resides in Conshohocken, PA, with her husband Joe Beck. Annmarie has been published in several *Chicken Soup for the Soul* books, *Reminisce* magazine, *Patchwork Path*, and many other anthologies. She also enjoys cooking, crocheting, and singing and recording Irish and American folk songs. E-mail her at irishbloom@aol.com.

Loretta Tschetter holds degrees in English and Accounting, neither one of which prepared her fully for all the twists and turns of life. She loves stories in all forms, making her children groan at her terrible jokes, and the ocean. She lives with her husband and two boys in Sioux Falls, SD, far from any actual oceans.

Melissa Valks is addicted to travel and other cultures. She has visited almost seventy countries, including many solo trips off the beaten path. Melissa is a previous contributor to the *Chicken Soup for the Soul* series, and has had several works published. E-mail her at melissavalks@ yahoo.ca.

Laura Ware's column "Laura's Look" is published weekly in the *Highlands News-Sun*. She is an author of short stories and novels in multiple genres. Laura lives in Central Florida, where she is active in her local congregation and enjoys reading and computer games. E-mail her at laura@laurahware.com.

Benny Wasserman, a retired aerospace engineer, began a second career as an Einstein impersonator. His book, *Presidents Were Teenagers Too*, was published in 2007. His stories have been published in *Reminisce*, *Good Old Days* and the *Los Angeles Times*. He is an avid reader and dedicated ping-pong player. E-mail him at wassben@aol.com.

Dorann Weber is a freelance photographer for a South New Jersey newspaper and a Getty Images contributor. She has a newfound love for writing, especially for the *Chicken Soup for the Soul* series. Dorann lives in the Pinelands with her family. E-mail her at Dorann_Weber@ yahoo.com.

Nicole Webster has been interested in writing since the age of eight. Her other interests include reading, scrapbooking, cooking, cross stitching, and being outdoors. She is a stay-at-home mom and currently resides in Utah with her husband and four children.

Leslie Wibberley loves the written word almost as much as her family. Her creative nonfiction essays are published in several literary journals, and her short story, "That Damn Pumpkin," in *Devolution Z*. She has won 6th place and an Honorable Mention in Writer's Digest's Annual Competitions. E-mail her at wibberleythewordsmith@gmail.com.

Aimee Mae Wiley is a wife, mother, writer, and editor living in historic Cedarburg, WI. She recently started her own writing and editing business, and for fun she also blogs about faith, family, and simple living. In her free time, Aimee enjoys frequenting local libraries and parks with her five children.

Dallas Woodburn is a writer, editor, teacher and literacy advocate living in the San Francisco Bay area. To date, she has been a proud contributor to more than two-dozen *Chicken Soup for the Soul* books. She regularly blogs about simple, joyful, healthy living at DaybyDayMasterpiece.com.

Woody Woodburn is a newspaper columnist and the author of *Wooden & Me: Life Lessons from My Two-Decade Friendship with the Legendary Coach and Humanitarian to Help "Make Each Day Your Masterpiece"* and *Strawberries in Wintertime: Essays on Life, Love, and Laughter*. Learn more at woodywoodburn.com.

Following a career in Nuclear Medicine, **Melissa Wootan** is joyfully exploring her creative side. She enjoys writing and is a regular guest on *San Antonio Living*, an hour-long lifestyle show on San Antonio's NBC affiliate, where she shares all of her best DIY/decorating tips. Contact her through facebook.com/chicvintique.

Sandra Wright loves to write to inspire others. If she's not writing she enjoys the outdoors, spending time with her family and travelling. E-mail her at sandrawright@a1.net.

Jennie Wyatt is a student at Eastern Washington University.

Jennifer Zink received her Bachelor of Arts degree from Rowan University, Glassboro, NJ, in 2012. She is married with three children: Mike, age twenty; Kimmy, age eighteen; and Daniel, age sixteen. Jen loves to read and write, spend time with her family, and travel.

Meet Amy Newmark

Amy Newmark is the bestselling author, editor-in-chief, and publisher of the *Chicken Soup for the Soul* book series. Since 2008, she has published 136 new books, most of them national bestsellers in the U.S. and Canada, more than doubling the number of Chicken Soup for the Soul titles in print today. She is also the author of *Simply Happy*, a crash course in Chicken Soup for the Soul advice and wisdom that is filled with easy-to-implement, practical tips for having a better life.

Amy is credited with revitalizing the Chicken Soup for the Soul brand, which has been a publishing industry phenomenon since the first book came out in 1993. By compiling inspirational and aspirational true stories curated from ordinary people who have had extraordinary experiences, Amy has kept the twenty-three-year-old Chicken Soup for the Soul brand fresh and relevant.

Amy graduated *magna cum laude* from Harvard University where she majored in Portuguese and minored in French. She then embarked on a three-decade career as a Wall Street analyst, a hedge fund manager, and a corporate executive in the technology field. She is a Chartered Financial Analyst.

Her return to literary pursuits was inevitable, as her honors thesis in college involved traveling throughout Brazil's impoverished northeast region, collecting stories from regular people. She is delighted to have come full circle in her writing career — from collecting stories "from the people" in Brazil as a twenty-year-old to, three decades later, collecting stories "from the people" for Chicken Soup for the Soul.

When Amy and her husband Bill, the CEO of Chicken Soup for the Soul, are not working, they are visiting their four grown children.

Follow Amy on Twitter @amynewmark. Listen to her free daily podcast, The Chicken Soup for the Soul Podcast, at www.chickensoup. podbean.com, or find it on iTunes, the Podcasts app on iPhone, or on your favorite podcast app on other devices.

Thank You

We are grateful to all our story contributors and fans, who shared thousands of stories about random acts of kindness that they experienced in their own lives. We had more than 5,000 submissions and it was all hands on deck to read them, with Susan Heim, Ronelle Frankel, Mary Fisher, Barbara LoMonaco, Kristiana Pastir, and D'ette Corona narrowing down the list to a few hundred finalists.

As always, we had way more great stories than would fit in this volume, and many of them will end up appearing in future Chicken Soup for the Soul titles.

Associate Publisher D'ette Corona continued to be Amy's right-hand woman in creating the final manuscript and working with all our wonderful writers. Barbara LoMonaco and Kristiana Pastir, along with outside proofreader Elaine Kimbler, jumped in at the end to proof, proof, proof. And yes, there will always be typos anyway, so feel free to let us know about them at webmaster@chickensoupforthesoul.com and we will correct them in future printings.

The whole publishing team deserves a hand, including Senior Director of Marketing Maureen Peltier, Senior Director of Production Victor Cataldo, and graphic designer Daniel Zaccari, who turned our manuscript into this beautiful book.

Changing the world one story at a time®
www.chickensoup.com